He Sent His Word

and

Healed Them

OTHER BOOKS BY DR. VICTOR PAUL WIERWILLE

(Published by American Christian Press)

Power for Abundant Living

Receiving The Holy Spirit Today

Are the Dead Alive Now?

Studies in Abundant Living Series

    Volume I, *The Bible Tells Me So*
    Volume II, *The New, Dynamic Church*
    Volume III, *The Word's Way*
    Volume IV, *God's Magnified Word*
    Volume V, *Order My Steps in Thy Word*

Jesus Christ Is Not God

Jesus Christ Our Passover

Jesus Christ Our Promised Seed

(Published by Eternally Blessed)

A Lot of Things Kids

Christ in You

Holy Spirit—Pneuma Hagion

How to Enjoy the Bible

HE SENT HIS WORD

AND

HEALED THEM

BY

DR. VICTOR PAUL WIERWILLE

ISBN 978-1-948987-22-6 (softcover)
ISBN 978-1-948987-23-3 (ebook)

The scriptures used throughout this book are quoted from the King James Version unless otherwise noted. All explanatory insertions within a scripture verse are enclosed in brackets.

While limited grammatical editing has been done to enhance contemporary readability, care has been taken to preserve the integrity of Dr. Wierwille's work.

Dedicated to those who desire, believe, and have the will to be made whole (sōzō) in every category of life: spiritually, mentally, and physically.

TABLE OF CONTENTS

HE SENT HIS WORD

FOREWORD

The essence of life in all of its exuberance is the most precious asset anyone can have outside of eternal life through Jesus Christ. In the scripture the term for this is wholeness (*sōzō* is the Greek word translated "*saved, healed, delivered*" which is to be made whole in every facet of life; having health and a sound mind socially, physically, spiritually, etc). As many experience health issues and know others struggling with sickness, they may question what the will of God is for them. Does God bring about sickness? Can I be healed by the power of God? What kinds of healings are in the Bible? How does one seek healing from the Creator-God?

The answers are in the Bible and can be found. This book, *He Sent His Word and Healed Them*, is a combination of teachings regarding healing and wholeness. It is being presented for those seeking answers to these questions, and for those in need to be made whole; for those that desire to believe that all things are possible to those that believe.

Matthew 19:26:
But Jesus beheld them, and said unto them, With men this is impossible; but with God all things are possible.

Therefore, let us dive into the scripture and let our doubts be removed cultivating a heart in which the fountain of life within springs forth into life with exuberance.

Victor Paul Wierwille had a remarkable ability to make the Bible fit like a hand in a glove. So often, the reason that people do not enjoy the Bible is simply because they do not understand it. Dr. Wierwille's life was dedicated to helping people attain that understanding.

As a young minister fresh out of seminary, Reverend Wierwille found himself ill-equipped to really take care of his people. That led to a fervent quest to intimately know God through His Word and to manifest His power in his life and ministry; and then in turn, to teach others also. For over forty years, Wierwille enlightened people all over the world through classes, books, live teachings, and radio and television broadcasts. He imparted to his students and listeners a deep understanding of the Word of God. But he accomplished even more than that as he opened up the Scriptures. He made it live!

Dr. Wierwille was a master teacher in every regard. He electrified audiences of over 30,000 people with his dynamic presentation of the Word, while at the same time elucidating substantial doctrinal matters. He stood alone in the field of Biblical research for his unmatched ability to put the whole Word of God together so that it cohesively fit without any contradiction from Genesis to Revelation. Moreover, as a teacher, he excelled at making even the most difficult verses easily understood. With an extra-ordinary ability to communicate simply, Victor Paul Wierwille made tenets of doctrine that theologians have strenuously wrestled with throughout the course of Christianity easily accessible to even the youngest neophyte.

He connected with the common man so readily because he spoke on their level. Yet, while most modern-day preachers that aim to appeal to the masses never move beyond feeding them the milk of the Word, his plain speech manner allowed the everyman to easily digest the meat. With honesty and frankness, Victor Paul Wierwille never watered down the Word, nor shied away from controversial subjects or truths some might have found difficult to swallow. Yet, his disarmingly warm, paternal manner made even strong reproof and correction somehow palatable to the honest hearers.

To some extent, Wierwille's ability to communicate in simple terms may have obscured both his intellect and education to some people. Dr. Wierwille received his Bachelor of Arts and Bachelor of Theology degrees from present day Lakeland College, and conducted graduate studies at the University of Chicago and Princeton Theological Seminary. It was at Princeton that Wierwille earned the Master of Theology degree in Practical Theology. He later completed his Doctor of Theology degree at Pike's Peak Bible Seminary and Burton College in Manitou Springs, Colorado.

His greatest learning, however, did not come from his formal education but instead his personal quest for truth. A voracious reader, Victor Paul consumed two or three theological works a week, week after week for years, until he finally came to the place where he realized that the Bible must be the only rule for faith and practice. For nearly twelve years of his life, he then worked the Word, studying from fourteen to eighteen hours a day in his search for answers. Throughout his life, Dr. Wierwille extensively studied the primary Biblical languages of Hebrew, Greek, and Aramaic; figures of speech used in the Bible; Eastern manners and customs; and many other resources and disciplines relevant to Biblical research. As he searched for enlightenment, he consulted and worked with some of the most outstanding individuals in Biblical studies and Christianity of his day; including Karl Barth, Joseph Bauer, Glenn Clark, Karl J. Ernst, Joseph Friedli, Louis C. Hessert, Elmer G. Homrighausen, E. Stanley Jones, George M. Lamsa, Richard and Reinhold Niebuhr, K. C. Pillai, Paul Tillich, Ernst Traeger, and many others.

The scope of his major works irrefutably stands as proof of V. P. Wierwille's achievements in the field of Biblical research. Dr. Wierwille was the author of numerous books, including *Are the Dead Alive Now?; Receiving the Holy Spirit Today; Jesus Christ is Not God; Jesus Christ Our Passover;* and *Jesus Christ Our Promised Seed.* Additionally, he developed and taught several comprehensive classes directed toward helping people to understand the Bible and to increase the power of God in their lives, such as the *Power for Abundant Living* series, *Living Victoriously*, and the *University of Life* courses.

All of Dr. Wierwille's works contributed to people's understanding of the Bible. The collections in this book specifically share how healing wholeness affects all of our lives. As Dr. Wierwille taught:

> I am in favor of physical healing because God is, and His Word is. But I am in favor of all healing wholeness, the salvation: mental, physical, spiritual. And that will be basically most of your ministries too. You are the ones that are going to have to hold forth the totality of the Word.

The underlying theme to this collection of amazing, transcribed Sunday Night Services is the healing wholeness that is available by Jehovah God in Christ Jesus today.

EDITOR'S PREFACE

G reat care has been taken to preserve Dr. Victor Paul Wierwille's actual words and teaching style along with the logical content as much as possible during the editing process.

Like most speakers, the way that Dr. Wierwille spoke often differed from the way that he wrote. In general, his books especially were more formal than the usual style of his live presentations. Having been delivered in a teaching setting during Sunday Night Services, a fundamental decision was made to retain the informal tone of the audio teachings in the approach to editing the manuscript, rather than "polish" the words a bit more to better match the style found in his other books. In doing so, the atmosphere of the Sunday Night Service setting has been allowed to reverberate through the teacher's words onto the pages of the book, and the reader enjoys a sense of intimacy and familiarity with him that would otherwise be missing. Beyond that, the subject matter of healing wholeness is most effectively communicated through the narrative setting of the many teachings.

In keeping with that approach, certain remarks that were directly relevant to the immediate audience have been retained in the book. Although not commonly found in the pages of a book, the closing prayers in their entirety are included for the same reason. However, some comments and references are no longer pertinent to the present time, and they have been changed or eliminated. Additionally, the audience interaction with the teacher has been removed from the manuscript simply to improve the flow of thought.

Although brief in length, each of these expositions provide great illumination and inspiration to all those who continue to seek after truth.

A FEW OTHER NOTES OF EXPLANATION:

Unless otherwise noted, all Scriptures quoted in the transcript are taken from the King James Version (KJV) of the Bible, also known as the Authorized Version (AV).

Italic type is used in the KJV Bible to indicate words that have been added by the translators to the Scriptural text, for which there are no words found in the original language.

Italic type is additionally used for Greek, Hebrew or Aramaic words, as well as the names of figures of speech.

( ) Parentheses are used in the KJV Bible to indicate explanatory statements within the actual Scriptural text.

[ ] Brackets are used within quoted scriptures to indicate the teacher's explanatory comments.

WHOLENESS

I am in favor of all healing wholeness,
the salvation: mental, physical, spiritual.

A verse of scripture that really settled some things in my heart many years ago is in 1 Peter 2. I too had the same opportunity as anyone of my age and background would have had, or did have, because I was believing and thought that God could save anyone, but it was not His will necessarily to heal everyone. Sometimes God would heal, but not very much. That was always relegated to the doctors or other associated fields.

And then I read in 1 Peter, Chapter 2, verse 24:

1 Peter 2:24:
Who [in] his own self bare our sins in his own body on the tree, that we, being dead to sins, should live unto righteousness: by whose stripes ye were healed.

And as I continued working the Word, I discovered that in the Passover there were two basic elements. Then I saw it in the Communion, or what is called the Lord's Supper. I also saw it in other places of the Word. Finally, as I worked the Word, I was able to see that if God does save, if He is able to save to the uttermost, then He is able to heal to the uttermost. For you have both the covering for sin and the results of sin in 1 Peter 2:24:

1 Peter 2:24:
…bare our sins in his own body on the tree…whose stripes ye were healed.

So, you have both of those basic elements in the atonement or the redemption. The word "salvation" basically means wholeness—wholeness. And I believe that in the early church—around AD 70-90—that when people would be born again, time and time again they would be physically delivered as well.

The reason I believe that is because I know that when they were born again they did immediately speak in tongues. And knowing that the word "salvation" means wholeness, why should people not be healed physically if they are healed spiritually when they are born again? I believe the reason we are not seeing physical healing when they are born again is because it is not taught. And you cannot go beyond what you are taught.

Therefore, when you go to any type of meeting where salvation is advocated, they teach those scriptures that in their mind and opinion deal with salvation, getting saved, but they do not teach that it will heal also. And therefore when people do get born again, they get Christ in them the hope of glory, but they still have the same physical problems. I believe if the Word of God is taught more fully, like I believe it was in the first century, then when the people were born again, they got physically healed, mentally, spiritually, and they were just made whole.

Why not? If God can heal you now when you are a Christian, then He could have healed you when you became one, if you had the need at that time.

So, this whole field of healing just needs a lot of honest, open research in it and not to be too dogmatic about it. And by dogmatic, I mean you point your finger and say, "Look, what are you sick for? If you're a Christian, why don't you get healed?" You know, "Nothing's the matter with me. How come you're sick?"

Well, you just act like that. Sooner or later, the old bug is going to get you too, maybe. And when the old adversary hits you, then you will wish you had not been so adamant with people. You can be so right about everything all the time, until you find out later that you were not quite so right, and some of the rest of the people had a little bit of right too. And then you feel badly that you were so adamant about it. Why not just love people to begin with?

That is why I never mistreat or make accusations to people when they are sick. I never say to people, "Now look, you ought to have more faith," because I know that they have the faith of Jesus Christ so they could not get more. I do not tell them, "Now, have more believing;" or, "If your believing is up, you'd get delivered." I do not do that unless they really bug me and say, "Well look, I believe God, I do everything, but I still got it."

And I say, "Wait a minute, that cannot be right because the Word said as we believe we receive."

You see, I have to stop with that. But we do not point our fingers at people when they are ill or when they get hurt over something. We just love people. Because it does not help a bit to tell you to have believing. You know it? Most likely it makes you feel worse. That's right. When people have a sickness or something, that is no time to tell them to believe. That is the time to tell them how much you love them and how much you pray for them. If you are going to teach them to believe, teach that when they are healthy.

Just like when people are dead, you never talk about death; you talk about life. I have never done a memorial service for anyone that I have not talked about life. You do not want to talk about death, you want to talk about life. The time when people are sick, you do not want to mistreat them and say, "Now look, get your believing up." No. What you do is: you want to tenderly love them with the love of Christ in your heart. And you just join with them in prayer and believing and ministering, whatever you can do the best to help people.

This really gets sort of neat. The Word says, that which is born of the flesh is flesh. And that old flesh is programmed by the adversary to have the possibility of getting sick. Another thing, the Word says the flesh is weak. That's right. If our flesh is weak, and we are weak in the flesh, why should I want to jump on people? Because I am flesh too. If I jump on you, then you should have a right to jump on me because I am flesh too. We do not want to do that.

And that is basically what I have seen so many times from people who do believe in healing. They get so adamant—especially young people because they think they feel so good that they are never going to have an ache or pain. And lo and behold, ten years later you see them sick in the hospital; then they change their tune. You can be tender with God's people from the very day you are born again if you really want to be. Renew your mind. It has nothing to do with age and everything to do with putting on the mind of Christ.

And if there is any time you want to be tender with anyone it is when they are hurt, when they are sick, when there is a death in the family or something. I have never been in favor of preaching a salvation sermon when you have people in a memorial service. That is not the time. Do you want to scare them into heaven because someone has died?

You see, all of that has made Christianity the laughingstock of the world. It is not the wrong usage necessarily of the Word, but it is not the best—and we ought to be doing our best for all people.

You know, sometimes people take the *Power for Abundant Living* class and they are hotter than a firecracker for three months, and then they cool off. The reason for that is the flesh is weak. Their old buddies come back to them or something else happens. It is really just having a knowledge of God's Word and applying it. And I just do not like criticism, because who should be in the authority to criticize? No one. The Word of God says, Paul got to the renewed place and he did not even judge himself. I do that sometimes weeks on end, but I cannot say that I do it years upon end. I am going to get to the place that I do not even judge myself. Paul said that is what he did. And Paul has the same God as I do. Same Christ. Well, if you do not even judge yourself, then certainly you do not sit in a position to criticize or judge anyone else.

And that is why this healing ministry is so alive to me. If we would take our healing ministry and do nothing publicly, Sunday after Sunday, but teach on healing and then minister afterwards, we would have thousands and thousands of people come for the healing campaign. But that is not the ministry whereunto I have been called. My ministry is an unfoldment, as many of you know, of the Word; searching the Word, questing it. And it ties the whole thing together, not just healing.

I am in favor of physical healing because God is, and His Word is. But I am in favor of all healing wholeness, the salvation: mental, physical, spiritual. And that will be basically most of your ministries too. You are the ones that are going to have to hold forth the totality of the Word.

You see, I came out of a background in this field where salvation is the most important. This is what I was taught—to get a person saved so he does not go to hell, or something—and I believed it. Being taught this, I thought that salvation was the most important, until I began to read God's Word and study it. It is God's total

Word that is the most important, not just one segment of it.

If you are not born again right now, then the most important thing for you would be to get born again. But there are a thousand other things in life. And therefore, if it is not salvation you need now, but you need something else, then for you that is the most important at that time. The whole Word of God is important. And in this ministry of healing, it is fantastic.

The thing you stay focused at day after day and week after week is what you do the best. For instance, if our ministry week after week taught the positive side of healing, shared it from the Word, and then ministered to our people; we would become very adept, very sharp. It is just the way things work. The more you use the revelation manifestation in specific instances, the sharper you become in it. Because you renew your mind, and you put on the mind of Christ and you develop yourself.

But basically, our ministry is to cover the great outreach of God's Word all the way from Genesis to Revelation, and that people do not get sidetracked on healing or on speaking in tongues or on receiving word of knowledge, but that all of it is put together so they have a complete spiritual package to walk with.

Basically, I think the Christian church teaches that God gave us doctors. And they quote that Luke was a physician. I recognize that, but I happen to know what the physicians did in Luke's day. How would you like to try a hospital on Luke's ground? No, God did not give us doctors. God blesses doctors the same as He blesses a carpenter, or anyone else that is a believer. Understand that. So, we do not go to the doctor first, we go to God first. God always comes first in our life. No matter where we are, what we do, what has to come up, we always go to God first. If I broke my arm, I would go to

God first. But if that thing did not heal real quick, you know who I would go to? The best arm setter nearest.

Now I want to show you something else. People thank God for saving them in the automobile accident and that they did not die. When our believing gets to where it is supposed to be, why have the automobile accident to begin with? If God can save you inside of it, could He not have saved you before you had one? It would been cheaper all the way round. Same way with breaking my arm. I have to try to so walk by the spirit and believe that I do not even break it. That's right. But if I do, I always go to God first. And if by my believing and the rest of the Word does not get the desired results, I will do the next best thing I know how, and that is find a doctor who can set that arm.

Now, that is the position we hold. And I think it agrees with the Word, unless you want to throw the whole Word out and say, "Look, believe or die." It's okay with me. You can do it, but I have lived too long to know that no one ever believes that big. Paul believed, right? How about Peter? How about Moses—a man who talked face to face with God? Did they believe? Yes. Did Moses die? Yes, so I think that answers the question, doesn't it?

The reason I teach you along this line is because we have had people who in their hearts feel condemned if they ever take an aspirin, or if they have to go to a doctor to get something. I never teach that. I do not know why the adversary lays that on people. He seems to. I do not see anything in the Word why I should ever teach that.

No condemnation to them that are in Christ Jesus. Why should I then be condemned? See, I wouldn't be. But the only thing that could be condemned would be my ego; that would be the condemnation. Suppose the idea that I want to make such a good show in front of everyone, I just do not want to get sick. Get it? Therefore, I do not want them to say, "Well, he had to go to the hospital," or "She had to go to the hospital because if they believed, they would not have gone into the hospital." See? Well, that is ridiculous.

Look at Matthew 8:16:

Matthew 8:16, 17:
When the even was come, they brought unto him many that were possessed with devils: [Possessed. See the accuracy of the word again?] and he [Jesus] cast out the [devils] spirits with *his* word, and healed all [without any distinction] that were sick:

That it might be fulfilled which was spoken by Esaias the prophet saying, Himself took our infirmities [our infirmities are our shortcomings, our sins, our trespasses], and bare *our* sicknesses.

Two things again in that verse: the covering for sin and the consequences of sin. All sickness is basically due to sin. There it is again like it was in 1 Peter 2:24.

In Matthew, Chapter 10, verse 1:

Matthew 10:1a:
And when he [Jesus] had called unto *him* his twelve disciples, [Who are also apostles. You know, every apostle is a disciple, but not every disciple is an apostle.] he gave them power...

He gave to them power. When you were born again, he gave to you power of attorney. Remember? He gave power to you when you were born again. To these apostles...

Matthew 10:1b:
...he gave them power *against* unclean spirits, to cast them out, and to heal all manner [all types and kinds] of sickness and...[diseases].

I do not believe, biblically, there is any doubt about the will of God or the desire of God as far as salvation is concerned; that it is wholeness: mental, physical, spiritual, every which way. And it is all in what God wrought in Christ Jesus.

Also, I have told you that the basic nature of the human body is to heal itself. No one has ever done any appreciable amount of scientific experimentation that I know of on what happens to someone when they are born again—the reaction of that Christ in them on their physical body.

I, perhaps, have as fine a knowledge of this field as any man living, only because I have had the joy of doing the research and watching what happens to people after they are born again in their physical bodies. How their eyes will change if they have some difficulty. How other things will improve. How people who previously had looked sort of emaciated or sick take on a wholesomeness. I really do not know what happens on the inside.

I know that when they speak in tongues for the first time, something tremendous happens to them. Usually, if you feel their hands or touch their heads or something, they are cold. But there happens to be a little law in life when your physical body on the outside feels cold, you are usually nice and warm inside. Do you ever notice that?

For years, I have worked with, observed and watched what would happen to people; analytically, but not in the sense of being critical. They begin to take on something of the beauty of the Christ in them. Things begin to heal in them; things begin to mend. They feel better in almost every category of life. Well, why not? He is a complete savior.

So, I am real blessed when I have the privilege of teaching on the manifestation of healing, because there is so much more involved in this whole manifestation and the whole field of healing than any of us have ever taken the time really to work out.

I think I told you that sickness is death in part or in whole. Furthermore, healing is life. Healing is life in part or in whole, as the need requires. That is what it is all about.

REDEMPTIVE NAMES OF GOD

*Each name starts with the word Jehovah and
each one represents a complete whole.*

The redemptive names of God in the Bible are tremendous learning. God does not change. Malachi 3:6 says:

Malachi 3:6:
…I *am* the LORD, I change not;…

Now, I learned a great deal on healing from the seven usages of God in the Bible and all seven of these are redemptive. The true God is always presented in His redemptive relationship to man. I have checked these all the way through the Bible, and it is remarkable what you can learn about healing. Healing is a lot more than just getting rid of a headache. Healing is to be totally whole.

JEHOVAH-JIREH (*Jehovah Sees and Provides*).

In Genesis, Chapter 22, in verse 13 it says:

Genesis 22:13-14:
And Abraham lifted up his eyes, and looked, and behold behind *him* a ram caught in a thicket by his horns: and Abraham went and took the ram, and offered him up for a burnt offering in the stead of his son.
And Abraham called the name of that place *Jehovah-Jireh:* as it is said *to* this day, In the mount of the LORD it shall be seen.

Jehovah-Jireh means: the Lord sees, or the Lord provides. Someone sings that song, "His eye is on the sparrow." The Lord sees. Not even a hair can fall from your head, the Lord sees. He sees to the extent that He provides. Understand? And the word is *Jehovah-Jireh.*

So, you see, whenever the Word of God uses the word "*Jehovah,*" they never pronounce the vowels. In the old Hebrew the vowels are not there; they would just put a blank. It was too spiritual of a word for them or something.

Now the true God, His name as *Jehovah* always means His dealing with man on a horizontal level. Whenever God deals with you and with me on this level, it is always *Jehovah. Jehovah* is God in relationship to that which He has formed, made and created—in relationship to it.

You know, in Genesis 1, the first verse:

Genesis 1:1a:
In the beginning God...

That is not *Jehovah* because He has nothing to relate to. Therefore, by sheer logic, that word could not be *Jehovah*, or your Bible would fall to pieces. And it is not. It is *Elohim. Elohim* is only used for the greatness of the creation of God, of all of God's creation. And whenever the word "*Elohim*" as God is used, it means God the creator. God is our creator spiritually, but He is our *Jehovah* in our walk. These are redemptive names of God, like *Jehovah-Jireh:* the Lord will provide.

The Lord sees your every need. He is more anxious to answer our prayer than we are to receive it. The Lord sees. And if He does, is He interested in His progeny? Certainly, God is interested in His people. Am I interested in my people? If I have the ability, and you have a need, and you are part of me, and I am part of you; would

I not do my best to meet your need? Surely, God does that for us, His people.

That is why the first thing that appears in the Word of God is to Abraham, and that relationship is one where He tells him, "I am the Lord. I provide. I see your problem. I see where you are. I provide."

He still does. These have never changed. He is still the same *Jehovah* to His people today as He has been throughout all history and all time. And these seven, in all their perfection, make up a great body of healing.

JEHOVAH-RAPHA (*Jehovah Heals*).

In Exodus, Chapter 15, verse 26:

> **Exodus 15:26:**
> …If thou wilt diligently hearken to the voice of the LORD thy God, and wilt do that which is right in his sight, and wilt give ear to his commandments, and keep all his statutes, I will put none of these diseases upon thee, which I have brought upon the Egyptians: for I *am* the LORD that healeth thee.

That is fantastic. He said, if you will diligently hearken to the commandments, and you do not bust them, you will never need it. That is what it says. But if you break the commandments, He said, then you are going to get the diseases. Then He ends up by saying, "I am the Lord that healeth thee." I call that a pretty good Lord.

First, He tells them if they keep all the commandments, they are never going to get sick. Then He says, I will heal you, knowing all the time that man's flesh was weak, and he would flip out on it; and He would still be the healer. Isn't that beautiful?

"I am the Lord." And the word "Lord" here is *Jehovah*. I am *Jehovah* who healeth thee—who healeth thee.

I should explain something to you. A lot of you know

it, but none of you ever know it too well. None of us do. Statements like: I will bring so-and-so on you if you do so-and-so. The reason for that is very simple if you want to understand it. If you want to blame the true God, then nobody can help you. Because when you blame the true God, you contradict a lot of other scriptures. So the simplest thing I know that explains this is an illustration and then people can make up their own mind.

God sets a law. After all, He is the creator, He ought to have a right to make the decision to set the law. And let's say this is the law that he set for Egypt: "Let my children go. If you do not, then you are going to have frogs for breakfast and grasshoppers for dinner. Finally, you are going to have the first born dead." It was not the will of God for Egypt to have frogs, to have the waters turn to blood, or the grasshoppers eat up the place, or the first born to die. But God had set the law. Now, all the Egyptians needed to do was be obedient to God. But they were not. And so those immutable laws of God came to be. Boom!

Suppose I bumped my head up against a wall, a ceiling or something, and I hit it with my unbelief. Then if that represented God, you could say, well, God brought it on me. That is how the old English usage, biblical usage, was understood. God did it—sure, God did it, because He told you to keep your nose clean, and then you bucked up against God. That is why the Word says God brought it on people. Understand? He really did not. He just set the law. They brought it on themselves by disobeying His commandments. We do the same thing today.

God is a God of goodness. If you understand that, as well as a little about the foreknowledge of God, then you can understand predestation and all those other things that come up in the Word. For whom He foreknew, He predestinated.

In His foreknowledge, God knew Egypt would not let the people go. But because He is a God of love and a God of care and could not possess the Egyptians and make them let God's children go—He could not possess them—He gave them the privilege of making up their mind. But in His foreknowledge, He already knew they would buck up against it.

That is predestination. Because of His foreknowledge, He knew you would be here. He knew you were going to be born again. Before the foundations of the world, He knew it. Yet, He never possesses you. He gives you the freedom. It is His foreknowledge that makes God so fantastic. That is the explanation for "I will put none of these diseases upon thee" in verse 26. And that is the explanation for all of men and women everywhere who really want to know. And for those who do not want to know, you cannot do a lousy thing about it.

You have to understand freedom of will, and that the true God does not possess. The adversary does.

Well, that is the Lord who healeth.

JEHOVAH-NISSI (*The Lord Our Banner/Canopy—
God Covers Completely*).

In Exodus, Chapter 17, verse 8:

Exodus 17:8-14:
Then came Amalek, and fought with Israel in Rephidim.

And Moses said unto Joshua, Choose us out men, and go out, fight with Amalek: to morrow I will stand on the top of the hill with the [staff] rod of God in mine hand.

So Joshua did as Moses had said to him, and fought with Amalek: and Moses, Aaron, and Hur went up to the top of the hill.

And it came to pass, when Moses held up his hand,

that Israel prevailed: and when he let down his hand, Amalek prevailed.

But Moses' hands *were* heavy [got tired of being up]; and they took a stone, and put *it* under him, and he sat thereon; and Aaron and Hur [took each one of his arms and] stayed up his hands, [they held them up for him] the one on the one side, and the other on the other side; and his hands were steady until the going down of the sun.

And Joshua discomfited Amalek and his people with the edge of the sword.

And the LORD said unto Moses, Write this *for* a memorial in a book, and rehearse *it* in the ears of Joshua: for I will utterly put out the remembrance of Amalek from under heaven.

We have had a lot of histories that have been found in archaeological work. They have never found anything on Amalek to this day, and I just bet they won't.

Exodus 17:15:
And Moses built an altar, and called the name of it Jehovahnissi:

Jehovah-Nissi. "The Lord our banner" is the center reference in many King James Version Bibles. That is the way it is translated in other translations too, but that is not really it. It does not communicate to our mind in our culture. When you think of a banner, you usually think of a state flag on a little stick that you parade around saying, "Here is my banner, I want to strike. I want to march on Washington." That is my banner, just a little triangular type of thing.

Nevertheless, this banner is a canopy. The Lord is our canopy. Our covering over the top. He is our roof. "Canopy" is the word that is really used. And that is wonderful because in the marriage ceremony, when the groom leads his bride to the wedding party, there are men who hold over the top of them a beautiful woven cloth. And he and she walk under that cloth. That is the covering; that is the canopy. And that is the Oriental, biblical culture of God's covering over that particular husband and wife.

God is our canopy, our banner. He is the one who covers for us. Isn't that beautiful? God our covering. And God's only begotten son, Jesus Christ, when he died for our sins, he covered for us.

Someday, people are going to see that greatness of the Word and how it all fits. When Jesus Christ covered for us, that canopy is totally over that husband and wife; totally over it, completely over them.

And that day, when Moses, Hur, and Aaron did that, God covered Israel. He covered Joshua while he was out there fighting. God covers us. That is *Jehovah-Nissi;* our canopy. Always covering for us.

Jesus Christ always did the Father's will. Therefore, what was he doing here upon earth? Peeling potatoes? Hauling peanuts? No, he was doing the Father's will. Look, the same redemptive things of God, you see in Jesus Christ. For example, they had no food, then a few loaves and fishes—now lots of food. The Lord will what? provide. He healed a whole multitude of sick. The Lord that what? healeth. They were on that little old boat in a storm. Then the Lord Jesus Christ did what for them? covered them. Nothing could happen to them.

See, everything you can pattern back through this. I have never seen it done in any writing, any place, in any theological work. No place has anyone ever thought of really carrying these all the way through the Word; seeing the things that are in the Word, and relating them to this.

It all fits. Jesus Christ is a perfect savior, complete

savior; everything that God is in Christ Jesus (who always did the will of the Father), he just carried out and just made live.

See Moses in this last one; previous it was Abraham. In Jesus Christ, they are *all* tied together—complete savior.

JEHOVAH-SHALOM (*Jehovah Our Peace*).

Now Judges, Chapter 6, verse 21:

Judges 6:21-24:
Then the angel of the LORD put forth the end of the staff that *was* in his hand, and touched the flesh and the unleavened cakes; and there rose up fire out of the rock, and consumed the flesh and the unleavened cakes. Then the angel of the LORD departed out of his sight.

And when Gideon perceived that he *was* an angel of the LORD, Gideon said, Alas, O Lord GOD! for because I have seen an angel of the LORD face to face.

And the LORD said unto him, Peace *be* unto thee; fear not: thou shalt not die.

Then Gideon built an altar there unto the LORD, and called it Jehovahshalom: unto this day it *is* yet in Ophrah of the Abiezrites.

Here is Gideon having this experience. You know, to understand this whole record, go back to verse 16:

Judges 6:16-19:
...the LORD said unto him, Surely I will be with thee, and thou shalt smite the Midianites as one man.

And he said unto him, If now I have found grace in thy sight, then shew me a sign that thou talkest with me.

Depart not hence, I pray thee, until I come unto thee,

and bring forth my present, and set *it* before thee. And he said, I will tarry until thou come again.

And Gideon went in, and made ready a kid,...

Now you just do not make ready a kid in two seconds; they did not have that type of microwave oven. And to do all of this takes time.

Judges 6:19-21:

...and unleavened cakes of an ephah of flour: the flesh he put in a basket, and he put the broth in a pot, and brought *it* out unto him under the oak, and presented *it*.

And the angel of God said unto him, Take the flesh and the unleavened cakes, and lay *them* upon this rock, and pour out the broth. And he did so.

Then the angel of the LORD put forth the end of the staff that *was* in his hand,...

That is what had happened.

Judges 6:24:

[And] Gideon built [this] altar there unto the LORD, [the word "LORD" is *Jehovah*] and called it Jehovah-shalom:...

The Lord our peace—the Lord our peace. See, Gideon was instructed to tear up the Midianites because they were making a mess of things. They should not have been doing it. So, God said to Gideon, "We will go work on them." But Gideon had an opportunity just like a lot of us do; we just want to be sure that we are right, and be sure that we are not at loggerheads.

And so, he said, "Lord, if I have really found favor in your sight, you come on down; you talk with me a little, and you show me a sign. You show me a sign."

"But," he said, "Before you do that I want to bring you a present." So he goes in, and he makes this kid (a goat), getting it all ready. And he took that goat and presented it, plus the soup that he had made, the broth.

Judges 6:21a:
[And] Then the angel of the LORD put forth the end of the staff that *was* in his hand, and touched the flesh and the unleavened cakes; and there rose up fire out of the rock, and consumed the flesh and the unleavened cakes....

And I think that was a good sign to him of what was going to be done to those "Midianite goats." He was going to just burn them up for him. And because of that, he built an altar there, and he called it *Jehovah-Shalom;* the Lord our peace.

The Lord is our what? peace. The Lord is our peace. And that is what the word *"shalom"* means: peace. The Lord is our peace even in those fiery situations.

Jehovah our *Shalom*, our peace.

Sometimes you will hear the word *"salaam,"* which is Arabic. And *shalom* is of the Jewish background. The same words are used in the Far East, like in the Hindi language and others. When people are greeted, like in the King James, it says salute; which is the word *"shalom."* Peace. That is the salute. It is not this usage.

In the Bible, the Blood Covenant, the Salt Covenant and this word *"shalom"* are real interesting pieces of research and work. *Shalom* means "peace"; *bi* is "brother"; *aleichem* is "my." And if someone would say to you: *"Shalom aleichem bi,* peace to you my brother," you can trust him with your life. But as long as they just say *"Shalom,"* do not trust them with anything. But when they say *"bi,* brother," then they will protect whatever they are responsible for because they have called you brother. Once again, the Covenant of Salt, the Covenant of Blood, and this Covenant of Brother are real interesting in the Word.

JEHOVAH-RAAH (*Jehovah Our Shepherd*).

Now we go to Psalm 23. This one some of you know from memory if you went to Sunday school.

Psalms 23:1:
The LORD *is* my shepherd; I shall not want.

The word "Lord" is *Jehovah*. The Lord my shepherd. This is the fifth redemptive name for God in the Old Testament, and it is *Jehovah-Raah*. *Jehovah-Raah:* the Lord my shepherd.

Now, I know that we are not the Lord's sheep, we are Sons of God. But understanding what Jesus Christ came to do for Israel, and what worked out for our good because Israel rejected it, the Lord is still our caretaker.

1 Peter 5:7:
…[Cast] all your care upon him; for he careth for you.

The Lord is our caretaker. He is our shepherd in that sense. Not that we are His sheep, but that we are His sons. And this psalm is really great because the shepherd gives you a beautiful picture of what Jesus Christ did when he was here upon earth. How he took people and he led them in green pastures, or pastures of tenderness as one translation added—which means tender grass. New grass in the spring is always tender. After, it has the hot sun beating on it, and it just subsists. Then it gets hard. But in the spring, the grass is tender. This is what that verse is talking about—tender grass.

Psalms 23:2:
He maketh me to lie down in green pastures: he leadeth me beside the still waters.

He takes us, in other words, to the tender places to feed us. And he leads us beside still waters. A sheep cannot drink from a bouncy creek. If the water has waves, it cannot drink. A sheep will only drink when the water is still. I mean really drink. They go up, and if it is bouncy, they do not get much. But when the waters are still, then the sheep can put its little mouth down there and get something to drink.

That is how wonderful God is! He is our shepherd, and He watches over every sheep. And the ninety-nine that are safely in the fold, remember that one? He goes out in the wilderness looking for that one and brings that one back.[1]

And being our shepherd is also really great, in my mind, because the sheepfold has no door on it. The master, the shepherd, is the door of the sheepfold. He lays across the entrance to the sheepfolds when he rests. And if any enemy is going to come in, they have to walk over him. If anyone is going to get to the sheep, they have to cross over him and get to him first. That's right. He is the door of the sheep gate, the sheepfold. He is the sheep gate.

Jesus Christ, he is the shepherd. The shepherd lays down his life for his sheep. He lays across the entrance-way. He is the door to the sheepfold.

Psalms 23:3:
He restoreth my soul:…

Did you see that one? He restores it.

---

1. Matthew 18:12-14: How think ye? if a man have an hundred sheep, and one of them be gone astray, doth he not leave the ninety and nine, and goeth into the mountains, and seeketh that which is gone astray?
And if so be that he find it, verily I say unto you, he rejoiceth more of that sheep, than of the ninety and nine which went not astray.
Even so it is not the will of your Father which is in heaven, that one of these little ones should perish.

Psalms 23:3:
…he leadeth me in the paths of righteousness [because of his name]…

And his name is my name, therefore, he does not want me in all that unrighteousness, so he leads me in paths of righteousness. Wouldn't you do it for your children?

Psalms 23:4-6:
[Even], though I [would] walk through the valley of the shadow of death, I [would have no] fear no evil: for thou [the shepherd are] with me; thy rod and thy staff…comfort me.

[You even prepare] a table before me in the presence of mine enemies: thou anointest my head with oil; [which is a blessing] my cup runneth over.

Surely goodness and mercy shall follow me all the days of my life: and I will dwell in the house of the LORD for ever.

What a psalm! The Lord, my shepherd—Jesus Christ, the door. He is our protector, the one who takes care of us. I think you understand.

JEHOVAH-TSIDKENU (*Jehovah Our Righteousness*).

The uniqueness of where these appear is also significant in the Word. Now, Jeremiah 23:

Jeremiah 23:1:
Woe be unto the pastors…[who] destroy and scatter the sheep of my pasture! saith the LORD.

Isn't that something? Pastors who destroy and scatter.

Jeremiah 23:2-5:
Therefore thus saith the LORD God of Israel against the pastors that feed my…[sheep]; Ye have scattered my flock, and driven them away, and have not visited them: behold, I will visit upon you the evil of your doings, saith the LORD.

And I will gather the remnant of my flock out of all countries whither I have driven them, and will bring them again to their folds; and they shall be fruitful and increase.

And I will set up shepherds over them which shall feed them: and they shall fear no more, nor be dismayed, neither shall they be lacking, saith the LORD.

Behold, the days come, saith the LORD, that I will raise [up] David a righteous Branch, and a King shall reign and prosper, and shall execute judgment and justice in the earth.

It would be great to have a little more of that today!

Jeremiah 23:6:
In his days Judah shall be saved, and Israel shall dwell safely: and this *is* his name whereby he shall be called, THE LORD OUR RIGHTEOUSNESS.

And that is the sixth one, which is *Jehovah-Tsidkenu:* the Lord our righteousness, *Jehovah* our righteousness. And certainly, there must come verses of scriptures from the epistles into your mind about Jesus Christ being our righteousness. The righteousness of God unto all and upon all that believe.[2] See? Just fantastic!

The Lord, our righteousness—righteousness that executes judgment and justice. And the Lord, as our righteousness, relates itself to the government of the people. That it is to be a righteous government, a righteous justice, a righteous judgment.

The people had been scattered, they were being destroyed. And the reason they were being scattered and destroyed is because the pastors were doing it. They were not laying the Word of God on the people. They were

---

2. Romans 3:22: Even the righteousness of God which is by faith of Jesus Christ unto all and upon all them that believe: for there is no difference:

not rightly dividing the Word. Even though it is addressed to Israel and to Judah, you could take this section of scripture and really work this; applying it in the truth of our times, and have a fantastic teaching.

Jehovah, in relationship to His remnant, His believers, is always righteousness to them. The Lord our righteousness. And He wants the judgments of the people to be in righteousness.

Being written in Jeremiah is quite significant. They called him the Weeping Prophet because he was said to always be crying about something. Had he lived today, they would have said, "You're always negative, Jerry." That is what they would have said in the newspaper about him. "Don't listen to old Jerry. He's always negative. He's always against everything."

He wasn't. He was just highly in favor of God. He had to tell the truth that he got by revelation, and they did not like what he said. Well, he still said it: the Lord our righteousness. And he was right, and all his critics were wrong.

Truth is never a question of the amount of people; it is always a question of quality. Truth is quality, not quantity. And if one person speaks the truth, and the whole world would say he was wrong, he would still be right. It is not in numbers. It is in truth! That's right.

JEHOVAH-SHAMMAH (*Jehovah is Present to Bless*).

Number seven is in Ezekiel. Ezekiel 48:

Ezekiel 48:30-35:
And these *are* the goings out of the city on the north side, four thousand and five hundred measures.

…the gates of the city *shall be* after the names of the tribes of Israel: three gates northward; one gate of Reuben, one gate of Judah, one gate of Levi.

And at the east side four thousand and five hundred: and three gates; and one gate of Joseph, one gate of Benjamin, one gate of Dan.

And at the south side four thousand and five hundred measures:...[then you put] three gates; one gate... [for] Simeon, one gate...[for] Issachar, one gate... [for] Zebulun.

[And] At the west side four thousand and five hundred,...[there you put] three gates; one gate of Gad, one gate of Asher, one [for] of Naphtali.

It was round about eighteen thousand *measures:* and the name of the city from *that* day *shall be,* The LORD *is* there.

The Hebrew is *Jehovah-Shammah*. The Lord is present. *Jehovah* in relationship to His people, He is present —present in that city.

When you study the Word: the arrangement of the city, the walls, and the gates that are in it, even the placement and the names of the different gates are significant in their usage. The walls were placed as a protection for the people on the inside, not as a protection for the people on the outside. That is why the wall is called in the Greek *polis*, which is transliterated into the English word "police."

The *polis* around the city was built to protect, guard, and watch over the inhabitants inside, because these are the people in the fold. These are the people who belong to our city, or our ministry, our work. And they need protection from the outside, from the enemy. That is why they built the wall.

And that is why it is called the *polis*. And the job of the police is to protect the people on the inside from the enemy on the outside. The job is not to whitewash the enemy at the expense of the inhabitants.

These words have continued in usage in the United States: in cities like Annapolis, Maryland and Indianapolis, Indiana. Any city that has a "polis" at the end of it means that it is supposed to be the wall to protect those inhabitants.

The Lord is present. He is present. Present to do what? to take care of His people. But the people of the Lord must also help to take care of themselves. He said, "Build the wall." He said, "Put in the west gates." I think he started out on the north side, and he just keeps going. North, east, south, west—all the way around.

The Lord is present. That is what I want you to see. But the Lord will only be present if you build the wall and put the gates right. That is His promise. He said to go out of the city so far, build a wall four thousand and five hundred measures away, and then put three gates in there after the names of the tribes of Israel: three gates northward; one gate of Reuben, gate of Judah, gate of Levi.

If we build and take care of what we are supposed to do, then the Lord takes care of what He is supposed to do, which means He is present to bless those people.

That is why I am so interested in the household. Because when that household is tight (not the family, the household), the Lord is present. When there is only the family left, He is still present; but not in the sense that He would be if we would built the fence and walls, and had them all intact. For when that household is tight, and they all speak the same thing with the same mind, the Lord is present to bless exceeding, abundantly, above all that we can ask or think. And it is in that household that you have to be tight. It is the household that has the greatest joy in it—greatest blessing.

The Lord is present. The Lord is present. And that is why you see so many blessings, signs, miracles, and wonders. Because when the Lord is present, that is just axiomatic. They come to pass, because the Lord is present!

Those are the seven great redemptive names of God, each one starts with the word "*Jehovah*" and each one represents a complete whole. Like, "the Lord will provide" is complete. "The Lord that healeth" is complete. "The Lord the canopy," he covers completely. "The Lord our peace"; the Lord is peace.

It is significant that love and joy are not mentioned. Because in the fruit of the spirit, there is love, joy, peace. It is because the Lord will provide, He healeth, and He is the canopy, which is all love of God. And the joy of God doing it, therefore He is our peace.

When the Lord is peace, there will be joy, there will be love, for the Lord is the peace. And it is the love of God where He provides. It is a great joy. The Lord is my shepherd. The Lord our righteousness. And the Lord is present—never leave thee nor forsake thee. Isn't that beautiful? The Lord is present; first to the individual, then to the household, the family. Whatever is in there, the Lord will still be present to the faithful. It is just the way God set it up.

TWO PART REDEMPTION

The Passover of the Old Testament was the atonement of which the bread and cup are the token in the Church of grace. In the Old Testament it was the lamb representing the flesh and the blood of that lamb. In the Church of grace, it is Christ who is our Passover, representing his flesh and his blood.

Today, there is an abundance of teaching regarding the shed blood of our Lord and Savior Jesus Christ and its accomplishment for the believer. But, by comparison, there is little teaching today regarding the broken body of our Lord and Savior Jesus Christ and its significance for the believer.

You recall Malachi 3:6 God said:

Malachi 3:6:
For I *am* the LORD, I change not;...

What God was, He is. What He did, He does. What He said, He says. Because He is the same God today as He was to Abraham, to Isaac, and to Jacob, and has been to all of His people through the years.

The fruitfulness of what God accomplished in Christ Jesus for us as believers depends to a marked degree on whether we as believers desire deliverance from sin and sickness, or if we simply want a rationalization of excuses for sin and sickness. Multitudes of Christian believers scattered across the world today still believe that it is God's will for people to be sick. Yet, by the same token, they cry loudly against it ever being God's will for people to sin. They believe that God is the author of sickness and disease, and they proclaimed loudly that sickness basically is only a "dis-ease."

Sickness is more than a "dis-ease." It is either death in part or in total.

I wonder how believers, calling themselves Christians, are ever capable of reconciling the Word of God with such a testimony. Look at the Word of God, for instance, in 1 John, Chapter 1, verse 5, where it says:

1 John 1:5:
...God is light, and in him is no darkness...

How can God be the author of sickness? How can He be the author of sin and disease if God is light, and in Him is no darkness? And any of us who have ever been sick, we know that sickness is more than just a "dis-ease." We know that it is something that makes us less than what God really wanted us to be.

In Galatians, Chapter 3, in verse 13 is a verse of scripture which should become most knowledgeable to all of us who are questing in the integrity and the accuracy of God's Word.

Galatians 3:13a:
Christ hath redeemed us from the curse of the law, being made a curse for us:...

Christ hath redeemed—past tense—Christ hath redeemed us.

Well, ladies and gentlemen, if Christ has redeemed us, then as far as God is concerned, we are redeemed. If I do not manifest it, I am still redeemed. Because what God did does not depend upon my feelings; it depends upon the reality of the presence and the power of God, of that which He wrought in Christ Jesus.

Feelings will come and go, but the Word of God liveth and abideth forever. And when He declares that Christ redeemed us from the curse of the law, then every curse that is under that law we have to be redeemed from, even if we never manifest it. In the will of God, in the work of God, in Christ Jesus; we are redeemed. And it is our opportunity to learn that Word and to so jell it within our lives, to so effervescently endeavor to make it a living reality, that these things come into concretion in our day by day living, according to His revealed Word.

I want to take you now to Deuteronomy 28, to set before you some of these great truths and the greatness of God's Word. It is really the fifteenth verse of Deuteronomy 28 where it all begins; but in order to put this whole thing together and make it living and real for everyone, even people who perhaps do not have a Bible in their hands, I begin with verse 1:

Deuteronomy 28:1-61:
And it shall come to pass, if thou shalt hearken diligently unto the voice of the LORD thy God, to observe *and* to do all his commandments which I command thee this day, that the LORD thy God will set thee on high above all nations of the earth:

And all these blessings shall come on thee, and overtake thee, if thou shalt hearken unto the voice of the LORD thy God.

Blessed *shalt* thou *be* in the city, and blessed *shalt* thou *be* in the field.

Blessed *shall be* the fruit of thy body, and the fruit of thy ground, and the fruit of thy cattle, the increase of thy kine, and the flocks of thy sheep.

Blessed *shall be* thy basket and thy store.

Blessed *shalt* thou *be* when thou comest in, and blessed *shalt* thou *be* when thou goest out.

The LORD shall cause thine enemies that rise up against thee to be smitten before thy face: they shall come out against thee one way, and flee before thee seven ways.

The LORD shall command the blessing upon thee

in thy storehouses, and in all that thou settest thine hand unto; and he shall bless thee in the land which the LORD thy God giveth thee.

The LORD shall establish thee an holy people unto himself, as he hath sworn unto thee, if thou shalt keep the commandments of the LORD thy God, and walk in his ways.

And all people of the earth shall see that thou art called by the name of the LORD; and they shall be afraid of thee.

And the LORD shall make thee plenteous in goods, in the fruit of thy body, and in the fruit of thy cattle, and in the fruit of thy ground, in the land which the LORD sware unto thy fathers to give thee.

The LORD shall open unto thee his good treasure, the heaven to give the rain unto thy land in his season, and to bless all the work of thine hand: and thou shalt lend unto many nations, and thou shalt not borrow.

And the LORD shall make thee the head, and not the tail; and thou shalt be above only, and thou shalt not be beneath; if that thou hearken unto the commandments of the LORD thy God, which I command thee this day, to observe and to do *them:*

And thou shalt not go aside from any of the words which I command thee this day, *to* the right hand, or *to* the left, to go after other gods to serve them.

But [in contrast] it shall come to pass, if thou wilt not hearken unto the voice of the LORD thy God, to observe to do all his commandments and his statutes which I command thee this day; that all these curses shall come upon thee, and overtake thee:

Cursed *shalt* thou *be* in the city, and cursed *shalt* thou *be* in the field.

Cursed *shall be* thy basket and thy store.

Cursed *shall be* the fruit of thy body, and the fruit of thy land, the increase of thy kine, and the flocks of thy sheep.

Cursed *shalt* thou *be* when thou comest in, and cursed *shalt* thou *be* when thou goest out.

The LORD shall send upon thee cursing, vexation, and rebuke, in all that thou settest thine hand unto for to do, until thou be destroyed, and until thou perish quickly; because of the wickedness of thy doings, whereby thou hast forsaken me.

The LORD shall make the pestilence cleave unto thee, until he have consumed thee from off the land, whither thou goest to possess it.

The LORD shall smite thee with a consumption, and with a fever, and with an inflammation, and with an extreme burning, and with the sword, and with blasting, and with mildew; and they shall pursue thee until thou perish.

And thy heaven that *is* over thy head shall be brass, and the earth that is under thee *shall be* iron.

The LORD shall make the rain of thy land powder and dust: from heaven shall it come down upon thee, until thou be destroyed.

The LORD shall cause thee to be smitten before thine enemies: thou shalt go out one way against them, and flee seven ways before them: and shalt be removed into all the kingdoms of the earth.

And thy carcase shall be meat unto all fowls of the air, and unto the beasts of the earth, and no man shall fray *them* away.

The LORD will smite thee with the botch of Egypt, and with the emerods [hemorrhoids], and with the scab, and with the itch, whereof thou canst not be healed.

The LORD shall smite thee with madness, and blindness, and astonishment of heart:

And thou shalt grope at noonday, as the blind gropeth in darkness, and thou shalt not prosper in thy ways: and thou shalt be only oppressed and spoiled evermore, and no man shall save *thee*.

Thou shalt betroth a wife, and another man shall lie with her: thou shalt build an house, and thou shalt not dwell therein: thou shalt plant a vineyard, and shalt not gather the grapes thereof.

Thine ox *shall be* slain before thine eyes, and thou shalt not eat thereof: thine ass *shall be* violently taken away from before thy face, and shall not be restored to thee: thy sheep *shall be* given unto thine enemies, and thou shalt have none to rescue *them*.

Thy sons and thy daughters *shall be* given unto another people, and thine eyes shall look, and fail *with longing* for them all the day long: and *there shall be* no might in thine hand.

The fruit of thy land, and all thy labours, shall a nation which thou knowest not eat up; and thou shalt be only oppressed and crushed alway:

So that thou shalt be mad for the sight of thine eyes which thou shalt see.

The LORD shall smite thee in the knees, and in the legs, with a sore botch that cannot be healed, from the sole of thy foot unto the top of thy head.

The LORD shall bring thee, and thy king which thou shalt set over thee, unto a nation which neither thou nor thy fathers have known; and there shalt thou serve other gods, wood and stone.

And thou shalt become an astonishment, a proverb, and a byword, among all nations whither the LORD shall lead thee.

Thou shalt carry much seed out into the field, and shalt gather *but* little in; for the locust shall consume it.

Thou shalt plant vineyards, and dress *them*, but shalt neither drink *of* the wine, nor gather *the grapes;* for the worms shall eat them.

Thou shalt have olive trees throughout all thy coasts, but thou shalt not anoint *thyself* with the oil; for thine olive shall cast *his fruit.*

Thou shalt beget sons and daughters, but thou shalt not enjoy them; for they shall go into captivity.

All thy trees and fruit of thy land shall the locust consume.

The stranger that *is* within thee shall get up above thee very high; and thou shalt come down very low.

He shall lend to thee, and thou shalt not lend to him: he shall be the head, and thou shalt be the tail.

Moreover all these curses shall come upon thee, and shall pursue thee, and overtake thee, till thou be destroyed; because thou hearkenedst not unto the voice of the LORD thy God, to keep his commandments and his statutes which he commanded thee:

And they shall be upon thee for a sign and for a wonder, and upon thy seed for ever.

Because thou servedst not the LORD thy God with joyfulness, and with gladness of heart, for the abundance of all *things;*

Therefore shalt thou serve thine enemies which the LORD shall send against thee, in hunger, and in thirst, and in nakedness, and in want of all *things:* and he shall put a yoke of iron upon thy neck, until he have destroyed thee.

The LORD shall bring a nation against thee from far, from the end of the earth, *as swift* as the eagle

flieth; a nation whose tongue thou shalt not understand;

A nation of fierce countenance, which shall not regard the person of the old, nor shew favour to the
young:

And he shall eat the fruit of thy cattle, and the fruit
of thy land, until thou be destroyed: which *also* shall
not leave thee *either* corn, wine, or oil, *or* the increase of thy kine, or flocks of thy sheep, until he
have destroyed thee.

And he shall besiege thee in all thy gates, until thy
high and fenced walls come down, wherein thou
trustedst, throughout all thy land: and he shall besiege thee in all thy gates throughout all thy land,
which the LORD thy God hath given thee.

And thou shalt eat the fruit of thine own body, the
flesh of thy sons and of thy daughters, which the
LORD thy God hath given thee, in the siege, and in
the straitness, wherewith thine enemies shall distress
thee:

So that the man *that is* tender among you, and very
delicate, his eye shall be evil toward his brother,
and toward the wife of his bosom, and toward the
remnant of his children which he shall leave:

So that he will not give to any of them of the flesh
of his children whom he shall eat: because he hath
nothing left him in the siege, and in the straitness,
wherewith thine enemies shall distress thee in all thy
gates.

The tender and delicate woman among you, which
would not adventure to set the sole of her foot upon
the ground for delicateness and tenderness, her eye
shall be evil toward the husband of her bosom, and
toward her son, and toward her daughter,

And toward her young one that cometh out from between her feet, and toward her children which she shall bear: for she shall eat them for want of all *things* secretly in the siege and straitness, wherewith thine enemy shall distress thee in thy gates.

If thou wilt not observe to do all the words of this law that are written in this book, that thou mayest fear this glorious and fearful name, THE LORD THY GOD;

Then the LORD will make thy plagues wonderful, and the plagues of thy seed, *even* great plagues, and of long continuance, and sore sicknesses, and of long continuance.

Moreover he will bring upon thee all the diseases of Egypt, which thou wast afraid of; and they shall cleave unto thee.

Also every sickness, and every plague, which *is* not written in the book of this law, them will the LORD bring upon thee, until thou be destroyed.

What a tremendous record from God's Word! And in many respects, how timely! How it would speak to our day and our time!

Perhaps we need to clarify that when it says that God brings it on them, it is simply because of the first part of the chapter where we read where God sets the law, to keep His commandments. Notice that the one great truth He gave to them in verse 14: "thou shalt not go aside from any of those commandments or any of the words which I command thee this day, either to the right hand or to the left, just stay put," He said, "on my Word." Basically, because the moment you turn to the right or the left, you get off of God's Word, you go after other gods to serve them. And the first commandment that God ever gave was that we were to love God and have no other gods before Him.

Exodus 20:2, 3:
I *am* the LORD thy God, which have brought thee out of the land of Egypt, out of the house of bondage.

Thou shalt have no other gods before me.

He had set this law. And when the people began to break that law, they broke themselves upon God's law.

And all of that record, from verse 15 on, is a record of the curse upon the people who broke the law of God. And yet in Galatians 3, it said:

Galatians 3:13:
Christ hath [past tense] redeemed us [past tense] from the curse of the law,...

If we are redeemed, then we are redeemed. What a glorious walk it should be to the Christian! What a declaration of boldness! What a declaration of the greatness of what God wrought in Christ! We as Christian believers ought to manifest across our nation, in our state, in our communities, wherever we live; he hath redeemed us.

This record from Deuteronomy you can see for yourself that the vast majority of the curse was sickness, was disease. And from those things, Christ redeemed us. But those children of Israel, as long as they obeyed God's command, they were a tremendous people.

Between two-and-a-half to three million of them wandered in the wilderness under the most adverse conditions, without all of these things that we feel today we need; they did not have. As it says in Deuteronomy 29:5:

Deuteronomy 29:5:
And I have led you forty years in the wilderness: your clothes are not waxen old upon you, and thy shoe is not waxen old upon thy foot.

They wandered for 40 years, and then this wonderful record in Psalms; listen to verse 37:

Psalms 105:37:
He brought them forth [out of Egypt] with silver and gold: and *there was* not one feeble *person* among their tribes.

Not one feeble person among all of those two-and-a-half to three million. And the record in the Word of God is that they wandered for 40 years in the wilderness. Not one person was ever sick.

Ladies and gentlemen, when I read that kind of word from God's Word from Deuteronomy, realizing what I read from Galatians, I know what a tremendous God He is! And since He is the Lord who does not change, He has to be the same way today as He was then. It then becomes our privilege and our joy to find out exactly what did God establish at that time, and what is placed for us as believers that we could walk before God without one feeble knee among us.

Now Exodus, Chapter 2.

God raised up a man who was 80 years old before he began his life's work. His name was Moses. And the record in verse 23 of Exodus 2 says:

Exodus 2:23-25:
And it came to pass in process of time, that the king of Egypt died: and the children of Israel sighed by reason of the bondage, and they cried, and their cry came up unto God by reason of the bondage.
And God heard their groaning, and God remembered his covenant with Abraham, with Isaac,...with Jacob.
And God looked upon the children of Israel, and God had respect unto *them.*

God had made a covenant. That which God has promised, He is not only able, but He is willing to perform. And when the people turned to Him in the bondage in Egypt, and they cried to the true God, then God heard their cries, and He raised up a man by the name of Moses who was 80 years old. And it was he to whom God gave the responsibility of leading them out of Egypt towards the Promised Land.

In Exodus, Chapter 3, in verse 10, He says:

Exodus 3:10:
Come now therefore, and I will send thee [Moses] unto Pharaoh, that thou mayest bring forth my people the children of Israel out of Egypt.

Chapter 12 of Exodus, we begin with verse 3:

Exodus 12:3-11:
Speak ye unto all the congregation of Israel, saying, In the tenth *day* of this month they shall take to them every man a lamb, according to the house of *their* fathers, a lamb for an house:

And if the household be too little for the lamb, let him and his neighbour next unto his house take *it* according to the number of the souls; every man according to his eating shall make your count for the lamb.

Your lamb shall be without blemish, a male of the first year: ye shall take *it* out from the sheep, or from the goats:

And ye shall keep it up until the fourteenth day of the same month: and the whole assembly [the whole congregation, the whole church] of Israel shall kill it in the evening.

And they shall take of the blood [of that lamb], and strike *it* on the two side posts and on the upper door post of the houses, wherein they shall eat it.

And they shall eat the flesh in that night, roast with fire, and unleavened bread; *and* with bitter *herbs* they shall eat it.

Eat not of it raw, nor sodden at all with water, but

roast *with* fire; his head with his legs, and with the purtenance thereof.

And ye shall let nothing of it remain until the morning; and that which remaineth of it until the morning ye shall burn with fire.

And thus shall ye eat it; *with* your loins girded, your shoes on your feet, and your staff in your hand; and ye shall eat it in haste: it *is* the LORD'S passover.

It is the Lord's Passover. God had said He was going to send Moses to pharaoh to lead His children out of Israel, where they had been enslaved for almost 400 years. When the children of Israel cried to God, God heard their cry. He sent a man to lead them out of that captivity, and He told them exactly what to do.

He told them to get a lamb, kill that lamb and to sprinkle the blood on the two side posts and the upper post to the door. Then He told them to eat the flesh of the lamb. Ladies and gentlemen, the eating of the flesh of the lamb you could say would satisfy their hunger, but he did not feed it to them because they were hungry.

And it seems really silly when you think of God Almighty saying to them, I want you to take the blood of the lamb and sprinkle it on the side posts and on the upper post of the door. What good is it? Well, I will tell you what good it is. It is the word of the Lord. That is what makes it good, because the Lord said do this. And I suppose the people had been in enslavement so long, they decided they might as well do it, for the Word of God says they did.

In this lamb you have two things represented: the flesh of the lamb and the blood of the lamb. Both the blood and the flesh are equally important in this record to the children of Israel. People, if God, under the law, can take approximately three million people, and for 40 years have them to wander under the most adverse conditions in a desert land with no sickness and no disease —if God did that under law, certainly, under grace, God could take two-and-a-half or three million and wander under the most adverse conditions for more than 40 years.

Believing is acting upon God's promise. God said, "Take this lamb, sprinkle the blood on the door posts and on the lintel at the top, then eat the flesh of the lamb." And it was when they ate that they were healed completely. Not before they ate, but when they ate the flesh of the lamb. The flesh of the lamb was given for their healing. The blood was put on the door posts and so forth so that it would cover them, that no evil could touch their lives.

These words were spoken to the children of Israel by a man named Moses. A man who had formerly killed someone, and for 40 years had to leave his people to save his own neck. A man who was slow of speech, who had to have a brother to speak for him. But somehow or other, he was a mighty man of God because he had turned to God. And God had blessed him, and God had honored the believing of this man Moses.

Yes, I know that these words were spoken by Moses. And I have heard it a thousand times through the years, "If only we had a Moses back. If only we had a Peter back. If only we had a Paul back. What a great day it would be for the church if we had men like that—like Moses, like Peter, like Paul, like John."

We have Moses. We have the prophesy. We have the Word of God. And any man of God today who speaks God's Word is as much a man of God as Moses was. The Word is as much God's Word today as it was when Moses spoke it, as long as it is the Word. This is why, note verse 11 again:

Exodus 12:11:
…thus shall ye eat it; *with* your loins girded, your

shoes on your feet, and your staff in your hand; and ye shall eat it in haste: [because it is what?] it *is* the LORD'S passover.

What a tremendous record! Down through the years, people have tried to tell me that the Last Supper Jesus ate was the Passover. The Bible says they sat down, they ate. This one here said, stand up—no sitting down. Why? Because they always eat the Passover standing up. They were getting ready to flee before the children of Egypt. The children of Israel were getting ready to flee before the armies of Pharaoh. And so, God said "This night, you sprinkle the blood over it, you eat the flesh of the lamb, you stand up. You have your shoes on your feet, your loins girded, your staff in your hand, you are ready to move out." And they moved out.

And again, ladies and gentlemen: 40 years, not one feeble knee among the entire bunch because of two great things. The flesh of the lamb which they ate, and when they ate it, they ate it with believing that what God had said, God had meant. God reckoned wholeness to their physical body, and for 40 years they wandered in the wilderness without one feeble knee.[1]

And they got out of Egypt because of the covering of the blood which had been sprinkled on the door posts and on the lintels. This is the Lord's Passover. Remember that.

Look at 1 Corinthians, Chapter 5, verse 7; the last part of the verse:

1 Corinthians 5:7b:
...For even Christ our passover is sacrificed...

---

1. Deuteronomy 29:5: And I have led you forty years in the wilderness: your clothes are not waxen old upon you, and thy shoe is not waxen old upon thy foot.

Sacrificed—past tense. To the children of Israel, the sprinkling of the blood, the eating of the flesh was the Lord's passover. But unto us we have something better, for it is Christ. Christ is our Passover. He is the one who was sacrificed for us. This is why Christ has to be the end of the law.

Turn to Matthew, Chapter 8; see what Christ, our Passover, really accomplished for us in verse 17:

Matthew 8:17:
…Himself took our infirmities, [our sicknesses, as the text reads]…

Himself—Jesus Christ took our sins and bare our sicknesses himself—Jesus Christ. Himself, Jesus Christ, took our sins and he bare our, what? sicknesses. Two things he did: He took our sins upon himself, and he bore our sicknesses.

Ladies and gentlemen, if Jesus Christ himself took our sins and he bore our sicknesses, then your sins and mine are they any longer upon us? Your sicknesses and mine are they any longer upon us? He bore them. He took them. What a tremendous revelation!

We have, for the most part, only taught one side of redemption. And that is that he took our sins; that he bore our sins. Like it says in Corinthians:

2 Corinthians 5:21:
…[he] who knew no sin [became sin]; that we might [become] the righteousness of God in him.

This is what we have lauded to the sky. This is what we have taught for the most part among Christian believers, which I call the teaching of only one side of redemption. And we have taught this at the expense of the other side, where he said he bore our sicknesses.

In 1 Peter, Chapter 2, verse 24, listen to this:

1 Peter 2:24:
Who his own self bare our sins in his own body on the tree [the cross], that we, being dead to sins, should live unto righteousness: by whose stripes [by whose stripes] ye were healed.

In the Old Testament, they looked forward to the coming of the Lord Jesus Christ. Those of us who live after the day of the resurrection and the day of the fullness of the holy spirit, we look back to it. By his stripes we were, past tense, healed.

Well, ladies and gentlemen, if I never manifest it in my life, as far as God is concerned, I was still healed in Christ Jesus. What a tremendous foundation! What a solid rock this puts under the believing of a son and daughter of God today!

Look at the book of Psalms:

Psalms 103:3:
Who forgiveth all thine iniquities [sin];…

Who forgiveth all—not 99 and 44/100th, but all.

Psalms 103:3:
Who forgiveth all thine iniquities [sin]; who healeth all thy diseases…

Ladies and gentlemen, we either have to say this is God's Word or we have to say God lied. This is the declaration of the Word. These are the Word pictures from the Word as to what God wrought for us in Christ Jesus; when he who knew no sin became sin, so that we might become the righteousness of God. Who in his own self bore our sins, and by his stripes we were healed.

In the book of Isaiah, Chapter 53, listen to this tremendous record in verse 5:

Isaiah 53:5:
…he *was* wounded for our transgressions, *he was* bruised for our iniquities: the chastisement of our peace *was* upon him; and with his stripes we are healed.

Always two elements. Always two things in the redemption; like the flesh of the lamb, like the blood of the lamb. Always two things. The covering for sin, and the covering for the consequences of sin, namely sickness.

In the Gospel of Mark, Chapter 2 in verse 5, listen to this:

Mark 2:5:
When Jesus saw their faith, [their believing] he said unto the sick of the palsy, Son, thy sins be forgiven thee.

Verse 11:

Mark 2:11:
I say unto thee, Arise,…take up thy bed, and go thy way into thine house.

Again, two things Jesus declared; that his sins were gone, and that he would take up his bed, his pallet, and go home healed. Always two in the Word.

In Matthew, Chapter 4, the later part of verse 23 talking about:

Matthew 4:23:
…Jesus went about all Galilee,…healing all manner of sickness and all manner of disease among the people.

Was Jesus Christ doing God's will? Definitely. Therefore, if it would be God's will to send sickness and disease, then Jesus Christ went against God's will. And this Jesus could not do, because Jesus was God's only begotten Son. He always did the will of the Father.

In the Gospel of John, verse 7:

John 19:7:
The Jews answered him, We have a law, and by our law he ought to die, because he made himself the Son of God.

In verse 6, going back up:

John 19:6:
When the chief priests therefore and officers saw him, they cried out, saying, Crucify *him*, crucify *him*. Pilate saith unto them, Take ye him, and crucify *him*: for I find no fault in him.

Here also in this chapter, it talks about that Jesus Christ bore the cross, verse 17:

John 19:17:
And he bearing his cross went forth into a place called *the place* of a skull, which is called in the Hebrew Golgotha:

He, Jesus, bearing his cross went forth into a place called the place of the skull. Remember, we read that he is our Passover. Here it said, "…he bearing his cross." The cross Jesus Christ bore was not the wooden one, because the record in God's Word says that the wooden cross was born by Simon of Cyrene. It was he who bore the cross to Calvary.

But what cross did Jesus bear? The cross Jesus Christ bore is that he was our Passover. Everything that is upon us, he took it upon himself. That was the cross he bore for you and for me.

The great declaration, of course, is in that wonderful verse of scripture in Colossians, Chapter 2. In Colossians 2:14 when he bore his cross, which is your sin and mine, your sickness and mine, he did what verse 14 says in Colossians 2:

Colossians 2:14:

Blotting out the handwriting of ordinances that was against us, which was contrary to us, [he, Jesus Christ] and took it out of the way, nailing it to his cross;

That explains his cross. His cross was that which he bore for us. He bore our sins and he bore our sicknesses. This was nailed to the cross. It was doubled. Our names written on the outside with anything against us.

In the Gospel of Matthew in Chapter 26, look at the record in verse 28:

Matthew 26:28:

For this is my blood of the new testament, which is shed for many for the remission of sins.

The blood was shed for many. All who believe, his blood was shed for their remission. And you know what remission is? Remission is for the unsaved sinner. When he gets saved, he gets remission. Everything up until that day is totally remitted. All sin is wiped away. As far as the east is from the west, and as deep as the deepest sea. And he will remember them no more.

That is what he is saying to us here in this verse 28. Remember this as we look at something in John, which gives the other side of the redemption coin in a word picture. In Matthew, we were talking about the blood; in John, we are talking about the bread of God.

In John, Chapter 6 and in verse 33:

John 6:33:

For the bread of God is he [Jesus Christ] which cometh down from heaven, and giveth life unto the world.

And in verse 35:

John 6:35:
And Jesus said unto them, I am the bread of life:…

I am the bread of life. He is both the bread of life for us and to us. He is also the shed blood to us and for us. Back to Matthew:

Matthew 26:26, 27:
And as they were eating, Jesus took bread, and blessed *it*, and brake *it*, and gave *it* to the disciples, and said, Take, eat; this is my body.

And he took the cup, and gave thanks, and gave *it* to them, saying, Drink ye all of it;

He is our Passover. He said, "This is my body." He said, "This is my cup."

Verse 28:

Matthew 26:28:
For this [cup] is my blood of the new testament, which is shed for many for the remission of sins.

Only two things—from the very day that God instituted the Passover, before Moses led the children of Israel out, all the way through the Word of God up until this time.

Now turn to a church epistle in 1 Corinthians; after the day of Pentecost, addressed to us.

1 Corinthians, Chapter 11, verse 23:

1 Corinthians 11:23-30:
For I have received of the Lord that which also I delivered unto you, That the Lord Jesus [Christ, the Lord Jesus] the *same* night in which he was betrayed took bread:

And when he had given thanks, he brake *it*, and said, Take, eat: this is my body, which is broken for you: this do in remembrance of me.

After the same manner also *he took* the cup, when he had supped, saying, This cup is the new testament in my blood: this do ye, as oft as ye drink *it*, in remembrance of me.

For as often as ye eat this bread, and drink this cup, ye do shew [proclaim] the Lord's death [what he accomplished for us, until his return] till he come.

Wherefore whosoever shall eat this bread, and drink *this* cup of the Lord, unworthily, shall be guilty of the body and blood of the Lord.

But let a man examine himself, and so let him eat of *that* bread, and drink of *that* cup.

For he that eateth and drinketh unworthily, eateth and drinketh damnation to himself, not discerning the Lord's body.

For this cause [because they were not discerning the Lord's body] many *are* weak and sickly among you, and many sleep [or die prematurely as the text gives it].

Why was the Corinthian weak and sickly? Why were the people dying prematurely? The Word of God says that they were carnal Christians.

In Chapter 1 of Corinthians, in verse 10, the Word says:

1 Corinthians 1:10:
…I beseech you, brethren, by the name of our Lord Jesus Christ, that ye all speak the same thing, and *that* there be no divisions among you; but *that* ye be perfectly joined together in the same mind and in the same judgment [same opinion].

They were not all speaking the same thing. There were divisions among them because some said, "Well, we have a great Apollos here, or we have a great Cephas.[2] We have this following, we have that following."

That is why in Chapter 3 and in verse 3 we read:

1 Corinthians 3:3:
For ye are yet carnal: for whereas *there is* among you envying, and strife, and divisions, are ye not carnal, and walk as men?

Ye are yet carnal, not working at all according to the revelation of God's Word. The Christian church is well aware today of what the blood of Christ means to the believer, but they have failed to properly discern the Lord's body. The Passover of the Old Testament was the atonement of which the bread and cup are the token in the Church of grace. In the Old Testament it was the lamb representing the flesh and the blood of that lamb. In the Church of grace, it is Christ who is our Passover, representing his flesh and his blood.

That is why we read in 1 Corinthians 10:16:

1 Corinthians 10:16:
The cup of blessing which we bless, is it not the communion of the blood of Christ? The bread which we break, is it not the communion of the body of Christ?

Two things he is to us and for us. Remember in Exodus 15:26, we have one of the seven redemptive names of God. Namely, the name *Jehovah-Rapha*. In Malachi, I gave you the record:

Malachi 3:6:
…I *am* the LORD, I change not;…

One of those seven redemptive names of God—there

---

2. 1 Corinthians 1:12: Now this I say, that every one of you saith, I am of Paul; and I of Apollos; and I of Cephas; and I of Christ.

are only seven—one of them is found in Exodus 15:26 where he says:

> **Exodus 15:26:**
> I *am* the LORD [who]…healeth thee.

In Hebrews 13:8, it says:

> **Hebrews 13:8:**
> Jesus Christ [is] the same yesterday, and to day, and for ever.

If the Lord changes not, if He is the one who heals us and He set up the lamb in the Old Testament for the children of Israel; He set up something much better for us when He set up his only begotten Son as the lamb of God who is to be slain from the foundation of the world.

This is why Jesus Christ is called the Lamb of God, for he took upon himself that which formerly was represented by the lamb in the children of Israel. He was the lamb of God. He is the one who became sin. He is the one; by his stripes we were and are healed.

When we come to the table of the bread and cup, you never depend upon your own feeling. Nor do you depend upon your own need. But you and I must come depending upon His Word and what He wrought for us in Christ Jesus with believing.

It is not just the doing of it. It is not just the doing of taking the bread and the cup, but as the Word says, "do this in remembrance of me." It is not the doing, it is doing it in remembrance. It is doing it in remembrance of what he accomplished for us.

That is why he said, "This is my body, which is broken for you: this do ye in remembrance of me. This is my blood which is shed for you: this do you in remembrance of me."

It is in the remembrance, thereof, as to what God wrought in Christ that we bring to ourselves the deliverance; not only from sin, but from the consequences of sin—sickness and disease.

This is why he bore our sicknesses, and he bore our sin. It is by his stripes that we were healed. Not by something that any other individual may have wrought.

And, ladies and gentlemen, we have these great truths in the same verse of scripture. How can we boldly declare one and deny the other? For it is that same God who wrought this for us in Christ Jesus, our Lord. Therefore, the bread represents his broken body, and the cup represents his shed blood for the covering of our sin.

My friends, when we have our sins covered and cleansed within; when we have our sicknesses, the consequences of sin removed; we have redemption—the wholeness of that redemption which God gave to us in Christ Jesus our Lord.

PARTAKERS OF DIVINE NATURE

In God's sight, as partakers of divine nature, you are righteous, you are justified, and you are already glorified.

I would very much like for our people around the nations of the world to understand and appreciate the greatness of the subject that I want to share with you entitled: "Partakers of Divine Nature."

Just because you cannot feel something or you cannot explain it, does not mean something cannot be real, genuine, or experienced. My being seated at this desk and you seated out there, can you feel the air around you? No. But it must be real and genuine for we are still experiencing life, and we are still breathing. How about light? We cannot feel it, and yet we can see, we can make our notes and look at our Bibles.

You know we have, from birth, been so conditioned by our five senses that we have erroneously come to believe that only what we can see, hear, smell, taste, or touch is real; when in truth it is not.

2 Corinthians, Chapter 4, verse 18:

2 Corinthians 4:18:
While we look not at the things which are seen, but at the things which are not seen: for the things which are seen *are* temporal; but the things which are not seen *are* eternal.

The man of the five senses—the natural man—no matter how intelligent, has never produced a civilization that it did not ruin; nor has it developed an educational system of philosophy and metaphysics that did not corrupt and destroy.

And the reason for that is given in 1 Corinthians, Chapter 2, verse 14:

1 Corinthians 2:14:
[For] the natural man receiveth not the things of the Spirit of God: for they are foolishness unto him: neither can he know *them*,...

The natural man—the man of body and soul—who gets all of his information via the five senses; seeing, hearing, smelling, tasting or touching; he just cannot know God. He cannot know. He cannot receive things of the Spirit, of God.

As a matter of fact, all of those things are:

1 Corinthians 2:14:
...foolishness unto him: neither can he know *them*, because they are spiritually discerned.

Things in the natural realm can be known by the five senses, but things that are of the spirit must be known spiritually.

Our day and time, our civilization in which you and I are living, has failed because of Churchianity and religious Christianity. Metaphysical and philosophical religions do not have, and they cannot offer, eternal life. They, from generation to generation, revamp the wrappings only.

So, the man of the five senses is left with his unworthiness, a sense of sin, and an inferiority complex. And that is why natural man has jealousies, bitterness and hatred.

But man was never made to be this way. God wanted winners; He wanted spiritual athletes. He wanted His own family, His own children. And because of God's great love from even before the foundations of the world, God conceived a second birth; which in the Word of God is called the New Birth in 2 Peter.

2 Peter, Chapter 1, verse 4:

2 Peter 1:4:
Whereby [or by which] are given unto us exceeding great and precious promises: [in order] that by these ye might be partakers of the divine nature, having escaped the corruption that is in the world through lust.

And the word "corruption" means where you were getting worse and worse and worse. By these great and precious promises: in order that by these (the great and precious promises of God) ye might be partakers (share fully of the divine nature) having escaped the corruption of that (of getting worse and worse and worse).

Because in verse 3, preceding this great verse 4, it says:

2 Peter 1:3:
…through the knowledge of him that hath called us to glory and virtue:

And the word "virtue" means superior excellence. God has called us to glory and superior excellence. So by His own glory and superior excellence we are given —there is given to us the exceeding great and what? precious promises. That great truth almost leaves me breathless. Who of us has really believed this to the end of magnifying it in our daily living? We cannot feel the new birth, so it makes such little difference in most people's lives.

And yet in the new birth, we have Colossians 1:27:

Colossians 1:27:
To whom God [desired to] would make known what *is* the riches of the glory of this mystery among the Gentiles; which is Christ in you, the hope of glory:

He has called us to glory and superior excellence. And then this verse talks about that glory again; which is Christ in you, the hope of glory. What a tremendous truth! We were natural men, but now we are sons of God.

1 John, the epistle, Chapter 3, verse 1:

1 John 3:1:
Behold, what manner of love the Father hath bestowed upon us, that we should be called the sons of God: therefore the world knoweth us not, because it knew him not.

Verse 2:

1 John 3:2:
Beloved, now are we the sons of God, and it doth not yet appear what we shall be:...

Right now, we are sons of God. We are not friends of God as Abraham was. That would have been wonderful, if you think of what Abraham accomplished and how God worked with him, yet Abraham was just a friend of God. It says so in the book of James.

Chapter 2 of James, verse 23:

James 2:23:
And the scripture was fulfilled which saith, Abraham believed God, and it was imputed unto him for righteousness: and he was called the Friend of God.

We are not friends of God as Abraham was; we are sons of God. And the reason this has been so hard for people to believe and to admit to is because of our sense-knowledge upbringing. Because we only believed in what we could see, hear, smell, taste, or touch. And as I said at the opening, just because you cannot feel something or explain it does not mean something is not real or genuine; or that it cannot be experienced.

We are not only not friends of God, we are sons of God; and we are not servants of God either.

Galatians, Chapter 4, verse 1:

> **Galatians 4:1-5:**
> Now I say, *That* the heir, as long as he is a child, differeth nothing from a servant, though he be lord of all.
> But is under tutors and governors until the time appointed of the father.
> Even so we, when we were children, were in bondage under the [tutors or ordinances] elements of the world [the elementary things]:
> But when the fulness of the time was come, God sent forth his Son, made of a woman, made under the law.
> To redeem them that were under the law, that we might receive [sonship]…

Not adoption—we are not adopted; we are born again. And to be born again means you have the seed of God in Christ in you. You are partakers of God's divine nature through Jesus Christ.

Verse 6:

> **Galatians 4:6, 7:**
> And because ye are sons, God hath sent forth the Spirit of his Son into your hearts, crying, Abba, Father [Father, Father].
> Wherefore thou art no more a servant, but a son; and if a son, then an heir of God through Christ.

We are sons of God in a perpendicular relationship. We are servants to our fellow men, but I hear people pray or talk about being servants of God. We are not; we are sons of God. If you say that you are a servant of God, thinking this way, that is contrary to God's Word.

Now, I know it is a shocker when you talk to people

how we are not friends nor servants of God. Because all
they have ever thought about is that if they could even
be a friend of God, they would be tickled. Or if they
could just serve God as a servant, they would be grateful. We have never magnified in our hearts and lives
that we are partakers of God's divine nature. And that
we have His glory and His superior excellence within
us. As natural men, we were fully failure conscious; condemnation conscious. Now, we must become God and
Son conscious. You have to get a new sense of God. You
have to get a new vision in your mind.

Look at Colossians, Chapter 1, verse 11:

Colossians 1:11, 12:
Strengthened with all might, according to his glorious power, unto all patience and longsuffering with
joyfulness;
Giving thanks unto the Father, which hath [or who
has] made us meet [adequate] to be partakers of the
inheritance of the saints in light:

"Made us meet" is adequate; He has made us adequate.
"Partakers" is to enjoy our share. He has made us adequate to enjoy our share of the inheritance of the saints
in the light, because we are partakers of His divine nature.

Verse 13:

Colossians 1:13:
Who hath [past tense] delivered us [past tense] from
the power of darkness, and hath translated [and the
word "translated" is has given us citizenship]...into
his kingdom [by the work] of his dear Son:

God has delivered us of the power of darkness—that
is the adversary or the negative—and He has given us
citizenship. And if you are a citizen like in the United
States, you are a citizen, you have certain citizenship
rights. God—because we are born again and partakers

of the divine nature of God in Christ in you, the hope of glory—He has given us citizenship in His kingdom (in God's kingdom) through, or by way of, the work of His dear Son.

Verse 14:

Colossians 1:14:
In whom we have redemption through his blood ["through his blood" is omitted], *even* the forgiveness of sins:

Not forgiveness, it is the word "remission." Remission is for the unsaved sinner; forgiveness is for the saved one. So, in God, in Christ we have our redemption. And to have redemption you have remission of sins.

Colossians 1:15:
Who is the image of the invisible God, the firstborn of every creature ["all creation" is the text]:

Look at Romans. This is terrific! Bless your hearts. We have to just become God conscious and Son conscious. We have to get a new vision; a new sense of God in Christ in us in evidence. Romans 6:11:

Romans 6:11-14:
Likewise reckon ye also yourselves to be dead indeed [to] unto sin, but alive unto God through Jesus Christ our Lord.

Let not sin therefore reign in your mortal body, that ye should obey it in the lusts thereof [in the five senses thereof].

Neither yield ye your members *as* instruments of unrighteousness unto sin: but yield yourselves unto God, as those that are alive from the dead, and your members *as* instruments of righteousness unto God.

For sin shall not have dominion over you: for ye are not under the law, but under grace.

Another translation of verse 14 that I like very much reads: "For sin shall no longer lord it over you [it is not going to be your lord]....for you are not under law but under grace."

Look at Romans 8, verse 16:

Romans 8:16, 17:
The Spirit itself beareth witness with our spirit, that we are the children of God:

And if children, then heirs; heirs of God, and joint-heirs with Christ;...

We are what? heirs. We are children of God because of His divine nature; partakers of His divine nature in us with Christ in us, the hope of glory. And if we are children of God then we are heirs of God; and we are joint heirs with Christ. Not with Jesus in his humiliation, but in the Christ—the messianic promise, and the one who has been raised from the dead, seated at God's right hand.

In the Gospel of John, Chapter 5, verse 24:

John 5:24:
Verily, verily, I say unto you, He that heareth my word, and believeth on him that sent me [on God who sent Jesus Christ], hath everlasting life, and shall not come into condemnation; but is passed from death unto life.

To pass from death to life is to be rescued. It is taken out of the Kingdom of Satan and put into the Kingdom of God by the works of His son, as we read in Colossians 1:13.

I think, again, I ought to explain to you the difference between the usage of the words "everlasting life" and "eternal life" in the scriptures. It is eternal life from God's point of view. It is everlasting life from your experiential point of view. Let's say you were eighteen or twenty years old when you were born again. Did you have eternal life before that? No. But once you got born again, from that moment on it is everlasting. If you would have had it from the beginning, you could have said, "Well, it was eternal from before I was born"; but the everlasting means it had a starting point. Eighteen, twenty, or thirty years old; whenever you got born again, from that time on it is everlasting. But from God's point of view, that everlasting life that you have is eternal.

You have to think a little bit about what it means for you to have His divine nature in you. Well, it means sonship; it means you are an heir of God; you are a joint heir with Christ. It means you have eternal life. It is everlasting but it is eternal because you got born again, and from that day on it is everlasting—but it is eternal life from God's point of view. And we have never measured the greatness of that eternal life because we get talked out of it by our feelings or by our environment; or what we see, hear, smell, taste or touch. But, people, we are what the Word of God says we are; we have what the Word of God says we have. It does not depend upon your feeling or mine, because we had nothing to do with the sacrifice of God's only begotten son. God so loved that He gave. You and I did not so love that we gave; God gave.

This eternal life, this sonship, is so fantastic that in a marriage situation if the husband is a believer and the wife is not; his eternal life just sort of sets her aside. Vice versa: if she is a believer and he is not; her eternal life, Christ in her, sets him aside.

It says so in 1 Corinthians 7. Listen to verse 14:

1 Corinthians 7:14:
For the unbelieving husband is sanctified [set apart] by the wife [the believing wife], and the unbelieving

wife is [set aside] sanctified by the [believing] husband: else were your children unclean; but now are they holy.

That is tremendous! That is part of the greatness of this: partakers of divine nature—sonship, eternal life, joint heirs; that the children are holy that are born where there is one member that is a born-again believer.

You see, this eternal life, this being partakers of divine nature, gives us the potential to change habit patterns. It gives us the potential to form new habit patterns; the potential to change our conduct and our living. It gives us the potential to manifest a new kind of love, which is the *agapaō:* the love of God in the renewed mind. For we are living in God's class as His children; for we are a new creation.

2 Corinthians 5:17:
Therefore if any man *be* in Christ, *he is* a new creature ["creation" is the text]: old things [the old man nature] are passed away; behold, all things [in Christ] are become new.

That is why we can manifest a new kind of love. It is not *phileō. Phileō* love is selfish love. This is *agapaō.* It is the love of God. Because we are partakers of His divine nature. That is why you and I can love the unlovable. Even as God in Christ loved us when we were dead in trespasses and sin, without God and without hope. And it is the love of God that draws people to repentance. I think it says that in the Word. It is the love that draws. There is no other way people can see the love of God except in your life and mine. And that is why God made it possible for us to be partakers of His divine nature, so we could manifest a new type of love.

According to Philippians 2:13, being a partaker of the divine nature:

Philippians 2:13:
For it is God [who is at work within us] which
worketh in you both to will and to do of *his* good
pleasure.

Why do we keep forgetting this? Because of our old
man training, we only believe what we can see, hear,
smell, taste, or touch. The Word says God is at work
within us.

So, tomorrow morning at the shop, factory, farm, or
business—wherever you are tomorrow morning—God
is going to be at work within you to will and to do His
good pleasure. So, you have the potential to change your
habit patterns. You have the potential to change your believing, change your conduct and living. And you have
the potential to manifest this new kind of love.

The mind of the believer must be renewed to come
into harmony and fellowship with God's divine nature in
us. This experience, plus concentration and commitment,
are the ingredients to spiritual success. And then compe-
tence leads to confidence.

The Word of God gives to every believer a deep sense
of affection, love, pride, self-esteem, and responsibility;
the reason for your living and doing something satis-
fying and worthwhile.

In Romans, Chapter 8, verse 28:

Romans 8:28:
And we know that all things work together for good
to them that love God,...

Not all things work together for good, but all things
work together for good to those who do what? love God.

I have seen a card that just had the first part of the
verse on it. That is a lie. All things do not work together
for good. But all things work together for good to those

who love God—to them, or those, who are called according to His purpose.

Verse 29:

Romans 8:29, 30:
For whom he did foreknow, he also did predestinate *to be* conformed to the image of his Son, that he might be the firstborn [Jesus Christ might be the firstborn, his Son] among many brethren.

Moreover whom he did predestinate, them he also called: and [those] whom he called, [must have called you because you heard, or you responded by confessing with your mouth the Lord Jesus; believe God raised him from the dead—you got born again.] them he also justified [so are you justified because you are partakers of His divine nature]: and whom he justified, them he also glorified.

So, in God's sight, as partakers of divine nature; you are righteous, you are justified, and you are already glorified.

Just think of what a wonderful time this can be for us as believers; knowing these great truths of God's Word, and going by the Word rather than our past experiences. Knowing that we are partakers of His divine nature.

That is why verse 31 is so tremendous!

Romans 8:31:
What shall we then say to these things? If God *be* for us...

And let me ask you, is God for us? Yes. We are his sons and daughters. We are not servants, we are not friends of His; we are sons of God. We have been made righteous; we have been redeemed; we have been justified; we have been glorified.

So,...

Romans 8:31, 32:

If God *be* for us, [and He certainly is] who *can be* against us?

He that spared not his own Son, but delivered him up for us all, how shall he not with him also freely give us all things?

And that is why one of the greatest truths in God's Word that we as believers need to recognize and build in our hearts and lives is that we are partakers of God's divine nature. And thereby we have His great, glorious, and precious promise.

No Condemnation

When you are born again of God's spirit, Christ in you, this Christ in you which is eternal life cannot come into condemnation. We have passed from death unto life as Christ is the end of condemnation.

Jesus Christ came that we might have life and have it how? more abundantly. But when you look around you, there are very few who are really manifesting even an abundant life, let alone a more abundant life—a life which is more than abundant.

The possibilities that are latent within the Christian believer seldom come into manifestation because we are talked out of it all the time. The people with whom we fellowship, the environment in which we live, the surroundings with which we are engulfed, are of such a nature that instead of lifting us up and really developing the potential which is within us and making this into a kinetic form of manifestation; instead of bringing it out, it usually gets darkened. However, there are absolute limitless limits that are latent within the believer because it is Christ in you, the hope of glory.

First you have to realize that if you are going to take the potential which is in your life, you are going to have to build this potential in manifestation upon the accuracy of God's Word and forget about your feelings or your past teaching. You have to come to believe God's Word and just say, "Thus saith the Lord," and that settles it.

All the waters of Niagara Falls are only potential until they run over the dynamos and move the dynamos to develop the electricity. Then that potential energy becomes kinetic. There are people who go through life born again of God's spirit, the potential within them, but it is never manifested. It is never in the form of kinetic energy. What you and I need to do is to find out what we have in Christ, know what we have, and then develop ourselves to bring it into manifestation.

You talk about developing the mind of man. We hear so much about this, developing their potential. You can develop the spirit within you. When you are born again of God's spirit, you can develop that spirit with the same effectiveness, and I would like to say even with a greater effectiveness and with a greater ability, than you can develop the mind.

But you have to apply spiritual things to develop the spirit, and very few people ever spend time to develop the spirit. They develop their mental abilities, they develop their abilities to work in the fields that they are interested in, but what about our spiritual potential? When you develop this spiritual ability then the potential will become kinetic.

We are what the Word of God says we are, we have what the Word of God says we have, we will be what the Word of God says we will be. So, the scripture says that when we are born again of God's spirit, we are in Christ. Well, if we are in Christ and born again of God's spirit, Christ is where? in us. And if we are in him, look at the limitless limits of that new life, that power that is latent within the believer.

In Romans 8 we read:

Romans 8:1:
There is therefore now no condemnation to them which are in Christ Jesus,...

The limitless limits of the new life in Christ Jesus, the first thing you learn is that there is an end of condemnation. Most of the good people, the sincere people, the honest people, the religious people are usually living under condemnation. They have been condemned so long that they just accept this. They just cannot fathom that God really did what He said He did in Christ Jesus; that there is no condemnation. There is no condemnation. Well, if the Word of God says there is no condemnation, then there is no condemnation.

So, if you say what the Word of God says, then you and God make a majority. But if we go by what the environment says, the surroundings, the community may say and this contradicts what the Word says; no matter how you feel, no matter how men and women look in that society, they have to be wrong, because what they are saying and doing is a contradiction of what the Word says.

There is now no condemnation. So, when you are born again of God's spirit, Christ in you, this Christ in you which is eternal life cannot come into condemnation. The wrath of God is no longer upon these believers. We have passed from death unto life as Christ is the end of condemnation. What a tremendous truth this is!

And to make these limitless limits of the new birth, the new life within the believer, manifested in a kinetic way in the senses world; you have to get to the place that you get over the condemnation under which you have been living a lifetime. And this applies to every segment, every facet in your believing walk of your life. You just have to get out of that condemnation.

And if you have developed this spiritual potential within you once, you have walked this way, you can hardly stand to be with people who are the other way. Only Christ Jesus and the knowledge of his word within us will ever make any individual positive. Otherwise they will always be under condemnation.

The reason for this is, basically, that man has magnified sin above redemption. We have magnified sin. And so, we have talked about sin until we are just "sinned out." We keep at it all the time.

Now sin is a fact, I know that. But what Christ was for us is a reality. And I am confident that he is able to do more than all the hosts of Satan were ever able to put together. And the scripture says there is no condemnation to them which are in Christ Jesus. And the moment you are born again, it is Christ in you; and at that moment, we are in him. And as we walk in the light as he is the light, we stay in that fellowship with him, and you can go through life without any condemnation anywhere in your life.

That is the potential. That is the limitless limits that are available to the new creature, the new birth and the person who is born again of God's spirit. Just think of it. It is unbelievable, but it is true, and therefore we believe it.

2 Corinthians 5 teaches this same truth in a wonderful way because this thing is alive. It is vital. It means what it says, and it says what it means. And this is what sets men and women free.

Verse 17 of 2 Corinthians 5:

2 Corinthians 5:17a:
Therefore if any man *be* in Christ, *he is* a new creature:…

I believe the root word of this is that he is a new species. He has something new within him, which is Christ in him, and this makes him a different person than he has been before spiritually. Because he is body, soul, and spirit.

2 Corinthians 5:17b:
Therefore…old things are passed away;…

All these old things that we have had in our minds—all the condemnation, all the disruption, all of that which we have magnified above redemption—all of that is gone.

2 Corinthians 5:17b:
...old things are passed away; behold, all things are become new.

Then what do you put into your mind? After you are saved, you put in your mind what you have within the spirit. What God has wrought in Christ. That you are passed from death unto life. This is the kind of thing you put into your mind. Then the old disappears and we have something new up in our minds to walk on. And no man walks beyond what he thinks. As a man thinketh, the Bible says, so he is or so is he.[1] That's right.

And you cannot go beyond what you think, and you cannot think beyond what you are taught. Old things are passed away. Behold, all things are new to the end that we renew our mind. This is why I teach our people in every Foundational class, the key to power is the renewed mind. To the end that we renew our mind and put on the mind of Christ, then these limitless limits of that new life come into manifestation. Look at the tremendousness of that!

2 Corinthians 5:18a:
And all things *are* of God, who hath [past tense] reconciled us to himself by...

...my good works? By my attendance faithfully? By my praying for hours and hours? By my confessing my sins? Nope. All things are of God who has reconciled us to himself by whom?

2 Corinthians 5:18b:
...Jesus Christ,...

---

1. Proverbs 23:7: For as he thinketh in his heart, so is he:...

Isn't that wonderful! You see why there is an end of condemnation? For he hath reconciled us. To reconcile means to bring back together that which has been separated.

If there is anything that I could do to reconcile myself to God and to put myself back in God's favor, then it would have to be of works and Christ died in vain. Right? Sure it is right, bless your heart. He has reconciled. And if you are reconciled then you are back on talking terms. There is no condemnation left. You are reconciled. You are brought back in. Reconciled us to himself by whom? Jesus Christ.

And the reason the word Jesus appears first in the texts and Christ secondly is because, whenever the Bible wants to manifest the greatness of the humility of what God wrought in Christ, the word "Jesus" is always used first in the Bible. Whenever it manifests the greatness of his messianic mission, the word "Christ" will always be used first. That is why the scripture teaches that when you are born again of God's spirit, you are in whom? in Christ.

And many times, you hear people talking about being in Jesus. Every time I hear that it sends chills up and down my spine because you cannot go far enough there. It is he who went that far. It is he who died upon the cross. It is he who was humiliated. It is he in whose face they spit, so that you and I might become righteous in God in him. Therefore, we are not in his humility, we are in his messianic glory.

This is why it says we are in Christ. When you are born again of God's Spirit you are in Christ, the glorified one who was the Messiah. Isn't that wonderful! The accuracy with which the Word is said is just tremendous!

2 Corinthians 5:18a:
...all things *are* of God, who hath reconciled us to himself by Jesus Christ,...

And then comes this tremendous statement that just shakes people when they first see it: "And he has given to us." Who is us? us, the reconciled ones in Christ. That's right. To those of us who are reconciled and in Christ, He has given the ministry of condemnation? No! Well, we sometimes act like it, don't we? People condemn this person, condemn that one. But the scripture says there is no what? condemnation to them that are in Christ. Well, if we are in Christ then we ought to get off of that old theme of condemnation. We ought to magnify what the Word of God magnifies, the redemption that we have in Christ Jesus, above everything else.

2 Corinthians 5:18b:
…hath given to us the ministry of reconciliation;

He has given it to us—the reconciled ones, the believers. Did he give it to Peter? Yes, but Peter only? Nope. Peter, because he was a born-again believer, and he was in Christ.

When you and I are in Christ, we also have the ministry of reconciliation. And most of the teaching across the nation is that the minister takes care of the spiritual needs of his congregation. Just like you go to a dentist to have your teeth fixed; if you have lots of trouble you go to a dental specialist. So, we think, in the ministry if we just have a little bit of trouble we go to the minister, because he is supposed to take care of the spiritual end. He has the ministry of reconciliation—this is what at least the Protestants believe, other groups believe differently. Then if you are in real trouble you go to a specialist of a minister, who turns out to be a psychiatrist or a psychologist, who has had a little bit of training in nothing.

I did not write it, but the Word says that God reconciled us to Himself by Jesus Christ and has given to us, (plural) the reconciled ones, the ministry of reconciliation. That is what it says; that is what it means.

If people are going to be reconciled today, if they are going to be born again of God's spirit, if they are going to be shown what they are in Christ—that they have passed out of condemnation and such, who is going to do it? We are. For He has given to us the ministry. He has given it to us.

What does that verse of scripture do with the teaching, for instance, of the Gospels that people always bring up where Jesus Christ builds the Church? They refer to the Church as a she; they refer to the Church as the bride, today. In the Gospels the Church was the bride because Jesus was the bridegroom. And in the Gospels, it said he would build his Church. Not Peter. Jesus said, I will build my Church. That is what he said; that is what he meant.

But in the Church Epistles addressed to the believer, born again of God's spirit on the Day of Pentecost He says that to us, He has given the ministry of reconciliation. Therefore, the Church of the Body is going to grow; men and women are going to again hear the Word of God. As He lives within you, you renew your mind, and God will be made manifest; men and women will be reconciled unto God to know what they have in Christ.

There is no greater lack of knowledge in the spiritual field than the knowledge of what men and women have in Christ. He has given to us the ministry of reconciliation. And then He describes it a little further in verse 19:

2 Corinthians 5:19a:
To wit, that God was in Christ,...

It does not say God was Christ; it says God was where? in Christ. That is what it means.

2 Corinthians 5:19b:
...reconciling the world unto himself, not imputing their trespasses [or their sins] unto them;...

Not imputing them. You see what He has done with

sin? He has not imputed this unto those of us who are born again. We no longer carry it. When you get born again of God's spirit, you get remission of sins. After you break fellowship, you confess the broken fellowship, you get forgiveness of sins.

He has not imputed their sins unto them. Then how can we be under condemnation if we do not have any? The only reason we can be under it is because people bring us under it. Because of the environment, or the society, or the fellowships we seek with others. They are the only ones that can obstruct us and bring us under it.

Then He makes this tremendous statement:

2 Corinthians 5:19c:
…and hath committed unto us…

Hath committed—Well, if He has committed it unto us, then who has it? We have it, the born-again believer. Committed unto us:

2 Corinthians 5:19d:
…the word of reconciliation.

Isn't that wonderful! The Word of reconciliation is committed unto those of us who have been reconciled. He has given it unto us. God reconciled everyone in Christ Jesus. Therefore, whosoever will, could get saved. They are already reconciled as far as God is concerned, but it becomes a reality to the individual when we believe.

Now, to get people to believe is the ministry of reconciliation. And to get people into this ministry, they must have the Word and nothing but the Word. For faith cometh by hearing and hearing cometh by what? The Word.[2] And the knowledge that we have of our abilities and of the things that we can do, that God wants us to

---

2. Romans 10:17: So then faith cometh by hearing, and hearing by the word of God.

do, we get from the Word. So, He has given us not only the ministry, but He has given us the Word. Without the Word, you could not have the ministries operating anyway. He has given us the Word of reconciliation.

2 Corinthians 5:20a:
Now then we are ambassadors...

How can you live under condemnation and be an ambassador? That would be terrible. How can you manifest the limitless limits of the new life in Christ Jesus and constantly be under condemnation? It would be impossible, because you cannot get sweet and bitter water out of the same vessel at the same time. It is impossible.

2 Corinthians 5:20a:
Now then we are ambassadors for Christ, as though God did beseech *you* by us...

Now we are ambassadors, see? God beseeched you by us, Paul says.

2 Corinthians 5:20b:
...we pray *you* in Christ's stead, be ye reconciled to God.

And then that tremendous verse:

2 Corinthians 5:21:
For he hath made him [God made Christ Jesus] *to be* sin for us, who knew no sin; that we might be made the righteousness of God in him.

Isn't that something! We are in whom? Christ. And Christ is in who? God. God is in Christ, we read a little while ago. We are in Christ. Jesus always did the Father's will. He never sinned. Therefore, being in him, being in Christ, we have that same righteousness. See? That we might be made the righteousness of God in him—the righteousness of God.

How can you live under condemnation and believe this scripture? If we have the righteousness of God, how much righteousness do we have? How righteous is God? Do you think you can improve on it? No. He is all righteousness. He is completely righteous. And the scripture says that when we are born again of God's spirit and in him, he has made us in Christ the righteousness of God.

It is just too big for the human mind to fathom with the first hearing. You see, when people are born again their sins are wiped out, even if in their mind they do not know it, because of the work which God wrought in Jesus while he was here upon earth. It is a wonderful thing!

The reason we have manifested so many condemnations in our lives is because we have allowed this to build within ourselves because of the ignorance of the Word. We have not been taught the Word. And not being taught the Word, being ignorant of the Word, we have just allowed this condemnation to so infiltrate our entire beings that just thousands upon thousands of Christians are constantly living in condemnation.

Look at Romans again. Chapter 8, verse 31:

Romans 8:31:
What shall we then say to these things? If God *be* for us, who *can be* against us?

That is right. Well, is God for us? Absolutely. Surely, when we are born again of God's spirit we are His children, and are you not for your children? When your child has a need, you call up for prayer or you write, or you ask others to pray. Why? Because it is your child.

Well, we are God's children when we are born again. Can you for one moment conceive of the human parent loving his child more than God loves His child? I cannot; not if God is the God that I read about who was in

Christ Jesus. But the "God" that people talk about, he is a mean critter many times, because the very people he loves who are his children, he kills them all. That kind of God I do not know, outside of Satan.

But the true God that we are talking about here, the scripture says He is more anxious to answer our prayer than we are even to ask Him. You see, He is for us all the time. He is always wanting us to move. But God cannot move, basically, until this limitless limits within us becomes manifested, because God is limited to His ability that lives within the believer.

Now that is unbelievable, but it is true. And it is tremendous when you rightly divide the Word and understand it, because in the satanic field, Satan who is the god of this world, he possesses. He makes people do. People become channels for him. They become instruments. They become tools in his hands. They become mediums, and they only know what Satan possesses them in.

But you, born again of God's spirit, operating the greatness of the power of God, you manifest the greatness in your life as you and I believe. Anyone that is possessed does not have to believe—he is possessed. The Word is accurate. But you and I are not possessed by God. When we are true Christians, born again of God's spirit—by true Christian I mean one who is born again of God's spirit and walking with a renewed mind —we are not possessed. We have freedom of will.

God having committed unto us the Word and the ministry of reconciliation, we have it. How can God get any work done? Only if you and I work it. Only if every Christian believer recognizes what they have in Christ, and they go out and tell the world. If they do not want to hear it, tell them anyway. Because the scripture says you have to witness to them twice; after that, you do not have to anymore. That just came to my heart and mind. It is in the book of Titus, Chapter 3, verse 10.[3] You ought to mark this because some people are always condemned because they are not out witnessing to Johnnie Joe for the 111,000 time, or something. They are so afraid that if they do not witness to him every time they see him, they are condemned. You see, that is what they have been taught; everyone you come to, if he is unsaved, you be sure to witness to him. Be sure to witness to him so that you do not get condemned for not witnessing to him. You see how we keep driving people many times into this type of condemnation? It is real devilish all the way through.

So, look what verse 31 says in Romans, where I was a moment ago:

Romans 8:31:
What shall we then say to these things? If God *be* for us, who *can be* against us?

That is tremendous! If God is for us, then who in the world can be against us? Then do we need to be negative? No. Do we need to be defeated, frustrated and full of fear? No. God is for His children.

You know, God has reconciled us and given us the ministry; Jesus Christ became sin so that we might become the righteousness of God. You know what righteousness is? It is the God-given ability whereby you stand before the presence of God right now without any

---

3. Titus 3:9-11: But avoid foolish questions, and genealogies, and contentions, and strivings about the law; for they are unprofitable and vain.
A man that is an heretick after the first and second admonition reject;
Knowing that he that is such is subverted, and sinneth, being condemned of himself.

sense of guilt, sin, defeat, frustration, worry, anxiety, or any other negatives. No condemnation—you just stand before Him as His son.

Romans 8:32a:
He that spared not his own Son, but delivered him up for us all, how shall he not with him also...

Reluctantly? No. Hesitantly? No. But what? Freely.

Romans 8:32b-33:
...freely give us all things?
Who shall lay any thing to the charge of God's elect?...

Yes, pray who will? People try it all the time but the scripture says, who is going to lay anything to God's elect? If you are born again of God's spirit, you are God's elect. Who shall lay anything to the charge of God's elect? How can you lay anything to the charge of God's elect if God has already covered them? God has already forgiven them. God has already passed them from death unto life. You cannot.

That is why it said:

Romans 8:33b:
...*It is* God that justifieth.

It is God who justified man. And when God justified man, He did not lay anything to his account; therefore, no other man can lay it either. But people sometimes really try to put this and that on you, or make you do this and that. All baloney, if the Word of God is right.

Romans 8:34a:
Who *is* he that condemneth?...

The word "*it is*" is "shall" in the text.

Romans 8:34b:
...*It is* [Shall] Christ [who] died, [no]...who is even

at the right hand of God, [does not condemn us, but he] who also maketh intercession for us.

Isn't that wonderful—a tremendous truth! Who shall separate us? Verse 35:

Romans 8:35a:
Who shall separate us from the love of Christ?...

Yes, who shall? Who will? Nobody can.

Romans 8:35b:
...*shall* tribulation, or distress, or persecution, or famine, or nakedness, or peril, or sword? [no war, nothing.]

Romans 8:37:
...in all these things we are more than conquerors through him that loved us.

We are more than what? conquerors! Isn't that wonderful!

Romans 8:38, 39:
For I am persuaded that neither death nor life, nor angels, nor principalities nor powers, nor things present nor things to come,

Nor height nor depth, nor any other creature shall be able to separate us from the love of God which is in Christ Jesus our Lord.

Amazing! Nothing shall separate us from the love of God. When you are born again of God's spirit, can anything separate you from the love of God? Nothing. Because you are His child. You are His son. You are His daughter. Nothing can separate us from the love of God which is in Christ Jesus, and you are in Christ.

That is why, people, it is the greatest Word of God in the world. It is the greatness of God's tremendous ministry; that He has committed unto us to go forth to show men and women the limitless limits that is possible because these abilities are within them potentially.

What a tremendous walk this truth is! It is wonderful when you see the greatness with which these things are set in the Word. It just blesses your heart.

OLD TESTAMENT HEALINGS: NAAMAN AND THE FOUR LEPERS

It is not important who delivers the Word; it is important that it is the Word. It is not important how you get the information from God; it is important to get it.

The history of our times are on so many occasions like records in the Word of God. The Word of God is always an eternal now; it is not a "has been" type of thing. It is God's Word living *now!* It is an eternal now. It is always a present reality. Any individual who would know enough of God's Word to believe God's Word, to confess with their mouth the Lord Jesus, believe God raised him from the dead; that individual would be saved. For God's Word is faithful; it is yea and amen. His Word endureth forever. It is always an eternal now. Anyone who wants to can get saved *now.* Deliverance is always a now. Eternal life is a one-time deal. Staying healthy is a minute-by-minute trip. It is a day-by-day walk. You only get saved once, but you can get delivered physically and mentally, time and time and time again. Because it is a day-by-day believing and walk in it.

There is an old hymn of the Christian Church which I have reworked in what I believe is the accuracy of God's Word. And before I share from 2 Kings, one of the great records in God's Word of deliverance, I would like to share this hymn.

> Man's feelings come, and feelings go;
> Feelings are senses man deceiving.
> My life is the Word of God,
> Nothing else is worth believing.

Should mankind the Word belittle,
And all the world the Word condemn.
I'll trust in God's unchanging Word,
Nothing else, until my very end.

Who and what is man against God?
Man's words succeed? Never.
Man's days are as grass and the flowers of the field,
But the Word of the LORD endureth forever.

Should man my soul and body sever,
And life offer no more sweet tokens,
I'll trust to the end my saviour,
For God's Word cannot be broken.

That's the hymn. And I would like to take you to
God's Word and show you that it cannot be broken, in
2 Kings, Chapter 5.

About 580 BC, there lived a mighty king who was
head of the mightiest empire of its day called the Syrian
Empire. The record that I want to look at is regarding
one of this king's great men. His name was Naaman.

2 Kings 5:1:
Now Naaman, captain of the host of the king of Syria,
was a great man with his master, and honourable,
because by him the Lord had given deliverance unto
Syria: he was also a mighty man in valour, *but he
was* a leper.

He was captain of the host to the king of Syria,
which perhaps would mean in our day that he would
have been a "five-star general." There was no one above
him. He was the leader of the greatest army of its day
and time. He was a great man with his master and honourable, because by him, the Lord had given deliverance
unto Syria. He was also a mighty man in valour. He
was not only a great man whom you could honor his
word when he said something, but also, he was not a

coward. He was a mighty man of valor. And I tell you mighty men of valor dare to believe!

It reminds me of David in the early days of his questing while fighting with the Philistines, when David just casually said, "If I could just have a drink of water from the well at Bethlehem." Now, he could not have it because the Philistines had the whole city outside of Bethlehem surrounded. But about four hours later, two men showed up with a drink of water for David. They had crashed through the lines of the great Philistine army, gone to the well, got King David a cup of water, and brought it to him. It is in the Word. That's right. I want to tell you, those men were not cowards; they were not men full of fear; they were men who dared to believe. And David did something that just turns your heart hot; David looked at the water, and he said, "For me to make such a request that these men risked their lives, I cannot drink the water." After they went all the way to get it, he could not drink it. And the Word said he poured it out as an offering to the Lord.

Naaman was a mighty man of valor, but he was a leper. Now, to be a leper in Israel put you outside of the pale, but if one was a leper among the so called Gentile or pagan nations, they did not throw you out. That is why Naaman was allowed to stay; and to the best of my knowledge, as I have worked the Word, this perhaps was in the early stages of what we know as leprosy.

2 Kings 5:2:
And the Syrians had gone out by companies, and had brought away captive out of the land of Israel a little maid; and she waited on Naaman's wife.

When Syria had gone in to capture Samaria, the capital of the ten northern tribes of Israel, they brought out many of the men and women. One little maid whom they brought out became the helper to Naaman's wife.

2 Kings 5:3:
And she said unto her mistress [unto Naaman's wife], Would God my lord [that is Naaman] *were* with the prophet that *is* in Samaria! for he would recover him of his leprosy.

She was just a little maid who had been captured. She had been brought in as a slave, a little maid in the house, a servant to the great Naaman's wife. And this little maid, in that extraordinary situation, said to her mistress, "Would to God my lord, Naaman, were with the prophet that is in Samaria, for he would recover him of his leprosy." That is a bold statement! How did she know the mind of the prophet back in Samaria? She did not know the mind, but what she had was revelation—word of knowledge, word of wisdom—one of the nine manifestations.

Verse 3 says "recover"; in order for you to recover from sickness you had to have health to begin with. You cannot recover something if you do not have it to begin with. If you are going to retread an automobile tire, you have to have a tire to start with right? That is a tremendous thing about healing!

Naaman had not always been a leper; he *became* a leper. Therefore, if he was going to be delivered, it has to be a recovery.

2 Kings 5:4:
And *one* went in, and told his lord [Naaman], saying, Thus and thus said the maid that *is* of the land of Israel.

And the king of Syria heard about this.

2 Kings 5:5a:
And the king of Syria said, Go to, go, and I [the great king of Syria] will send a letter unto the king of Israel....

Just stop right there. That was not what the little maid had said. The little maid had said, "Would God my lord were with the prophet that is in Samaria! for he would recover him of his leprosy." But do you know what that sharp king figured out? He figured out if that prophet in Samaria could deliver him, the king had more power than the prophet; so instead of sending him to the prophet, he would send him to the king. He was smart, and it was great protocol as well.

So, the king of Syria wrote a letter.

> **2 Kings 5:5b-7:**
> …And he [Naaman] departed, and took with him [Naaman took with him] ten talents of silver, and six thousand pieces of gold, and ten changes of raiment.
>
> …And he [Naaman] brought the letter [from the king of Syria] to the king of Israel, saying, Now when this letter is come unto thee, behold, I have *therewith* sent Naaman my servant to thee, that thou mayest recover him of his leprosy.
>
> And it came to pass, when the king of Israel had read the letter, that he rent his clothes, and said, *Am I God*, to kill and to make alive, that this man [the king of Syria] doth send unto me to recover a man [Naaman] of his leprosy? wherefore consider, I pray you, and see how he seeketh a quarrel against me.

"He knows that I cannot recover Naaman, therefore he sends the letter, saying, 'Recover him.' I cannot recover him, and that will give him an excuse so he can send his armies down and destroy us." That was what the king of Israel said.

> **2 Kings 5:8a:**
> And it was *so*, when Elisha the man of God had heard that the king of Israel had rent his clothes,

that he [Elisha] sent to the king [by way of a messenger], saying, Wherefore hast thou rent thy clothes? let him [Naaman] come now to me, and he shall know that there is a prophet in Israel.

That is telling the king! And, the king did not wait very long to tell Naaman about this.

2 Kings 5:9:
So Naaman came with his horses and with his chariot, and stood at the door of the house of Elisha.

He is a five-star general, and he stood at the door waiting for that prophet to come out to him—because after all he is a five-star! Do you know what Elisha did? I think Elisha was sitting in the kitchen, and his servant had baked some chocolate chip cookies. He was having himself a cup of tea and chocolate chip cookies! And there was that five-star standing outside. I can just see this thing: Elisha reached over; he took a sip; and while he took a sip he signaled with his eyes to his servant; the servant came over and he said, "Go tell the five-star out there:"

2 Kings 5:10a:
...Go and wash in Jordan seven times, and thy flesh shall come again to thee, and thou shalt be clean.

And then, he took another sip of tea! Naaman, of course, stood outside waiting for the man of God to come out, which was the respect that was needed, according to his thinking. But, the man of God never moved out of the kitchen. He just poured himself another cup of tea, gave a messenger the information, sent the messenger out; the messenger delivered the report to Naaman, and the messenger came back in.

What a great, tremendous lesson! It is not important who delivers the Word; it is important that it is the Word. It is not important *how* you get the information from

God; it is important *to get* it. And I learned many years ago that often times the information is delivered through the most unlikely vehicle. That's right. The Word of God was from the Prophet Elisha to Naaman via the messenger, "Go and wash in Jordan seven times, and thy flesh shall come again to thee, and thou shalt be clean."

2 Kings 5:11:
…But Naaman was wroth [angry], and went away, and said, Behold, I thought, He will surely come out to me, and stand, and call on the name of the Lord his God, and strike his hand over the place, and recover the leper.

Naaman had it all figured out, but it did not quite work that way!

2 Kings 5:12:
Are not Abana and Pharpar, rivers of Damascus, better than all the waters of Israel? may I not wash in them, and be clean? So he turned and went away in a rage.

The Jordan is very narrow, usually very dirty; it is not mountain water. You know, the logic of a man's mind really tricks him. He was told, "Go dip in the Jordan seven times."

But his mind said: "Why Jordan? Why that dirty Jordan? Are not the rivers of Damascus clean and nice? I might as well go there and dip seven times."

But you see, the Word of God is the will of God; it means what it says and it says what it means. The prophet said, "Jordan"; and what did he mean? Jordan. Had he meant the rivers of Damascus, he would have said Damascus. That is how simple the Word is.

2 Kings 5:12b, 13:
…So he turned and [he] went away in a rage.

> And his servants came near, and spake unto him, and said, My father, if the prophet [Elisha] had bid thee *do some* great thing, wouldest thou not have done it? how much rather then, when he saith to thee, Wash, and be clean?

What a servant Naaman had! If Elisha had said to him, "Look, I will take all those gifts you have. Go back and get twice as much, and God will heal you of your leprosy," do you know what Naaman would have done? You know what he would have done. He would have gone back, and he would have gotten all the money that he needed. He would have begged it; he would have borrowed it; he would have gotten it any which way he could to come back to get deliverance. For when a man is really hurting physically, he will pay everything he has, if necessary. Naaman would have done the same.

And his servants said to him, "If he would have asked you, you would have done it, right? If he would have asked you to crawl barefooted up the steps to the highest pinnacle, you would have done it. But, since he said the simple little thing to you, 'Go wash in the Jordan seven times,' it upset you. What is the matter?"

2 Kings 5:14a:
Then went he down [to the Jordan], and dipped himself seven times in [the] Jordan, according to the saying of the man of God...

He dipped himself how many times? seven. That was exactly what the prophet had said via his messenger. He had delivered the Word of God via a messenger and said, "Go and wash in Jordan seven times, and thy flesh shall come again to thee, and thou shalt be clean."

In order to dip seven times, he had to dip the first time. When he dipped the first time, he was a leper when he went in; when he came up, and he looked, he was still as much a leper as he was before he went down the first time. He went down the second time; came up, looked at himself, and he was still as much a leper because he had not yet fulfilled the Word of God, which is the will of God. The Word of God was to dip seven times. Even if he had no improvement after six times, which he did not, that did not invalidate God's Word because he had not yet fulfilled the Word. Most people start praying for their deliverance, and then they think about it, and they say, "Well, I do not see much improvement." He did not see any! He went down six times, and he did not see any improvement. But he went down the seventh time according to the word of the prophet, and when he came up from the seventh dipping...

2 Kings 5:14b:
...his flesh came again like unto the flesh of a little child, and he was clean.

The skin on him was like the skin of a baby, and he was clean—there it is.

The most important thing is to (1) get God's Word, then to (2) carry it out literally. If God would say, "Jump," you never ask, "How high?" you just jump.

2 Kings 5:15, 16:
And he returned to the man of God, he and all his company, and came, and stood before him [the man of God]: and he said, Behold, now I know that *there is* no God in all the earth, but in Israel: now therefore, I pray thee, take a blessing [a gift] of thy servant.

But he [Elisha] said, *As* the Lord liveth, before whom I stand, I will receive none. And he [Naaman] urged him to take it; but he [the prophet] refused.

The reason the prophet refused is because of revelation. God told him not to take it.

2 Kings 5:17, 18:
And Naaman said, Shall there not then, I pray thee, be given to thy servant two mules' burden of earth? for thy servant will henceforth offer neither burnt offering nor sacrifice unto other gods, but [only] unto the Lord.

In this thing the Lord pardon thy servant, that when my master [the king of Syria] goeth into the house of Rimmon [which is a pagan god] to worship there, and he [the king of Syria] leaneth on my hand, and I bow myself in the house of Rimmon: when I bow down myself in the house of Rimmon, the Lord pardon thy servant in this thing.

Oh, it is beautiful! Being the king of Syria's right-hand man, whenever the king walked into the house of worship of Rimmon, the king would put his hand on Naaman's arm; and he would walk with him down to where the altar was, and when the king would bow, Naaman the servant would have to bow. And yet God had just delivered Naaman of his leprosy. And Naaman asked the prophet, Elisha, "Do you think, maybe because I am the king's right-hand man—even though when I bow, I really won't worship Rimmon; I am only going to worship the true God—but in order for me to go with the king, do you think maybe the Lord, *Jehovah*, God would overlook this?"

Do you know what I would have said? "No, He won't. If God delivered you, why don't you take a stand out there in Syria?"

The average man would have said, "Look, God delivered you. It is my denomination; don't you get out of this denomination and go back to all those sinful things." There is fantastic learning in here.

2 Kings 5:19:
And he [the prophet] said unto him, Go in peace....

By revelation from the true God, the Prophet Elisha said to Naaman, "Go in peace. Whenever the king goes into worship Rimmon, let him lean on your arm." What a tremendous God of love we have!

We believe in healing—our God is able to deliver to the uttermost—all things are possible to him that believeth. Yet, we never speak disparagingly about the medical profession; we do not speak disparagingly about the chiropractors, the dentists, or any others. We are not in the business of speaking disparagingly about people or professions; we are in the business of teaching God's Word—God's deliverance—no matter what profession or business. I am just thankful when anybody gets delivered from anything in any which way, because no man can heal; no doctor can heal. All they can do at best is help to remove some of the cause. If your arm is broken, all the doctor can do is set it; he cannot heal it. The healing is still of God; I do not care who does it! It is still of God!

God had delivered Naaman of the leprosy. God delivered him. The Prophet Elisha had carried out the ministry that he was responsible for. And yet, the love of God is so tremendous that He allowed him to go back and go into the house of Rimmon. If God is that loving, why should I become critical? Why should I criticize people? Every man has to walk in his own shoes before God, for we are all accountable to God. He is our Creator. He is the One who gave us the new birth. We will all stand before Him, and therefore, there may be some things in your walk that you can do which I cannot do. There may be things in my walk I may be able to do that you cannot do. So, it is never that we criticize anyone, we just hold forth the greatness of God's Word, that whosoever will may come and get delivered and get what God's best is.

Elisha said, "Go in peace."—"Go in peace."

I would like to show you one more deliverance from 2 Kings, starting with the twenty-fourth verse of the sixth chapter:

2 Kings 6:24-31:

And it came to pass after this, that Benhadad king of Syria gathered all his host, and went up, and besieged Samaria.

And there was a great famine in Samaria: and, behold, they besieged it [the city of Samaria], until an ass's head was *sold* for fourscore *pieces* of silver, [about $25] and the fourth part of a cab of dove's dung for five *pieces* of silver [about $1.75].

And as the king of Israel was passing by upon the wall, there cried a woman unto him, saying, Help, my lord, O king.

And he said, If the LORD do not help thee, whence shall I help thee? out of the barnfloor, or out of the winepress?

And the king said unto her, What aileth thee? And she answered, This woman said unto me, Give thy son, that we may eat him to day, and we will eat my son to morrow.

So we boiled my son, and did eat him: and I said unto her on the next day, Give thy son, that we may eat him:... [but] she hath hid her son.

And it came to pass, when the king heard the words of the woman, that he rent his clothes; and he passed by upon the wall.... the people looked, and, behold, *he had* sackcloth within upon his flesh.

Then he said, God do so and more also to me, if the head of Elisha the son of Shaphat shall stand on him this day.

The king blamed the prophet, the man of God, for the great famine. Men of God have always taken blame for everything that somebody else does not want to blame themselves for. They always put it on men of God. This is what the king did. And so, the king said, "I am going to get the head of that prophet before this day is over. I am going to chop his head off."

2 Kings 6:32:
But Elisha sat in his house,...

Biting his fingernails up to his second knuckle? Scared to death? Not so. Elisha sat in his house, and he was still in the kitchen pouring himself another cup of tea. This did not shake the prophet any.

2 Kings 6:32:
...and the elders sat with him; and *the king* sent a man from before him: but ere [before] the messenger came to him, he [the prophet] said to the elders, See ye how this son of a murderer hath sent to take away mine head?...

Here comes this guy from the king, and the prophet is sitting there with the elders sipping tea. He is not reading out of the bottom of the teacup, but by revelation he sees this man coming.

2 Kings 6:32, 33:
...[and] he said to...[his] elders,...when the messenger cometh, shut the door, and hold him...[out]: ...[because] the sound of his master's feet [are] behind him...

And while he [the prophet] yet talked with them [the elders], behold, the messenger came down unto him: and he said, Behold, this evil *is* of the LORD; what should I wait for the LORD any longer?

The messenger throws blame, "This great famine is of the Lord. The Lord sent the famine. You're responsible for it, Elisha."

2 Kings 7:1:
Then Elisha said, Hear ye the word of the LORD;
Thus saith the LORD, To morrow about this time
shall a measure of fine flour *be sold* for a shekel,
and two measures of barley for a shekel, in the gate
of [the city of] Samaria [about $1.16].

A great famine. No food, ass's head, dove's dung. You
saw it. No food. People were really starving. Somebody
had boiled a kid. And here is that prophet, who stands
up and says:

2 Kings 7:1, 2:
…Hear ye the word of the LORD;…To morrow
[less than 24 hours] about this time [there is going
to be so much food in that city, you can buy] a measure of [barley and] fine flour [for $1.16]…
Then a lord on whose hand the king leaned…

"Hand" in the text is "arm," meaning that he laid his
hand on him. Hand, leaned—remember? We just read
that about Syria.

2 Kings 7:2b:
…*if* the LORD would make windows in heaven,
might this thing be?

He said, if God Almighty made windows in heaven,
you could not get that much food into Samaria in less
than 24 hours.

2 Kings 7:2c:
…And he [the prophet] said, Behold, thou shalt see
it with thine eyes, but shall not eat thereof.

If God is going to accomplish that which the prophet
just said, and not make the prophet look like a fool, God
has got to go to work because He has got a short time to
do it—less than 24 hours. That's right.

Now, how is He going to do it? Oh, it is wonderful!

2 Kings 7:3:

…there were four leprous men at the entering in of the gate: and they said one to another, Why sit we here until we die?

That is about the smartest thing those four ever said. Now, the reason they were sitting at the gate is because they had been thrown out of the city of Samaria. They were not allowed in. So here were these four lepers, not allowed in the city, sitting on the outside during this tremendous famine; and one of them said to the other three, what are we doing sitting here until we die?

2 Kings 7:3, 4:

And there were four leprous men at the entering in of the gate: and they said one to another, Why sit we here until we die?

If we say, We will enter into the city, then the famine *is* in the city, and we shall die there: and if we sit still here, we die also. Now therefore come, and let us fall unto the host of the Syrians: if they save us alive, we shall live; and if they kill us, we shall but die.

Often, I think of these things: "Why sit we here until we die?"

You see, if we walk into the mouth of the lion, all the lion can either do is chew on us, or get regurgitated and turn into a lamb or something. These four lepers said, "Why sit we here until we die?"

If we go back in the city, they do not have any food, we die. If we sit here, we die. We might as well get up and do something. Because if we start moving, all we can do is die. And if we stay sitting, we are going to die anyway. If you are going to die, you might as well die standing up as laying down. That's right.

And if I had any one message to cry out, it would be

that same message of truth, "Why sit we here until we die?" That's right. Why don't we as Christian believers stand up and get counted? Why don't we hold forth God's Word to every man and woman? The Word, the Word, the Word! We do not lack a knowledge in physics, chemistry, and a lot of others. The reason people are dying is because of a lack of the knowledge of God's Word.

So, if I were to cry out to our nation and the world, I would say, why do we as Christians sit here until we die? The only thing they can do to us if we get up and walk is kill us. But if we sit here, we are going to kill ourselves. Either way, we are going to die. So why sit we here until we die? Why don't we get up and move God's Word! Talk the Word. Walk the Word. Speak the Word. Move it!

Well anyway, every word of that prophet was true. In less than 24 hours they had all of it. These four men dared to believe God, and they were not even Christians. They dared to believe. They came to a decision: why sit we here until we die? They moved. And when they moved, God moved.

Ladies and gentlemen, God has (past tense) moved in Christ Jesus making available the power of the holy spirit on the Day of Pentecost. And God does not move today until you move! God moved in Christ Jesus, and any man can be born again. But that man has to move. He has to open the door. God has moved. He is waiting on us to move. God has moved. He is the first, prime mover. Now when you and I move, then God moves again. And we move upon the greatness of the Word!

Those men said, "Why sit we here until we die?" They got up, they moved, and God brought deliverance. Ladies and gentlemen, when we move God will bring deliverance!

Turn your eyes upon Jesus. Remember that great hymn?

Look full in his wonderful face; then the things of earth grow strangely dim, in the light of his glory and of his grace.

Ladies and gentlemen, we are on the move for God with the greatness of His Word. I thank God that you have the courage to move on the Word and no longer just sit and die.

GOSPEL HEALINGS:
MARK 3 AND JOHN 9

God has no hands but our hands with which to give peo-
ple bread. God has no feet but our feet with which to move
among the almost dead. We say that we are His and He is
ours—deeds are the proof of that, not words, and these are
the proving hours.

Many people wonder why I do not teach on Christian healing a great deal more; I really don't know why I don't. It is a field that I have pioneered in. I have been through every avenue of healing in extent, both from the spiritualist side, the psychiatric, as well as all the medical fields—not that I have done all of them, but I have been with great leading men who have opened their hearts and their lives; we have talked and worked healing.

The second most difficult subject in the Word of God that I have ever dealt with in research is healing. The most difficult one is the most terminating one, and that is death. I spent several years looking and working the subject of death—the explanation; and of course, when you touch death, you have to touch suffering. When you touch suffering, you get into the whole field of sickness and disease.

In the Foundational Class, in order to teach some of the great principles of God's Word, I handle the third chapter of the gospel of Mark. I do not want to handle it in that detail, I simply want to set some truths before you and then move on to the great chapter on healing.

In Mark, Chapter 3, verse 1, we read:

Mark 3:1, 2:
And he [Jesus] entered again into the synagogue; and there was a man there which had a withered hand.

And they watched him [Jesus], whether he would heal him [the man with the withered hand] on the sabbath day; that they might accuse him.

Now isn't that beautiful? Here was a man whose hand was withered. He had gone to the synagogue. And the synagogue represented the place where the Word should be taught; that is where the ministry of deliverance should have been carried out. Jesus Christ walked into that synagogue that day, and there was this man with the withered hand, and they watched him. They were not interested in the man at all. It was the Sabbath day, and they watched him to see whether he would deliver this man for one reason only: did he do it on the right day at the right time. That is not what I call love. They watched him to see if they could do one thing: accuse him. They were not concerned about the man. They were only concerned about whether Jesus Christ would do it, and if he did it, it would be the wrong day to do it on. How terrible! One should think that a person who has a need could go to the synagogue, and at least someone there would love you, right? Today, the same thing is true. We ought to be able to go to the church; and there in that church, there ought to be love. And if man has a need, that is where they ought to have the deliverance—it ought to be there.

Well, Jesus saith unto the man who had the withered hand:

Mark 3:3:
...Stand forth.

Now, that takes a lot of courage on the part of the man with the withered hand. Because the moment he is going to take this stand of standing forth on the word of Jesus Christ, it is going to separate him out from the rest, and the criticism is going to begin—you can guarantee it.

Mark 3:4, 5a:
…[then Jesus] he saith unto them [unto the people there], Is it lawful to do good on the sabbath days, or to do evil? to save life, or to kill? But they held their peace.

And when he had looked round about on them with anger…

It does not say compassion or love; it says "with anger" —Jesus Christ got really angry. Here, there was a synagogue where they should have loved that man; they should have been willing to have that man helped—if it was Sunday or Monday or Tuesday, what difference did the day make? Well, they said, it is the Sabbath day; on the Sabbath we are not supposed to do it. Well, bless God, Jesus Christ did it anyway in spite of them. He did, because people need help. It does not make any difference what kind of package the help comes in. If anyone has it, praise God for it, because we sure need it today.

Mark 3:5a:
…he…looked round about on them with anger, being grieved [hurt] for the hardness of their hearts,

My heart breaks of the hardness of the heart of people who call themselves Christian, who have no compassion for people, who are not willing to go to God's Word and let God's Word speak again and just try it out!

Mark 3:5b:
…he saith…to the man, Stretch forth thine hand.

He cannot do it because the man's hand is withered. But Jesus still said to him, "Stretch forth thy hand."

Now you have to explain something to me. How can a man do something he cannot do? That's right. Before you can get anything from God, there are three things you have to know: number one, what's available; number two, how to receive it; and number three, what to do with it after you've got it. You cannot receive anything from God until it is available. Now whatever God says is available, is available. And that day Jesus said to the man with the withered hand, "Stretch forth thy hand." He could not do it because his hand was withered. Then, how did he do it? It is very simple: there was a law involved; it is the law of believing. He believed that what Jesus Christ said was God's will, and his believing acted literally upon the Word—literally. He acted literally upon the Word. Jesus said, "Stretch forth thy hand"—four words, that is all the Word of God he had. But, ladies and gentlemen, that is all the Word he needed to meet his need.

You find that Word of God that meets your need; you stand on it literally and believe it; God will bring it to pass. He said to the man, "Stretch forth thy hand," and what does it say? It says he—and he, he, the man—that is a great key. Because in every prayer group that I have ever been with, they talk about healing, then always talk about Jesus doing it. They always talk about God doing it. My Bible says the man did it. Now you have to make up your mind whether what they are saying is right, or whether the Word is right. It is as simple as that.

Jesus said to the man stretch forth thy hand, and then it says:

Mark 3:5b:
...And he [the man whose hand was withered, he] stretched it out:...

He stretched it forth. How did he do it? By believing

that the Word of God was the will of God—that it meant what it said and said what it meant! That's right. When Jesus Christ said stretch forth thy hand, he literally believed it; he stretched it forth. He, the man, stretched it forth. That is the believing. Believing is action. To believe is a verb, a verb connotes action and when you believe, you act. He stretched it forth, and his hand was restored.

There are different kinds of healings in the Bible. This is one—when something is restored. You cannot restore something if you have never had health to begin with—like you cannot retread an automobile tire if you have never had an automobile tire to start with. You can restore it, if you had one to begin with. This man had healing—he was whole at one time, but he lost this (Satan robbed him of it), and his hand was withered. That is why the word "restored" is used.

Mark 3:5c:
…and his hand was restored whole as the other.

Now, this man found out what was available. The how of receiving is believing; he knew how to receive it. And naturally, you know what to do with it after you've got it; if your hand is withered, made whole, there is no problem of what to do with it after you have got it.

Another thing I know is that in order for him to do this, he had to get his need and want parallel. Also, he had to recognize that God's ability equals God's willingness. What God is willing to do, He is able to do; and what He is able to do, He is willing to do. This is not always true in my life or yours, perhaps. I am sometimes willing to help people, but I lack the ability. At other times, I am able to help people, but I am not willing to do it. But, in God and in His wonderful son Jesus Christ the ability and the willingness go together. The need and want are parallel in an individual. When you get your need and your want parallel, you know: what is available; how to receive it; what to do with it after you've got it; realizing that God's ability equals God's willingness—God's Word never fails. Now, those are the great principles set forth. And every place in God's Word where something happens (and in every individual's life today where something happens) those same five basic laws can be followed and can be seen—never fails. Every place in the Bible, every miracle, every record in the Bible all fits in the same pattern.

Now, I take you to the greatest miracle of all time, a healing miracle which Jesus Christ did. It was a prophecy, hundreds and hundreds of years before the birth of Jesus Christ. In the prophecy, this man of God had given the statement that when the true messiah would come, he would do one miracle that had never before been done in the history of the world; and that one miracle would be the proof that he was the son of God. Ladies and gentlemen, that is the miracle recorded in John, Chapter 9.

The historical position of this ninth chapter in the great Gospel of John is tremendously remarkable because Jesus Christ had just come out of the fight in the temple area with those who were born of the seed of the serpent (who were the head of the temple), the Pharisees. He had just told them that they were of their father, the devil.[1] And they had just informed him that he was born illegitimately, and that he did not know what he was talking about. They became so angry that they would have killed him, but he walked right out of the group.

---

1. John 8:44, 45: Ye are of *your* father the devil, and the lusts of your father ye will do. He was a murderer from the beginning, and abode not in the truth, because there is no truth in him. When he speaketh a lie, he speaketh of his own: for he is a liar, and the father of it.

And because I tell *you* the truth, ye believe me not.

And then begins that great ninth chapter. It starts with the conjunction "and"—tying together that which now follows with that which precedes.

John 9:1a:
And as Jesus passed by,...

He passed by these people who would have stoned him and gotten rid of him outside the temple, or in that area of the temple.

John 9:1b:
...he saw a man which was blind from *his* birth.

He was born this way—blind. Ladies and gentlemen, if you have never had sight, you cannot have a recovery. That's for sure.

And then Jesus' disciples asked him, saying:

John 9:2:
...Master, who did sin, this man, or his parents, that he was born blind?

There is an age-old question. As a matter of fact, this is the verse some shove at you to prove their belief of reincarnation, because it says in this verse: "who did sin, this man or his parents?" Now, if the man sinned, then it must be sort of like reincarnation, because you cannot sin before you are born—that is how they use it. Well, the background is the eighth chapter, and who had brought up all of this? Those who were born of the seed of the serpent (the head of the temple); they had questioned the disciples, and the disciples brought the question to Jesus.

And the punctuation in the King James is totally erroneous. Punctuation came relatively late. They were not in the original text, and therefore I pay no attention to them. I work the Word for truth, not punctuation because you can take a comma and change the whole meaning of God's Word. I would like to punctuate it and give you what it really says.

> **John 9:2, 3** [accurate punctuation]:
> And his disciples asked him, saying, Master, who did sin, this man, or his parents, that he was born blind?
> Jesus answered, Neither hath this man sinned, nor his parents. [period.][2]

Now verse 4:

> **John 9:4, 5** [accurate punctuation]:
> But [in contrast] that the works of God should be made manifest in him, I [Jesus] must work the works of him that sent me, while it is day: the night cometh, when no man can work. [period—one sentence]
> As long as I am in the world, I am the light of the world.

Now to go back and pick it up.

> **John 9:3** [accurate punctuation]:
> …Neither hath this man sinned nor his parents. [period]

That's the Word of God. The man who was born blind did not sin and naturally his parents did not sin. That is Jesus' answer to reincarnation on this verse.

> **John 9:3b, 4:**
> …but [in contrast] that the works of God should be made manifest in him.
> I must work the works of him that sent me,

---

2. John 9:3, 4: Jesus answered, Neither hath this man sinned, nor his parents: but that the works of God should be made manifest in him.
I must work the works of him that sent me, while it is day: the night cometh, when no man can work.

The man was not born blind so Jesus could go to work. Blindness does not come from God. God does not cause people to be born blind. That's right. But, here was a man who was born blind, but in contrast to his birth, that the works of God should be made manifest in him.

John 9:4:

I [Jesus Christ] must work the works of him that sent me,...the night cometh, when no man can work.

And ladies and gentlemen, if you know your Bible, and you have worked it, there is a day coming that nobody is going to get healed. Nobody is going to get delivered.

John 9:5:

As long as I am in the world, I am the light of the world.

That's right. He is here now because there are born-again believers here; whoever is born again of God's spirit, it is Christ in you the hope of glory, and he is the light. And as long as the church of the body to which you and I belong exists, there is going to be light. And as long as there is light, there is going to be deliverance available for believers. But there is a day coming when the church is going to be gathered up, taken out, it says. When that gathering day comes, the light is not here. And those remaining are not going to get delivered. As long as he is here in the world—"I am the light"—deliverance is available. That is the tremendous thing that he is saying.

You know:

John 9:3b:

Neither hath this man sinned, nor his parents: but that the works of God should be made manifest in him.

Have you ever taken a look at that sixth chapter of John, back a few chapters?

John 6:28:
Then said they unto him, What shall we do, that we might work the works of God?

The works of God—right. This is the question in John 9—works of him that sent me.

John 6:29:
Jesus answered and said…,This is the work of God, that ye believe on him whom he hath sent.

"…whom he hath sent"—that is the Word; to believe on him whom He hath sent. And that is to believe on the Lord Jesus Christ.

And that is why he said:

John 9:5, 6:
As long as I am in the world, I am the light of the world.
When he had thus spoken, he spat on the ground, and made clay of the spittle, and he anointed the eyes of the blind man with…clay,

I have been to healing meetings where people literally go outside, and they get dust, and they spit in it, and put it in the blind person's eyes; but I have not seen them delivered. This bothered me. With healing, I spent most of my time studying my failures and not the successes. I was thankful to God for what we were seeing in successes, but what bothered me was why wasn't everything we were doing a success; where were we failing? And I think if you are going to be honest in research, you have to look at those failures. That's right.

Same way with people getting born again—I just want to help people, and if you get help, you get help. But, I had to study and work and try to figure out where the problems were, on where the failures were because we had no visible results manifested. Therefore, you and I have to be honest enough to find out. And, this particular verse I can explain to you because I understand it.

There are nine manifestations of the spirit.[3] In the worship manifestations you have: speaking in tongues, interpretation of tongues and prophecy. And then there are three revelation manifestations. You do not squeeze them out of God, but God is able, and God is willing. He is more anxious to answer our prayers then we are, the Word says. So, I have no doubt about God's love. And these three revelation manifestations are called: word of knowledge, word of wisdom, and discerning of spirits. Those are the revelation manifestations; they are the informational manifestations whereby God can and does give revelation, from God to man, regarding any subject or any situation about which it is humanly impossible with you by your five senses to know anything about.

By word of knowledge God told Jesus, "Put clay in his eyes." That is how He told him. Word of wisdom is doing it. And you never treat any two cases alike because there are never any two cases alike. I have never seen any two identical, and I do not see any two alike in the Word of God. And I know every healing, every miracle in detail in the Word, and they are just not alike.

So, God gave revelation (word of knowledge) and told him to spit in the dust and put it in the eye. That's right. That is what He told him. Now there happens to be an Eastern biblical custom behind this that Bishop K.C. Pillai, as well as Dr. Lamsa and I discussed. Many peo-

---

3. 1. Worship or inspirational manifestations—speaking in tongues, interpretation of tongues, prophecy.

2. Instructional or revelation manifestations—word of knowledge, word of wisdom, discerning of spirits.

3. Action, power or impartation manifestations—faith, healing, miracles.

ple from this culture believe that there is healing power in the spittle of a holy man.

Now, God by revelation must have told Jesus, well, this is what the man believed, or this is what the man needed. And so, all Jesus did was took clay (which literally means he took the dust of the ground), he spit in it, made like a clay (like you make little mud pies), and he anointed the eyes of the blind man with the clay —word of knowledge and word of wisdom. And you see, the healing that I watched (or so-called, were-to-be healing), that never happened to blind people; they would just plunk it in their eyes. That is what I call mud in the eyes, ha-ha. That does not heal you. You have to walk by revelation. In this case, God said to Jesus, "Put it in his eyes." Now you do exactly what the word of knowledge and word of wisdom says.

John 9:7:
And [then he] said unto him, Go, wash in the pool of Siloam,...

This just blows my mind; seven words in translation here, "Go wash in the pool of Siloam." Now that is the craziest thing in the world to do when you are blind because the waters of the pool of Siloam are not healing. That's right. No more so than a lot of other waters. Sure, there may be some corrective things water can do—like just recently in Europe, I was at the place where just hundreds of people come to take baths for their rheumatism. They spend thousands of dollars because it is a certain type of water, it runs through a certain type of a filter, and that is supposed to do it. It does help them, because the heat helps them, and so forth, so they get some relief. Well, I praise God for it, but that is not Christian healing. That is not what I am talking about. And that is not what Jesus Christ sent him to the pool of

Siloam for. No more so than he told Naaman, the head of the army of the great Syrian Empire.

God, by way of the prophet, told Naaman, "Go dip in the Jordan seven times." And you know, Naaman was real irritated; it says he became wroth. And he said, "Why do you want me to dip in that stinking Jordan anyway? Are not the rivers of Damascus that come out of the mountains, pure mountain streams? They are clean up there; why should I go down to the Jordan and dip?"

Well, the prophet never left the kitchen and his teapot. He just poured himself another cup of tea. He had given the word once, and once the Word of God's given, that settles it. It is God's Word. And so finally Naaman goes down and dips in the Jordan six times, and he takes a look at himself—no improvement. He has not literally fulfilled the Word yet. Then he dipped the seventh time. When he came up the seventh time the Bible says the skin on him was like the skin of a baby.[4]

John 9 says he put clay on his eyes and he said, "Go wash in the pool of Siloam"—seven words.

There are over nine hundred and some promises in the Word of God for physical and material well-being of an individual. Once upon a time I counted them, worked them. Nine hundred and some—how many do you know? You cannot utilize or operate any more than you know. That's right. Now, suppose you can find just one that meets your need. You get your need and want parallel, know what's available, know how to receive it, know what to do with it, believe it; and what is God going to do? Bring it to pass. Nine hundred and some—how many do you know? Once again, you cannot utilize any more than you know.

Well, this man had one promise. That is all he needed.

---

4. The record of Naaman and his healing is in 2 Kings 5.

Seven words, "Go wash in the pool of Siloam." He had been born blind. Now, ladies and gentlemen, if you had been born blind, and you had not seen for thirty-five, forty, fifty years; how much believing would you have if somebody plunked some mud in your eyes and said, "Go wash in the Arkansas River"? Honestly, how much believing would you and I have after thirty-five, forty years of the same sickness? How much believing would you have to be healed now? I deal with people who if God does not heal them "right now" (they have only been sick about an hour), they turn their backs on God. That is honestly how they act. They have called me on the phone and said, "You believe in healing?"

I said, "Sure, don't you?"

They said, "Well, we'll try you out."

I said, "Goodbye." Ha-ha!—That's right. I am not in business to be tried out; I am to help people in the Word, that I know.

The reason I learned all these things is because I used to always fall for that stuff. Every time someone would call and need any help, I would run to them. I have driven over 150 miles one way to minister or pray for someone, yet they never thanked me or even paid for my gas—just nothing. Finally I came to the place to understand the Word and revelation, so now I just sit and brew myself another pot of tea. That's right. I wait until I get one thing—revelation. When I have revelation, that's it. Then I would go a thousand miles to help someone, but until I have that revelation—no use.

I had to learn this the hard way, because in life when you are honestly questing and really moving into these categories and fields, it takes a real discipline to stay there. Mrs. Wierwille was so angry at me we almost didn't talk for three days because we had a person who had just started coming to our church, and they had a child they had to take into the hospital. She thought if I went right then to visit that child in the hospital, that would bless Daddy and Mommy, and they would keep coming back to church. You know the deal. So, she asked me when I was going, and I said, "I don't know."

And then about supper time she asked me, "Did you go to the hospital this afternoon?"

And I said, "No."

And she said, "YOU DIDN'T?"

And I said, "Nope."

The next day I did not go, and it got worse and worse. But, you see, I was learning. I just did not want to do it. Then all at once, there it was, and I went to the hospital. Lo and behold, Daddy and Mommy were not in the room, nobody was there; and the little boy was just tickled I came to see him. And he said, "Sure glad you came now, because Daddy never would have believed if you would have come in because he doesn't believe God can do it. But I know God can do it, and I'm glad you came." That afternoon he walked out of the hospital.

You see, I have learned this stuff the hard way. It is something you work at honestly. If we do not know something, we just admit we do not know it. I have done it a thousand times. It is no disgrace to admit you do not know something. But, to me, it is a terrible disgrace to say you know something, and then you do not know it. And, people, there are a lot of things about God's Word we do not know. And when people bug you while you are trying to help people, and they think you should have all the answers, just tell them straight, "I haven't got it, but I know Him who is the answer." And then you begin moving. You see, if we just help one person, it would be worth a lifetime. If we just saved one person, it is worth a lifetime because the Bible says that a man's soul is worth more than all the wealth of the world. And God's Word has to be right. You cannot fail when you walk that way.

And so, he said to the man, "Go, wash in the pool of Siloam." The Word of God is the will of God. It means what it says, and it says what it means. So, what do you think this man had to do? Go wash in the pool. If he would have washed any other place, he would not have gotten healed. He literally had to go to the pool of Siloam. And that is exactly what he did.

Look what it says: he, the man—like Mark 3, the man —he did it.

John 9:7b:
...He went his way therefore, and washed, and came seeing.

The man was born blind. And this is the first time in the history of the world that anybody who was born blind was healed.

Now the neighbors are going to get involved. They are usually more interested in your life than you might think. Verse 8:

John 9:8, 9:
The neighbours therefore, and they which before had seen him that he was blind, said, Is not this he that sat and begged?

Some [neighbors] said, This is he: others said, He is like him: but he [the man] said, I am he.

The man said, I'm the guy. Beautiful neighbors, right?

John 9:10, 11:
Therefore said they [the neighbors] unto him, How were thine eyes opened?

He answered and said, A man that is called Jesus made clay...anointed...[my] eyes, and said unto me,

Go to the pool of Siloam, and wash: and I went and washed, and I received sight.

How did he get it? He received it; he took it. The *only* way you ever get anything from God and His promises—you have to believe, and you *take* it! You talk about truth. He went, he washed, and he received it. He took it. That is how you get delivered. How do you get saved? You believe, and you confess with your mouth. *You* do it—not your grandma; you do it. You confess with your mouth the Lord Jesus, you believe God raised him from the dead, and "thou shalt (absolute tense) be saved."[5] He went, he washed, and he received sight. That is the way you get it! You have to receive it. But you know what the human mind says to you? "Oh, you can't have it." Well, I guess you can't when you say that.

Verse 12:

John 9:12:
Then said they unto him, Where is he? I know not.

That is really something! He did not even know this Jesus man; he did not know where he had gone—nothing. Real tremendous!

Verse 13:

John 9:13:
They brought to the Pharisees him that aforetime was blind.

Now the synagogue, the church, the temple had to get involved—the religious ones, you know. And there is no persecution that equals the religious. That's right.

---

5. Romans 10:9, 10: That if thou shalt confess with thy mouth the Lord Jesus, and shalt believe in thine heart that God hath raised him from the dead, thou shalt be saved.

For with the heart man believeth unto righteousness; and with the mouth confession is made unto salvation.

Just check your history. If you want to see persecution that is vicious, go the religious route. They brought him to these men who were the heads of the temple, where God had said He would meet His people; they brought him there.

And verse 14 says it was the Sabbath. The man born blind was healed on the Sabbath. The first time in the history of the world that anyone who was born blind was healed, and it happened on the wrong day! That is terrible. That's right.

> **John 9:15, 16a:**
> Then again the Pharisees also asked him how he had received his sight. He said unto them, He put clay upon mine eyes, and I washed, and do see.
> Therefore said some of the Pharisees, This man is not of God, because he keepeth not the sabbath day. Others said, How can a man that is a sinner do such miracles? And there was a division among…[the top brass in the temple in the religious circles].

And where there is division there is every evil work.[6]

> **John 9:17:**
> They say unto the blind man again, What sayest thou of him, that he hath opened thine eyes?…[And the man] said, He is a prophet.

That takes some boldness for a layman to say to the top religious brass, "He's a prophet!" That's right.

> **John 9:18:**
> But the Jews did not believe concerning him, that he had been blind, and received his sight, until they called the parents…

---

6. James 3:16: For where envying and strife *is*, there *is* confusion and every evil work.

Now the parents get involved. First the neighbors, then the religious groups, now the parents.

John 9:19-22a:

And they asked them, saying, Is this your son, who ye say was born blind? how then doth he now see?

His parents answered them and said, We know that this is our son, and that he was born blind:

But by what means he now seeth, we know not; or who hath opened his eyes, we know not: he is of age; ask him: he shall speak for himself.

These words spake his parents, because they...

Loved their son, and what God had done for him? Well, one would think so. If God had saved your son or daughter, one would think you, as a parent, ought to be grateful and thankful and take a stand for God and the ministry that did it.

Verse 22 says: These words spake his parents because of one thing—fear. That is what it says, that is what it means! For fear of the Jews—they were afraid of the society in which they lived. They were afraid of the top religious echelon, what they would do to them. Ladies and gentlemen, wherever you have fear, you are encased, you are enslaved. Fear always encases; fear always enslaves. Fear always makes you less than what you really ought to be, and what you really want to be in the inner most depths of your soul, when you are yourself. These parents had a son born blind; here he sees for the first time, and his parents cannot say anything. I do not care who did it, but whoever did it, I praise God for it. They could not do it because they were full of fear.

And our society cannot take an accurate stand on God's Word because our society is full of fear. We are afraid of what they may say. We are afraid we may lose a business. We are afraid of the power. You believe God;

He will give it to you. He can open the windows of heaven and pour it out to you! He does not need us to wait on the arm of man to get something done. Our God is still God of the heavens and the earth. And ladies and gentlemen, I am convinced He can still feed five thousand with a few loaves and a few fishes if He must. And I am still convinced, He can get a man from Samaria down on a certain road where there is a man reading the Word of God who needs help. But you see we have such little believing in God because no one ever believed God can do what His Word says.

Those parents, for fear of the Jews, could not say, "Thank God our son is healed." Well, I know that I as a parent have to stand with my children. When my children take a stand, I as a parent stand with them. If my child makes a mistake, I do not agree with him on the mistake; but I want to tell you something, he is still my child. As far as I am concerned, I do not care how you got here, but God has a purpose for you. You are here because God has a need in this world for someone to understand God's Word again and hold it forth. I know that beyond a shadow of a doubt. And if you do not do it in your lifetime, it is not going to happen. You have to get over the fear and really stand. And you young people have to go back to your parents and try to love them and get them with you in the greatness of God's Word. You have to make it a choice. Is God first, or isn't He? Joshua said, "As for me and my house, we will serve the Lord." That is the decision you have to make. And so that tremendous thing here just tears the heart out of a man when he sees it.

John 9:22:

These *words* spake his parents, because they feared the Jews: for the Jews had agreed already [and he is talking about the religious leaders, they had agreed already], that if any man did confess that he was the Christ, he should be put out of the synagogue.

If anyone said that this man was Christ, do you know what they are going do to them? Put them out of the synagogue. That is just terrible.

John 9:23
Therefore said his parents, He is of age; ask him.

That is what they were afraid of. Now being excommunicated out of the synagogue meant something in that day; it does not mean anything today, compared to what it meant then. When the parents would be excommunicated from the synagogue they could not buy food, they could not get any clothing, nobody would talk to them. If they would walk down this side of the street, everyone else would walk on the other side. The excommunication was sort of sharp. Today, it does not mean anything. If one church at this corner throws you out, all you need to do is fly to the other side because there is usually a church on the other corner, and you drop in. You know, if this brand kicks you out, that brand will be glad to have you. That's right.

John 9:24a:
Then again called they the man that was blind, and said unto him, Give God the praise:…

"Give God the praise." That is what the heads of the temple (who were born of the wrong seed) said to this man, they said, "Give God the praise, brother. Give God the praise, give God the praise!" This fools most people because they just forgot to say which god! And my Bible says there are two gods: one is the God and Father of our Lord Jesus Christ, the other is the god of this world,[7] called Satan. Looks real religious: "Give God the praise, brother. Give God the praise, give God the praise."

---

7. 2 Corinthians 4:4: In whom the god of this world hath blinded the minds of them which believe not, lest the light of the glorious gospel of Christ, who is the image of God, should shine unto them.

John 9:24b:
…we know that this man is a sinner.

Wow! "Give God the praise; we know the man who did it is a sinner." A what? sinner. How do you like that one?

John 9:25:
He answered and said, Whether he be a sinner or no, I know not: [but] one thing I know, that, whereas I was blind, now I see.

Glory hallelujah! Once I was blind, but now I see. Once I was lost, but now I am born again. Take a stand! Once I was blind, but now I see. Amen! I want to tell you, that takes courage to say to the top religious echelon in that day!

John 9:26, 27:
Then said they to him again, What did he to thee? how opened he thine eyes?
He answered them, I have told you already, and ye did not hear: wherefore would ye hear it again? will ye also be his disciples?

Wow! Can't you just see it?

John 9:28:
Then they reviled him [they reviled him], and said, Thou art his disciple; but we are Moses' disciples.

You know, we are Moses' disciples. You are his disciple; he is a sinner.

Verse 29:

John 9:29:
We know that God spake unto Moses: as for this fellow, we know not from whence he is.

Wow! How do you like that?

John 9:30:

The man answered and said unto them, Why herein is a marvellous thing, that ye know not from whence he is, and yet he hath opened mine eyes.

Here is a layman talking to the top PhDs in the religious circles; the heads of the temple in Jerusalem, the men who made up the Sanhedrin, the ruling seventy of all Judaism. He said, herein is a most unusual thing, the man healed me, and yet you religious leaders do not know who he is?

John 9:31:

Now we know that God heareth not sinners: but if any man be a worshipper of God, and doeth his will, him he heareth.

Here it is, verse 32:

John 9:32:

Since the world began was it not heard that any man opened the eyes of one that was born blind.

And here is a layman quoting them God's Word from Isaiah 35. Isaiah prophesied years and years ago that when the true Messiah would come, he would open the eyes of a man born blind. The men in the top religious circles did not know God's Word. But a layman who was born blind said, "Herein is a real marvelous thing that you do not know who opened my eyes, because since the foundations of the world has it never been heard that any man opened the eyes of one that was born blind."

John 9:33, 34a:

If this man were not of God, he could do nothing.

They answered and said unto him, Thou wast altogether born in sins, and dost thou teach us?...

Oh, how do you like that one? You are altogether in

your sins, you poor, miserable guy. We run the outfit and you want to tell us?

And they did the most beautiful, loving thing in the world: they cast him out. Isn't that great love? Wonderful. A man born blind gets healed at a place where healing ought to be available to people, where they ought to be looking for answers. But instead, it is not on the right day, not done in the right way, not by the right people (as far they are concerned); and so it cannot be genuine, it has to be counterfeit. Let's get rid of him.

John 9:34b:
...And they cast him out.

And I want to tell you, when they cast him out, they just did not take him by the arm and say, "Now, pretty please, come on out." They turned him around, and they used some tremendous force, and they literally took him and threw him out!

John 9:35a:
Jesus heard that they had cast him out;...

This gets back to an accurate knowledge of God's Word where people are going to take a crack at you, they are going to throw you out. They are going to put you in jail for what you believe. Well, I would like to say to you, Jesus Christ will be there with you. He is going to stand right by you. The neighbors may cop out, the parents may cop out, the religious echelon may be copped out; but there is one that never cops out, and that is the Lord Jesus Christ. He will stand with his people. He never backs down one iota. Jesus found him; that is what I call love. Nobody else looked for him, nobody else cared about him, but Jesus found him.

Look what it says:

John 9:35b, 36:

...he said unto him, Dost thou believe on the Son of God?

He answered and said, Who is he, Lord, that I might believe on him?

He did not even know Jesus Christ was the son of God. Well, I would have never healed him unless he belonged to my gang. Ever heard that one? I have heard it a hundred times. Look, you first have to become a Christian, then God will heal you. Oh baloney. Everyone I read about in the Bible were all non-Christians. They received healing first, and then they wanted such a savior who would heal them. That's right. This man born blind did not even know who Jesus was, and yet Jesus healed him. Healing is not dependent upon whether you are a Christian or non-Christian; it is dependent upon believing. Believing! And I see more non-Christians healed than I have ever seen so-called Christians healed because the non-Christians still want (some of them) to at least believe. You show them the accuracy of the Word, and they believe. The so-called Christians always want to fight about it. He said, "Dost thou believe on the son of God." And he said, "Lord, who is he that I might believe?..."

John 9:37, 38:

And Jesus said unto him, Thou hast both seen him, and it is he that talketh with thee.

And he said, Lord, I believe. And he worshipped him.

Lord, I believe. That is a tremendous thing. That is the miracle (which the Bible says is the proof that Jesus Christ is the son of God) because he opened the eyes of a man who was born blind. And he did this for this man when this man did not know he was God's son, but he knew he was a prophet. And when they cast him out,

Jesus went and found him and led him into a great spiritual truth, "Dost thou believe on the son of God?"

And he said, "Who is he that I might believe?"

And Jesus said, "You have seen, I am the son of God."

And he said, "Lord, I believe." All things are possible to him that believeth.

It is a tremendous time, people! You cannot get too much of the knowledge of the accuracy of the Word, and it takes time to build this Word in our life. Get started on the principles, and then take the days of your life putting it into that Word. Let that Word begin to effervesce and live in your whole heart, soul, mind, and strength that people again may see the Lord Jesus Christ, because they will never see him unless they see him in you. Because God has no hands but our hands with which to give people bread. God has no feet but our feet with which to move among the almost dead. We say that we are His and He is ours. Deeds are the proof of that, not words, and these are the proving hours.

STEALING YOUR HEALING

God's Word, with your believing,
dominates circumstances.

Unbelief only utters words; it never utters the Word. It does a lot of talking, uses a lot of words, but never gets to the Word. Some of us have gone through experiences where we were taught as if we should touch the radio or television as our point of contact, or reach over and touch the individual nearby as a point of contact. Well, for those of us who love God and His Word, His Word is our point of contact with Him; not some radio, not some TV. It is His Word.

It is His Word that brings us to the place where we become utterly and completely one with Him. We become what that Word says we are when we believe what that Word says. Then we become utterly one with Him. I refer to it as union with God and His Word.

You see, when this happens in the life of a man or a woman, those weaknesses and those inabilities that mankind is so acclimatized to seeing in Christians just disappear in the presence of God and by the strength of God as He reveals Himself in His Word.

The Word of God IS. For most people, the Word of God is a has-been. But for believers, the Word of God is. It is a present tense, active verb, now. And if any man ever wills to know the will of God, he has to come to the Word of God to get the will of God.

The only way you can ever know the will of God regarding healing is you have to go to the Word. In Luke 8 there are a number of them, but the one I would like to handle and share with you begins in verse 43:

Luke 8:43, 44a:
And a woman having an issue of blood twelve years, which had spent all her living upon physicians, neither could be healed of any,
Came behind *him*, and touched the border…

The word "border" is the word "hem"—just the border. We understand what that means; a border is a hem.

Luke 8:44b:
…of his garment: and immediately her issue of blood stanched.

Which means it dried up. It terminated.

Here is a woman who has been very much afflicted for twelve years, and usually if you have been afflicted for any great length of time (like twelve years, or one man thirty-eight years in the Word) there is very little believing left that God is still able to do something. Here was this woman who had this sickness for twelve years. She had done everything she could, everything she knew how to do sense knowledge wise. She had not just sat around and prayed and done nothing; she had been praying, but she had also been taking action, doing everything she could. Yet somehow or other she was not delivered, because it said she "neither could be healed of any" or cured.

Verse 44:

Luke 8:44:
Came behind *him*,…

She came behind Jesus. She followed behind him. I do not know if I can paint a picture to you as vividly as I see it in the original text. She is coming behind him, and she is just pushing up through the crowd toward the front. She wants to push in on him and yet not really do it. She wants to do it, and she doesn't want to do it. That is the text. You know, in action—she came behind.

The word "him" in the King James Version is in italics. Well, if you are behind, you are behind him; that is axiomatic. But the depth of the word here is what intrigues me; came behind and touched. And in order to touch, she had to reach out. She had to reach out just to touch. She came behind and began thinking, well, I wonder what he will say if I just touch. Just touch. In that culture at that time, this was a real bold move on a woman's part. A real bold move, because the woman does not come to the front; she always stays behind. For this woman to break culture—and that is what she is doing—is real fantastic. She literally broke the culture because she was a woman. The men would follow; the women come behind, way behind. For example, if I went for a walk, all the men would walk right behind me, and then behind the men come all the women.

Now, this woman got up toward the front. And I want to tell you, I will bet that took a little boldness. That is what I see in the Word. She got right up there, and that is why she "came behind." Because she had finally made it in the front line with the men. Right at the front.

People, when your need gets big enough, and your want gets lined up with it, you are going to do anything that has to be done, if you have to break every cultural rule in the world. Because God is more important than tradition, and culture is nothing but tradition. God is more important than anything men ever say about Him. That's right. No man can say anything better about God than what God says about Himself in His Word. No man ever improves upon the Word. The best man ever does is to equal what the Word says, but usually men do less than what the Word says when they present it. They usually water it down.

This woman broke all culture, and she got right behind Jesus, and she reached out. She reached out and she just touched the hem of his garment. What a woman!

You see, it is hard for us in the Western world to understand this. Ordinarily a woman of the West will run up and say, "Hey, hug me." You do not do that in this woman's Eastern biblical culture. She did not run up to Jesus and say, "Hug me." No, no, no. Even to press way up to the front and then just to reach out and just to touch the hem of his garment was a fantastic act of believing. Listen, there are very few of us in the Western world that understand these things because we do not understand the order and the tradition of the Eastern world of biblical culture at that time. Quite a bold woman.

That woman had a fantastic need. Twelve years she had been suffering, and here was the one about whom she had been hearing. Maybe she had been following in the crowd previously when he ministered as talked about in those records in the Gospel of Luke. Maybe she saw these things and her believing was built up. Here was the man of God whom she believed could really help her. And she got so moved, she came all the way to the front. Then she just reached out and just touched the hem of his garment. Jesus did not minister to her, Jesus did not pray for her, Jesus did not put her under a psychiatric probe, Jesus did not do any one of those. Isn't that fantastic? And the moment she touched the hem, immediately—what does it say? *Immediately*, her issue, her problem with her blood situation was terminated, dried up, staunched, healed.

This is the case that I would like to refer to as "stealing your healing." It is something, isn't it? You know, she never said to him, "May I please touch the hem of your garment?" No. She just walked up and claimed what I know in our administration as legal sonship rights. She just walked up, and she believed. She believed that if she could but touch the hem of his garment, she would be made whole.

What a principle of believing! She believed if she could just touch the hem. She did not even believe that he had to pray for her. I have had people come to me and say, "Dr. Wierwille, I think if you pray for me, I'll be healed." Well, if you have your believing there, then I have to do it. But what are you going to do if I am not around and you are sick?

You see, there is no more strength within me than there is within you. For the same Christ that lives within me is the same Christ that lives within you. And God so made the Body of the Church that each believer could help every other believer when they had need. But we have to build our believing upon the integrity and accuracy of God's Word and not upon an individual.

Whether I am here or not, the fact is, the Word is here! That is what is important! That's right. It is not important *who* teaches it, it is important *what* is taught. And if you hold forth the Word, it is as much the Word as when I hold it forth.

This woman was so fantastic. She was so absolutely convinced that he did not even have to minister to her, he did not even have to pray for her, he did not even have to put any mud on her sores. She just reached out, believing if she could just touch the hem.

Now, ladies and gentlemen, there is no healing in the hem of a garment. That's right. There is no healing in the aprons of Paul. They took from his body, what was it? Apron? Handkerchiefs? And people were healed. There is no healing in a handkerchief. There is no healing in an apron. Then, why did they get healed? Believing.

Let me explain it another way to set it for you completely, as I understand it. In the Eastern world of biblical culture, they believe that whatever a man of God wore was a blessing if you could even touch it. That is what they believed. That is why this woman just reached out to touch his hem. Isn't that beautiful?

Well, people, it is in the believing. And the believing is built upon the integrity of God's Word. Is God's Word true, or is it not? Remember John 10:10?[1] Is it true, or is it not true? Is Corinthians true, or is it not true? Is Galatians true, or is it not true? You have to make up your mind whether the Word of God is true or not true.

When I talk about the Word of God, I am not speaking about a translation; I am speaking about that Word that fits like a hand in a glove—that Word that works all the way through. Work the texts until they fit without you squeezing them, then you are back to that original Word that holy men of God spake because they were moved by the Holy Spirit.[2] And that is God's Word. And God's Word is absolutely God's Word. You just have to make up your mind whether you believe it is.

This woman believed. She believed so utterly that she broke all the culture; she broke through the men, came up to the front, and finally reached down and just touched the hem of his garment. The healing was in the believing that if she could but touch the hem of this garment of this wonderful man, she would be healed. And she was, it says, immediately. And you know what immediately means? Right away—boom, quick, now, immediately— immediately. It is a miracle of healing.

---

1. John 10:10: The thief cometh not, but for to steal, and to kill, and to destroy: I am come that they might have life, and that they might have *it* more abundantly.

2. 2 Peter 1:21: For the prophecy came not in old time by the will of man: but holy men of God spake *as they were* moved by the Holy Ghost.

Verse 45:

Luke 8:45a:
And Jesus said, Who touched me?…

Isn't that beautiful? He did not know who touched him, but he knew something had happened. You know how I know he knew? By revelation. God showed him something had happened. He felt something in his body.

Luke 8:45:
And Jesus said, Who touched me? When all denied, Peter and they that were with him said, Master, the multitude throng thee and press *thee*, and sayest thou, Who touched me?

There was Peter and all of them that denied him, every one of them. They said, "Oh, nobody touched you, master, we're just going along with you." When all denied, Peter and they that were with him said, "Master, it's a very logical thing, very simple. There's a whole multitude here, and the multitude thronged thee. And the newspaper gang is here, the press; you know they always crowd in." Doesn't God have a wonderful sense of humor?

Peter was logical as crazy, wasn't he? His logic is good, but he is still dead wrong. That's right. Jesus said, "Who touched me?"

Peter said, "It is very simple, a whole bunch of people could touch you."

Jesus said, "Don't kid me—somebody touched me."

People, when you reach out to touch him, he will automatically and spiritually touch you.

Luke 8:46:
…Jesus said, Somebody hath touched me: for I perceive that virtue is gone out of me.

The word "virtue" is the Greek word *dunamis*. *Dunamis* is inherent power. It is potential power that is latent within; it has to be there before it can bless people on the outside. You cannot give anything away if you do not have it.

Well, Jesus said he had perceived what? virtue—*dunamis*. That inherent power within him had gone out. He got revelation. He knew something had happened.

Luke 8:47a:
And when the woman saw that she was not hid,...

She saw. I see this so very beautifully. It is so simple. Jesus was standing close to everybody with people on either side of him. All at once he turned around, and he said, "Who touched me?"

And Peter said, "Nobody in particular; the whole crowd is around."

And then those words, "when the woman saw..."; do you know what happened? Jesus looked right at her, that is what happened. He looked right at her, and she knew that he knew that she had been the one who touched the hem. That is why she came trembling. What does it say?

Luke 8:47b:
...she came trembling, and falling down before him, she declared unto him before all the people for what cause she had touched him, and how she was healed immediately.

How was she healed? Jesus saw by revelation who had touched him, but he did not know why. She came and told him why. What you can know by your sense knowledge, you do not need revelation. Isn't that beautiful? She just told him.

And she came trembling. One of the reasons she came trembling was not because of a negative fear, but of the excitement of the moment. I do not believe that she was full of fear. If you have ever been really sick and received deliverance, you might tremble just from the joy and rejoicing in your heart. I think that is this woman. She had gotten delivered. It would not have surprised me a bit if she was crying her eyes out. I know a gentleman who got healed once, and he jumped around; he was leaping and praising God.

This woman came:

Luke 8:47:
...falling down before him, she declared unto him before all the people for what cause [why] she had [reached out] touched him, and how she was healed...

And Jesus said:

Luke 8:48:
...he said unto her, Daughter,...

Isn't that beautiful? You talk about the tenderness of Christ. Jesus said to this beautiful woman, "Daughter." Do you know what the word "daughter" means? The same as the word "son" means; when it is used in the gospels, it means that she belonged to the household of that great, wonderful fellowship of the saints who are called out of Israel. A woman, a daughter of Abraham, like the Syrophoenician woman. This woman was a daughter, a believer.

Luke 8:48:
...be of good comfort:...

These words "be of good comfort" are omitted in all the texts. And of course, because it is here, I see her really excited and even thanking the Lord within her heart. And he says, "You are sweet, you are wonderful. Cool it. Just have a good time. Be of good comfort."

Then comes this tremendous phrase:

Luke 8:48:
…thy faith hath made thee whole; go in peace.

It is really something; "Daughter, thy faith hath made thee whole."

This word "faith" is the one that needs to be clarified, because I have consistently used the word "believing." And I have said as I have been teaching regarding this, that this woman believed. It was her believing when she touched the hem—her believing.

Now, here we have the word "faith." Those two words are not identical. Faith is a spiritual inside job. Believing is of the mind—or as the Bible says at times, of the heart. That does not mean the physical heart, but the renewed mind that is so completely renewed that with every fiber of one's being they just know it is true.

The Greek word "*pistis*" is translated "faith," and it is also translated "believing" or "to believe."

Go to Galatians, Chapter 3, verse 23:

Galatians 3:23:
But before faith came,…

Before what? faith; before faith came. Then there must have been a time when there was no faith. That's right. There was a time when there was no faith, but there has never been a time when men could not believe. The natural man of body and soul can believe, otherwise he could not be born again. The natural man of body and soul does not have faith, but he has the ability to believe.

Suppose I am a natural man of body and soul, and you teach me God's Word. Now, once I hear it, I have the ability and the freedom to either accept it or reject it. Which means I can either believe it or not believe it, right? So, the human mind has the ability to believe but the human mind does not have faith. Faith is an inside job.

There was a time before faith came. Now, it will tell you exactly when it was, if you just read what is written:

> **Galatians 3:23:**
> ...we were kept under the law, shut up [closed off] unto the faith which should afterwards [After what? the law. After the fulfillment of the law] be revealed.

That is the verse. Very simple. Look at it again:

> **Galatians 3:23:**
> But before faith came, we were kept under the law, shut up [or closed off] unto the faith which should afterwards [after the law] be revealed.

In Romans, it says that Christ is the end of the law.[3] He is the fulfillment of it. Before faith came, we were kept under the law. After its fulfillment—afterwards be what? revealed.

Verse 24:

> **Galatians 3:24:**
> Wherefore the law was our schoolmaster *to bring us...*

The law was not faith, the law was our schoolmaster. "...*to bring us*" is in italics—scratch it. The law never brought anybody to Christ. The law made you conscious of sin. Without the law, the scripture said there would be no awareness or knowledge of transgression. The law was the schoolmaster, the teacher,...

> **Galatians 3:24:**
> ...[until or] unto [whom?] Christ, that we might be justified by faith [*pistis*].

---

3. Romans 10:4: For Christ *is* the end of the law for righteousness to every one that believeth.

Verse 25, now watch it carefully:

Galatians 3:25:
But [in contrast] after that faith is come, we are no longer under a schoolmaster.

How many of us have not endeavored to live under something that was not even available to us? But everyone worked on us saying the law was our responsibility to be under.

You see, when you practice the law of life, the law of the spirit of life in Christ Jesus, the great law of love; you do not need the Ten Commandments. That's right. Christ is the end of the law. He was the fulfillment of it. And after that, faith came, which came with Jesus Christ. He is the one who made it available. After that faith is come, we are no longer under a schoolmaster. You are no longer under the law; you are living in a higher realm of spiritual adaptation to the greatness of the power of God and His Word. That is wonderful!

This is why faith came with Jesus Christ. It is a spiritual job. If you are born again of God's spirit you have Christ in you, the hope of glory. He is the one you have —Christ is in you.

People used to say to me, they wished they had my faith. You have the same amount I do. If it is Christ in you, then you have the same power in you that I have. Because I do not have any more of Christ than you have. That's right.

Believing varies among people who are Christian, but faith does not vary. God has given to every man, the scripture says, the measure of faith, which is Christ in you, the hope of glory. That is all wrapped up in that spiritual package. The same amount of faith I have, you have. The difference then is not in faith, it is in believing. If you believe God's Word, and I do not, you get the results of your believing, I get the consequences of my unbelief. That is why there is a difference.

Now, back to this woman in Luke 8. Jesus…

Luke 8:48:
…said unto her, Daughter, thy…[*pistis*]

Thy what? It cannot be faith, it has to be what? believing. Because Christ had not yet fulfilled what I read to you from Galatians. Christ came to make the new birth available. If any one person could be born again *before* it was completely complete, then everyone could be born again before it was complete. Then Jesus would not needed to have died, and God would not needed to have resurrected him.

Faith was not available until Jesus Christ had completed everything. And his completion was not just with his death, but with his resurrection, with his ascension.

So, if this Word of God is to be handled accurately, the text reads, "Daughter, thy believing hath made thee whole; go in peace." Go in peace. Isn't that beautiful! Her believing had made her whole. There were ten lepers who came to Jesus, all ten were healed. Only one, the Bible says, was made whole.

So to be made whole means biblically more than just to get healed. That's right. To be made whole is to really get it together in life: mentally sound, physically sound, spiritually whole, financially whole. This woman had spent all that she had. Jesus said, woman, your believing—your believing has made you what? whole. And then he said, just go in what? peace. Quite a record!

You see, God's Word, with your believing, dominates circumstances. And we have to be Word-conditioned rather than world-conditioned. And when this is true of our individual lives, then you and I are God's will in the adversary's world; and we take the place of Jesus Christ here upon earth, acting in his stead. That is power of attorney, legally, which he has given to every believer.

Jesus Christ is not upon the earth now. The Bible said God resurrected him, raised him, he ascended, and he sat down at the right hand of God. And from thence, he is coming back. He is not here now in all the effulgence, the beauty, the dynamic that we shall someday see. He is here now by what God wrapped up in that new birth of Christ in you; which is the faith of Jesus Christ—the love, the peace, the joy, all of that. But he is living within you spiritually. That is where he is—Christ in you.

You and I have to take the place right now of Jesus Christ here upon earth, and we have to act in his stead. Jesus said, "The works that I do ye shall do also." He said to the woman, "Daughter, your believing hath made you whole; go in peace." If Jesus can say that to people, then I as God's son, born again of God's spirit, I can say to you, "God bless you." And I think for most people they think that is just a flip of the lip. Not for me. It is the blessing of God. It is the power of God moving upon an individual.

Jesus said, "Daughter, go in peace." Look at the tremendous truth in that. She no longer had to fret and worry about getting this problem all over again. She did not have to wonder how long this would hold good, or if the issue would return. Jesus just quieted her beautiful heart and said, "Go in peace."

And that is what we need to do as God's people. We need to bless each other. We need to just quietly but dynamically put the peace of God, the love of God, the joy of God on people.

The Word of God says that those of us who are born again in God's spirit, we are to be *especially* good to the household of faith. Remember that? It is in the Word —especially good. Now, I can afford to be good to a lot of people, but I have to be especially good to the house-hold of faith. And you know who the household of faith is? Those that are born again of God's spirit, who have the faith of Jesus Christ. To those I have to be *especially* good. So do you.

You just have to sometimes feel this thing in your bones like it is written. You have to feel it throughout your whole being. That he should say to her, "Woman, you spent everything, do not worry about it. Just go in peace. Daughter, you've got it. Go in peace."

JUMPING AND LEAPING AND PRAISING GOD

Until people see the Christ in you,
you will never be able to deliver or help people.

Like so much in God's Word, this record in the Book of Acts is simply amazing; dynamically revealing of the greatness of the first century church, and a section of God's Word that has been pretty-well hidden. For the most part, it has just been another nice story to people —something that occurred in the first century, but it passed away with the apostles, and consequently this is the kind of thing you no longer believe for.

You see, I was trained in the theological seminaries that in Peter and John's day the first century church did not have the intellect of the medical profession, and therefore they needed Peter and John and God to help them. But since that time, we have developed science and the medical profession. And it is the medical profession that has replaced the power of God and the greatness of that which is made known in the Word. So, the medical professions with their hospitals took over the days of Peter and John.

You just cannot get rid of God's Word that easily. If one thing in the Book of Acts is dropped out—and you drop out anything you want to drop out—you lose the new birth, you lose everything. It is either the Church in action with the greatness of the power of God all the way through, or it is not.

The greatness of Jesus' ministry was manifested in

its maximum with the healing of the man born blind in John. The record is in John 9. The greatness of the power of God in the believers in the early church were made manifest here in the third chapter of the Book of Acts. This is the first record in the Word, after the birth of the church, regarding the deliverance of someone who was born incapacitated; or, as I say, who came from the factory with parts missing.

You see, when people were born again of God's spirit they immediately spoke in tongues. Having continued in the apostles' right-believing doctrine, they not only spoke in tongues, but they operated the manifestations. I believe that they interpreted and prophesied. I believe they operated word of knowledge, word of wisdom, discerning of spirits, faith, miracles and healing.

Before the Lord Jesus Christ ascended, when he was with the apostles, he must have taught them many things because they spent approximately forty days together. Things that, of course, are not recorded in the Word of God. They must have talked about something, and I am sure they did not spend much time talking about the social problems in Palestine. Nor about who was going to be the next governor elect of the Judea territory. By sheer logic, from the integrity and accuracy of God's Word, I would say that those were great days of instruction and teaching. He must have just opened his heart, spiritually speaking. Opened it to them and taught them things to look for, and what to do when certain things occurred, as you and I understand they did on the Day of Pentecost.

I would not be a bit surprised if he taught them how to operate the word of knowledge, word of wisdom, discerning of spirits, (believing) faith, miracles, and healing —all of that. You have no proof of it text-wise, but when you get into the inner depth of God's Word, and you see the greatness of that Word, you just know that nothing ever happens by chance or accident. You know that people are not good baseball pitchers because they read a book, but because someone instructed them properly and taught them. When you understand this, then you have to realize that certainly there must have been some fantastic teaching to a group of men.

I think the greatness of all of this shows up in the third chapter of Acts, where it says:

Acts 3:1:
Now Peter and John went up together into the temple at the hour of prayer, *being* the ninth *hour*.

These words, "Peter and John" together are used seven times, in the Book of Acts. Peter is always the one that is mentioned first. The "ninth hour" would be approximately three o'clock in the afternoon—the ninth hour of prayer. As you know, the first hour corresponds to our 6:00 a.m., then the third hour 9:00 a.m., the sixth hour 12:00 noon, the ninth 3:00 p.m., and the twelfth hour which was the fifth hour of prayer rather at 6:00 p.m.

Acts 3:2:
And a certain man lame from his mother's womb was carried, whom they laid daily at the gate of the temple which is called Beautiful, to ask alms of them that entered into the temple.

One would have thought that with such a tremendous occurrence, the least they could have done would be named the man. One would have thought that when Jesus Christ healed the man born blind, the least they could have done is put his name in the record.

I think some of the greatness of God's Word is in things like this. What difference does it make if you never know the man's name, as long as he received the deliverance? As long as he was a man who was committed to God, the things of God, what difference does it make?

History, for the most part, is unjust. Very brief in mind. The God we serve is just and long in remembrance of the good things, and He keeps the records.

I do not know this man's name, nor does anyone else. He was just a certain man. But he was not a second-rate certain man. He was a certain man who was laid at the temple gate Beautiful. He did not need money. According to the record here, in the inner depth of it, I would say he had plenty of money. For if he needed money, they would not have laid him at the temple gate Beautiful; they would have laid him at the entrance to the city where all the people more or less came in, the main gate. If you were poverty-stricken you would not go to the temple gate Beautiful, if you really needed money. That is why, from the context, I believe it indicates that this man, lame from his mother's womb, perhaps belonged to a very outstanding family and even had some great religious connection with the temple. But because he was crippled, he automatically could never have been of service in the temple, because those men who served in the temple could not be physically maimed.

Acts 3:2:

…[he was] laid daily at the gate of the temple which is called Beautiful, to ask alms…[from] them… [who] entered into the temple;

The asking of alms was not because he needed money, but because it indicated his humility. Because for you to go out and to beg, sense knowledge-wise, would be humiliating. Here was a man who came born lame from his mother's womb with a prestigious background, a family of note. So, in order to show how humble he really was, how badly in need he was of deliverance, he humbled himself to ask alms from those who entered into the temple.

Acts 3:3:
Who seeing Peter and John about to go into the temple asked an alms.

One of the great and wonderful things about this record is, why did Jesus Christ not pay any attention to this man? Didn't Jesus Christ love him? Whenever Jesus Christ went into the temple, and he went there frequently according to the Word, this man was laid at the temple daily. And when Jesus went in he must have seen him. He must have known he was there. I would not be a bit surprised if he called him by name, saying, "Good morning, Herman." That's right. Yet he never ministered to him, never delivered him.

What about the record in the Gospels with the multitude at Solomon's porch, and the other porches who were sick waiting for the moving of the water? John 5. Take a look at it for a moment.

John 5:2, 3:
Now there is at Jerusalem by the sheep *market* [or the sheep gate] a pool, which is called in the Hebrew tongue Bethesda, [that means mercy, like Bethesda Hospital] having five porches.

In these lay a great multitude of impotent folk,... blind, halt, withered,...

See, all of these believed in healing. That is why they were there. All of them.

Verse 5:

John 5:5-9:
...a certain man was there,...[who] had an infirmity thirty and eight years.

When Jesus saw him lie, and knew that he had been now a long time *in that case*, he saith unto him, Wilt thou be made whole?

The impotent man answered him, Sir, I have no man, when the water is troubled, to put me into the pool: but while I am coming, another steppeth down before me.

Jesus saith unto him, Rise, take up thy bed, and walk.

And immediately the man was made whole, and took up his bed, and walked: and on the same day was the sabbath.

Here were a whole multitude of sick and impotent, but they all believed in healing. Jesus Christ, God's only begotten Son, the greatest believer that ever walked the face of the earth delivering people was there. Why did he not deliver every one of them? No revelation. So, he delivered just one.

Here is a man in Acts, laid at the temple gate Beautiful daily. Day after day after day. Whenever Jesus walked in, there he was, humble, asking for healing, yet Jesus Christ never stopped to deliver him. Why? No revelation.

In the one instance Jesus had revelation to minister just to that one person. In this particular instance, Jesus Christ never had any revelation. And, by the way, this was not the first time Peter and John went by him. Why didn't they minister to him earlier? No revelation. But today is the day.

I do not know what it is that brings a man or a woman to that point of decision at that time, when it could have been there just as easily a year before, as far as God is concerned. But why is it that it takes some so long to get to this point? I don't know. I am sure Jesus Christ would have been delighted to heal him, had it been the time as far as the man was concerned, because it is always God's time. God's time is always a now. Man's times many times is future. But when man in the future gets to the now time, God is now presently available to meet that need.

Here was this man who saw Peter and John, and he asked alms.

Acts 3:3, 4:
Who seeing Peter and John about to go into the temple asked an alms.

…[But] Peter, fastening his eyes upon him with John, said, Look on us.

Look on us. This Peter "fastening his eyes upon him" means a lot more than just casting a glance over. It tells me that he had revelation. Peter fastened his eyes. He just did not cast them over, he looked straight at him. Looked him straight in the eye. You have the word "fastened" —tied to, fastened his eyes upon him. So did John. And then Peter said:

Acts 3:4:
…Look on us.

Peter said to the man, look at us, look on us. Quit trying to act so humble and be so humble, begging alms. Get your eyes up. Quit looking down, look up.

What a revelation! This is the first time in the history of the Christian church that this comes to pass because God in Christ is in Peter and John. So, when they look at Peter, and they see Peter with the greatness of that Word living in him, they see the living Christ! When they look at John, they see the living Christ! And we have to again let people see that living Christ.

Peter said, look up here, look at us; and what a tremendous thing! Because, until people see the Christ in you, you will never be able to deliver or help people. As long as they look halfway at the world, halfway at you, you are never going to get the job done. People have to start looking at you. Well, bless God, give them something to look at! Stand up, throw your shoulders back. Walk like a woman of God, like a man of God. Peter and John did not have to walk into that temple stoop-shouldered and ignorant. They walked toward that temple with the spring of God in their souls, and God said, "There's the guy." He looked at him and he said:

Acts 3:4:
...Look on us.

You have to get people's attention before you can help them! Before you can ever minister God's Word, you have to get their attention, or you are just spinning your wheels. Before you can set people free, you have to get their attention. If they do not believe that you can do it, you cannot do it.

There is a record in the Gospels, where the disciples were asked; and they could not heal him. Jesus said, "O, you of little believing."

Matthew 17:16, 17:
And I brought him to thy disciples, and they could not cure him.

Then Jesus answered and said, O faithless and perverse generation,...

And after everything had occurred, the disciples said, "Why did we have this problem?"

And Jesus said, "This cometh forth by nothing but by prayer and fasting."

Matthew 17:19-21:
Then came the disciples to Jesus apart, and said, Why could not we cast him out?

And Jesus said unto them, Because of your unbelief:...

Howbeit this kind goeth not out but by prayer and fasting.

By believing and doing the work—it comes forth no other way.

In the Book of Acts, this "look on us" is not an ego trip; it is the truth of the greatness of God's Word. Men and women have to have confidence in your ability to help them, with the God in Christ in you to help them. Understand? If they do not believe that, you cannot do a thing for them. That's right.

Acts 3:5:
...he gave heed unto them,...

He looked at them, but his expectation was way below par, because he needed healing; but he expected at this time to receive only alms. That is what he thought Peter was trying to say when he said, look on us we are going to give you something.

Acts 3:5, 6:
And he gave heed unto them, expecting to receive something of them.
Then Peter said, Silver and gold have I none; but such as I have give I thee: In the name of Jesus Christ of Nazareth rise up and walk.

The word "receive" is the Greek word *lambanō*, which is the matter of giving alms.

Acts 3:6:
...Peter said, Silver and gold have I none;...

They love that one, because now we can have a whole group of priests who have renounced everything. That group absolutely declares that they never own anything, and they do it upon this scripture. They want no material things, and they pattern their lives after, they say, Peter; because Peter said, "Silver and gold have I none."

Peter was not poverty-stricken. The Word does not say he was poverty-stricken. He just said silver and gold have I none. How many of you have no money with you at all? You can say the same thing. That's right. Does that mean you are poverty-stricken? No. You just do not have any with you. Peter and John were going to the temple to pray. You were not allowed to carry any money into the temple to pray. It is an old rabbinical law. You know, he just left his wallet home—no problem. The devilishness of teaching that Peter and John were poverty-stricken is just contrary to God's Word. God's Word says He never saw them begging bread.

Acts 3:6:
...such as I have...: In the name of Jesus Christ of Nazareth rise up and walk.

Silver and gold have I none. Not because they were poverty-stricken, but because they were on the way to temple to pray. And the man sat there for alms. Now, if this is true rabbinically, which I know it is because it is old Hebrew culture, why would they have laid the man at the temple gate Beautiful asking alms when nobody has any money? I told you they did not lay him there for money. He was laid there to indicate his poverty, his spiritual in-depth need, so to speak. He physically needed something.

Acts 3:6:
Peter said,...such as I have give I thee:...

You cannot give anything if you do not have it. And in the ministry of healing, which this is in operation, the man ministering has to always give of himself.

A woman walked up to Jesus Christ and stole her healing. The Word says she followed in the press behind and reached out and just touched the hem of his garment. Immediately, she was made whole. Jesus said, "Who touched me?"

And his disciples said, "Master, lots of people are around you. Somebody touched you but we do not know who touched you."

Jesus said, "Don't give me that stuff. Who touched me?"

Look, if you girls were standing up dressed in a long formal, and someone reached to touch just the hem of your dress, do you feel it? No? That is why I know it was not the touching of the hem. He felt revelation— revelation. Sure. He said, who touched me? She had just reached up, believing that if she could touch the hem of his garment, she would be made whole. That is why I say she just sort of stole her healing. He did not know anything about it until it was all over with, and then he said, who touched me? The disciples said, you cannot figure that out because there were too many people. Then the woman came, and it says she confessed. Which simply means she just came and said, I did, sir. Jesus said, great, go on, have a good time; sin no more.

It says in the text:

Luke 8:46:
…Jesus…[felt] virtue is gone out of…[him].

In the Gospels, the word "virtue" is the word "*dunamis*"—power.

Now back to Acts. Such as I have, I give thee. Never is there a time when someone believes for deliverance from you that it does not cost you something in your life to give. You have to give for them to receive. It is part of the law of deliverance. Their believing will draw it out of you, but your believing works with theirs in order to bring it to fruition. Really something.

Acts 3:6:
Silver and gold have I none; but such as I have give I thee: In the name of Jesus Christ of Nazareth rise up and walk.

Number one, that is an impossibility because the man came born lame from his mother's womb. Secondly,

Nazareth is a defamed city. Can any good thing come out of Nazareth?[1] All strikes against the man. Really something, isn't it?

Proverbs 3:27:
Withhold not good from them to whom it is due, when it is in the power of thine hand to do *it*.

When it is in the power of thy hand to do it, like in Acts, do not withhold it if you have revelation. Do it. Do it.

Acts 3:6:
Peter said, Silver and gold have I none; but such as I have give I thee: In the name of Jesus Christ of Nazareth...

In the name—in that name. Verse 38 of Chapter 2:

Acts 2:38:
...Peter [had] said unto them, Repent, and be baptized every one of you in the name of Jesus Christ...

In Chapter 2, verse 22:

Acts 2:22:
Ye men of Israel, hear these words; Jesus of Nazareth, a man approved of God...

Impossible. No good thing comes out of Nazareth. Well, maybe it is impossible with people, but it is not impossible with God.

Acts 2:38:
...Repent, and be baptized...in the name of Jesus Christ...

Acts 3:6:
...Peter [fastening his eyes] said, Silver and gold

---

1. John 1:46a: And Nathanael said unto him, Can there any good thing come out of Nazareth? Philip saith unto him, Come and see.

have I none;…In the name of Jesus Christ of Nazareth rise up and walk.

How fantastic! In the name. What name? Jesus the Christ. The word "Jesus" is put first because it emphasizes his humility, his earthliness, and that is exactly where the man needed healing; right here upon earth. That is where our Savior is to deliver people.

Jesus of Nazareth. Jesus Christ of Nazareth. It never says Christ Jesus of Nazareth, as far as I know, any place in the Word because the Christ part is the heavenly type. Jesus is the earthly type, the Messiah. So the two are put together here in a remarkable way.

Acts 3:6:
…In the name of Jesus Christ of Nazareth rise up and walk.

Impossible, but there is the Word. This is inspired utterance. This is a man having revelation and inspired utterance. He just simply said:

Acts 3:6:
…In the name of Jesus Christ…rise up and walk.

And verse 7 is inspired action:

Acts 3:7:
And he took him by the right hand, and lifted *him* up:…

There was Peter with the revelation: "Look on us." And in those things, I see the whole moving picture. God showed Peter everything in a moment of time. And there he is, ministering. He gives him the Word until he builds believing enough for the man to be delivered, and he says:

Acts 3:6, 7:
…In the name of Jesus Christ of Nazareth rise up and walk.

...[Then he reaches down, gets] him by the right hand, and [he] lifted *him* up: and immediately his feet and ankle bones received strength.

My oh my! Imagine—healed in a name which is a defamed type of name—Nazareth. No good out of Nazareth? Yet in that name, he was healed!

People laugh at the name of Jesus Christ today. Let them laugh all they want to. All they get is consequences. We believe, and we get the results of that beautiful name.

Acts 3:8:
And he [the man] leaping up stood, and walked, and entered with them into the temple, walking, and leaping, and praising God.

If this would occur today, they would call the psychiatrist or do something to throw you out. You just cannot afford to get that excited about your deliverance.

Here is a man who was only delivered physically, and look what he did. When his ankle bones strengthened and whatever else it needed; he leaped up, stood, and walked. He entered in the temple, walking and leaping and praising God.

When we get born again of God's spirit, filled with the holy spirit in manifestation, people think we are a little rocky if we sing loud and have a good time being with believers. They think we are off our rocker. It certainly is much bigger when you are dead in trespasses and sins to get born again than it is to get an ankle bone put in. This man only had an ankle bone put in, and he had the audacity to defame that famous temple by walking and leaping in it, and praising God? Well glory, hallelujah!

I suppose if you were about forty years old and had never walked, and then you walked, you might be happy too. But what about if you were about forty years old and get born again of God's spirit? Why can't we be just as happy? As a matter of fact, we ought to be happier because we were dead, now we are alive. That man was alive; he only was lacking a few pieces. We were not just lacking a few pieces, we were lacking all the pieces: dead in trespasses and sins, without God, and without hope!

Ephesians 2:1:
And you…,who were dead in trespasses and sins;

Ephesians 2:12:
…having no hope, and without God in the world:

Do you see how we have been talked out of the greatness of the new birth and what it is all about? But people get born again, then are around negative people, and become just as cold as the negative people a week or two later. When you are first born again, you sure like to go out and tell everyone, because you are hotter than a firecracker. When you are born again of God's spirit, you know it. You want to tell it. When you are filled with the power from on high, and the Book opens for you, for the first time, you want to tell it. Well, do not ever deny a person the joy and enthusiasm of believing and sharing the greatness of God's Word. They will grow up soon enough. Let them have the fun of children, holding forth the greatness of the Word.

And then that great verse where all the people saw him.

Acts 3:9-11:
And all the people saw him walking and praising God:

And they knew that it was he…[who had] sat for alms at the Beautiful gate of the temple: and they were filled with wonder and amazement at that which had happened unto him.

And as the lame man which was healed held Peter and John, all the people ran together unto them in the porch that is called Solomon's, greatly wondering.

Isn't that something? People are like this.

Verse 12 begins the second great sermon in the Book of Acts. In between the first great sermon, the operation and outcome of that ministry, and how it worked in the early church, there sits this record of the healing of the man born lame.

It says in the Book of Acts that on the Day of Pentecost, Peter and John and all those apostles spoke in tongues. They went from house to house, and they worshipped and prayed together. It does not say that they interpreted and prophesied, but it does not say they spoke in tongues either. But they did speak in tongues previously on the Day of Pentecost. Then when they went from house to house, by sheer logic what do you think they did? Less than what they did on their first day? I don't think so.

Now, speaking in tongues builds up the inner man, which is the Christ in you, the hope of glory. And the more you build up the inner man, the bigger and fatter you are spiritually to receive revelation. Interpretation and prophecy builds up the body of believers. And when the individual body is built up, when the body of believers are built up, then the signs and the miracles follow.

Word of knowledge: whereby to receive from God the facts concerning the situation, which he could not know via his senses. Word of wisdom: what to do about it. Discerning of spirits: to know whether this situation with this man was due to a spirit possession or not. Once he had the revelation of what it was all about, Peter had to operate the manifestation of believing, so that "such as I have, I give unto thee" would come to pass. He had to believe that when he said, "...in the name of Jesus Christ, rise up and walk," the man would rise up and walk. He had to believe that when he took him by the right hand, he would get up. That is the manifestation of believing.

It says, "...and immediately..."; verse 7:

Acts 3:7:
...immediately his feet and ankle bones received strength.

That makes it a miracle of healing. And it was a healing because his feet and ankle bones received strength.

In this first great record of the deliverance of a man born lame, you see very clearly throughout that all nine manifestations had to be an operation in Peter to do this one piece of work. He had to have spoken in tongues to build himself up. In a believers' meeting, he surely must have interpreted and prophesied. He had to have word of knowledge to know what the score is; word of wisdom, what to do about it; discerning of spirits to know whether it was spirit or non-spirit; the manifestation of believing to hold on until it comes to pass according to the revelation he received. It was a miracle because it was instantaneous, and it was healing because the man was born lame. All nine manifestations in the deliverance of one man.

That is why I know Jesus Christ must have taught a great deal more in those forty days than that which is recorded in the Word. And yet, here in this portion of this chapter, you can see that all those manifestations have to be evidenced for the deliverance of one person. Therefore, all those manifestations must have been latent within Peter and John from the day they were born again. And the same Christ is in you that was in Peter; therefore those manifestations, all nine, must be latent in every born-again believer.

FOUR TYPES OF HEALING

We should not be concerned how God does it,
we should be concerned about the reality that God does it.

Signs, miracles, and wonders should be commonplace among the Christian believer.

In the Book of Acts, as the Early Church moved out across the world in the first century, by AD 55, Bartholomew was in the Bombay area teaching the Word of God. These men, the march of twelve men, walked with great boldness and great power; where signs, miracles, and wonders were commonplace.

Today, to have signs, miracles, and wonders is almost uncommon, except in the spiritualist field where they get it from the wrong source. There they are producing what the church should legitimately have been doing all along.

Because of the way we feel in this ministry regarding testimonies and talking about the things that God does for us individually, perhaps this is the reason why very little is said from time to time about the greatness of the signs, the miracles, and the wonders that God does in our midst. Because it seems like every time we are together, there is always one thing predominant in our heart and in our life, and that is that we can get to the Word. Men's illustrations come and go. You cannot always trust a man, or a testimony, or a sharing. You cannot always trust it because you are not always sure if it is the Word of God.

But upon this Book, the Bible, this I can say to my people and declare boldly that this is the Word of God.

And when a story is told in here of a miracle of healing, or of a sign, or by a wonder that was wrought under the hands of the men and the women of God; then we can again say, "Thus saith the Lord." And yet, we have had many signs, miracles, and wonders among our people, as we always expect to have. We expect our God to be living and real and alive for the people.

We have had real opportunities where we really had to believe God or go down with the ship. But there is one thing for sure, that when we believe, and when this Word has preeminence, then God's wonderful matchless power is made known to His people.

Four Types of Healing:

1. *To Restore to Health.*

The Bible sets before us four different kinds or types of healing. To heal is to restore to health. You could not restore anyone to health had they not had health to begin with. To restore to health, biblically speaking, indicates that there is no cause to remove. But there is also healing in the Bible called to do a cure. To heal is not only to restore, but secondly it is to do a cure.

2. *To Do a Cure.*

To do a cure goes a step further than recovery or restoration. It goes a step further than restoration, because to do a cure you must remove the cause. When the cause is removed, the symptom will disappear.

3. *To Make Sound or Whole.*

I do not believe in faith healing; I believe in what the Word teaches—Christian healing. Well, someone will say, "Isn't that faith healing?" The answer is definitely, no. This is Christian healing that is talked about in the Word of God.

The third phase of Christian healing in the Bible is to make sound or to make whole. In Acts, Chapter 3 is the record of the man who was placed at the temple gate Beautiful ever since he was a child. He was there all the time, and yet he was never healed. Jesus walked by that man when Jesus went into a temple. So why did Jesus not heal that man? Did he not love him? Certainly, he loved him. Then why did he not heal him?

You see, these are the questions we deal with. And until you understand the answers to some of those questions, you do not know how God operates or what God's plan is in the life of an individual. Certainly, Jesus loved him, but why did he not heal him?

There is another record outside of the temple in a pool area wherein there lay a whole multitude of sick and impotent folk, the Bible says. They all believed in healing; every one of them believed in healing.

Not everyone believes in healing, Christian healing. You believe that if it is God's will, He might be able to do it. But, in that day that is written in the Bible, everyone at that place believes in healing. They were all there to be healed—every one of them. And yet, Jesus healed how many? only one. Why? There has to be a reason. Did he not love all of them? Were they not all there because they had a need, and they needed to be healed, and they believed in healing? Then why did he heal one?

You see, this is why you must understand the operation of the word of knowledge, the word of wisdom, discerning of spirits. Until you understand that, the Bible is a closed book to you. Oh, you will hit it here, you will hit it there, but you will miss it most of the time. You just will not be able to make it jell.

To make whole—to make sound—back to the man at the temple gate Beautiful. They had to put in ankle bones. They had to put those parts into his body that were not in his body when he was born. That is what the Bible talks about when it says, to heal is to make sound or to make whole.

4. *To Reconcile.*

And the fourth way that the Bible gives as Christian healing is to reconcile. To reconcile is to bring back together that which has been separated. For instance, if bones have been separated, then those bones are brought back together, that means to reconcile.

Now, these are the four different kinds of healing that are mentioned in the Bible. I believe that every honest medical man understands what I am talking about. Because the medical man knows that if he is to restore to health, he could not restore to health had they not had health to begin with. He knows what it is to do a cure, to remove the cause. And he knows that if that cause is satisfactorily removed, that the symptoms will disappear. He also knows what it is to make sound or to make whole —what it is to replace sections of the eye or of the body at other places; he knows what it is to put in, when it has never been before. And he also knows what it is to reconcile, to bring back together that which has been separated.

I would like to say very plainly that we as Christian believers never diagnose. We never diagnose—never. The medical profession, the scientists, that is their category. That is their field. These are the men and women who diagnose cases. This is what they are trained to do. This is what they must do. We who are born again of God's spirit, filled with the power of the holy spirit, and know how to operate the manifestations of the spirit—the word of knowledge, the word of wisdom, discerning of spirits, faith, miracles and healing—we do not diagnose, we must ascertain.

To ascertain is for God to give revelation. We do not diagnose; not at all.

Why should tremendous miracles not be normal? Why should they not just be the pattern in life? Why do we always have to believe that if someone got healed that is the extraordinary? Our God is able to meet needs. You know, I believe that as Christians we ought to try to build this Word within us. And when we have a need, I think the first place we ought to go is our heavenly Father. I think we ought to endeavor to go to Him and believe with everything we have for Him to set us free. And then if it is not done because we are not believing, then if you want to go to these other places that is your business.

Now in the eleventh chapter of the Book of Acts is a tremendous record that ought to just bless your heart.

Verse 19:

Acts 11:19-21:
Now they which were scattered abroad upon the persecution that arose about Stephen travelled as far as Phenice, and Cyprus, and Antioch, preaching the word to none but unto the Jews only.

And some of them were men of Cyprus and Cyrene, which, when they were come to Antioch, spake unto the Grecians, preaching the Lord Jesus.

And the hand of the Lord was with them: and a great number believed, and turned unto the Lord.

Would they have ever turned to the Lord if these men had not gone and really set forth the Word of God? No. It is their teaching of the Word of God that made it possible for these men and women to turn to the Lord.

Verse 22:

Acts 11:22, 23a:
Then tidings of these things came unto the ears of

the church which was in Jerusalem: and they sent forth Barnabas, that he should go as far as Antioch.

Who, when he came, and had seen the grace of God,...

And people, it is grace and nothing but grace.

Acts 11:23b-26:

...was glad, and exhorted them all, that with purpose of heart they would [should] cleave unto the Lord.

For he was a good man, and full of the Holy Ghost and of faith: and much people was added unto the Lord.

Then departed Barnabas to Tarsus, for to seek Saul: [Saul was his Hebrew name, Paul was his Greek name]

And when he had found him [in Tarsus], he [Barnabas] brought [Paul or Saul] unto Antioch. And it came to pass, that a whole year they assembled themselves with the church [with the believers], and taught much people. And the disciples were called Christians first in Antioch.

The word Christian means "Christ in." And they were called Christians first in Antioch. Before they were called Christians in Antioch, they were called followers of the way. Jesus said, "I am the way." And those who followed the Lord Jesus Christ were followers of the way.

But in Antioch, where Barnabas and Saul ministered among the people, the people began to call those believers, "the followers of the way"; they called them "Christ in"—Christians—because they were teaching that it is Christ in you. Christ in you. And therefore, they said because Christ is in us, therefore, they call them Christians.

In the twelfth chapter of this tremendous Book of Acts:

Acts 12:1-6:
Now about that time Herod the king stretched forth *his* hands to vex certain of the church.

And he killed James the brother of John with the sword.

And because he [Herod] saw it pleased the Jews, he proceeded further to take Peter also. (Then were the days of unleavened bread.)

And when he had apprehended him [Peter], he put *him* in prison, [when Herod had taken Peter, he put him in prison] and delivered *him* to four quaternions of soldiers to keep him; intending after Easter to bring him forth to the people.

Peter therefore was kept in prison: but prayer was made without ceasing of the church unto God for him.

And when Herod would have brought him forth, the same night Peter was sleeping between two soldiers, bound with two chains: and the keepers before the door kept the prison.

Isn't that something? He just could not get out of that. There is not much in that verse that disturbs me except one truth: how in the world can a man sleep? Here was Peter, one arm shackled to a soldier, another arm shackled to another one. And there he was lying on the floor, sound asleep, knowing that the next morning he was scheduled to be executed. Yet, he was having a good night's sleep.

Some of us cannot sleep when we think about going fishing or going to the hospital. Here was a man who was scheduled for execution at sunrise the next morning, and yet he was sound asleep, chained between two soldiers.

Ladies and gentlemen, a man either has something that

most of us do not have, or there is something we should learn about this. Well, I am going to show you a little later from the Word, God had already told Peter by word of knowledge and word of wisdom that this was not the hour, and this was not the time. And so, his God had, by revelation, told him by word of knowledge that this was not the time. This was not the day. This was not the hour. Peter decided, "Well, I might as well have a good night's rest." And so, he did.

It is like Daniel in the lion's den. He said, "Leo, get over." And Leo the lion went over to the corner, and he laid down; then Daniel walks over and puts his head on him and goes to sleep. Why? All because of the operation of revelation manifestations: word of knowledge and word of wisdom. And here Peter is scheduled for execution, but he is sound asleep, bound with two chains and so forth.

Verse 7:

Acts 12:7a:
And, behold, the angel of the Lord came [about midnight. And when this angel of the Lord came]..., and a light shined in the prison: and he smote Peter on the side,...

He said, "Pete, get up; come on." Can you get the picture? Maybe since he was lying down the angel did not stoop; he just took his toe and pushed him in the ribs a little bit or something. Arise, saying, get up quickly.

Acts 12:7b:
...Arise up quickly. [And when he rose up]...his chains fell off from *his* hands.

That's right. People say today, well, that does not happen today. Do you know why it does not happen? Because we are not believing, and we are not walking. We are expecting the arm of man to set us free. And if he does not, we are expecting some aspirin to help, or a little Bufferin maybe. That's right. You are not trusting the Lord. We are trusting on the arm of man. That is why we are not seeing anything.

These men are just as human as we are. They were bound in prison between two chains. He was scheduled for execution. Well, people, I want to tell you, either God's gotten weaker, or man's believing has gone underground. But the Bible says God does not change. Therefore, it is man's unbelief that produces the consequences, which we are so acclimatized to seeing today.

Well, read what the Word says:

Acts 12:8-10a:
And the angel said unto him, Gird thyself, and bind on thy sandals. And so he did. And he saith unto him, Cast thy garment about thee, and follow me.

And he went out, and followed him; and [Peter did not know] that it was true which was done by the angel; but [Peter] thought he saw a vision.

When they were past the first and the second ward,...

They were four deep, these fellas that were keeping him in prison. They had placed him in the inner prison, and then outside they had set these guards in four different sections.

Acts 12:10b-13a:
...they came unto the iron gate that leadeth unto the city; which opened to them of his own accord: and they went out, and passed on through one street; and forthwith the angel departed...

And when Peter was come to himself, he said, Now I know of a surety, that the Lord hath sent his angel, and hath delivered me out of the hand of Herod, and *from* all the expectation of the people of the Jews.

And when he had considered *the thing*, he came to

the house of Mary the mother of John, whose sur-
name was Mark; where many were gathered together
praying.

And as Peter knocked at the door...

The text reads, technically, "as Peter knocked at the
door." To knock at the door means he stood outside and
called. To knock at the door in the Bible is to call, because they do not have a door, so you cannot knock on
anything you do not have. But they stood outside the gate
and called.

> **Acts 12:13b, 14a:**
> ...Peter knocked at the door of the gate, a damsel
> came to hearken, named Rhoda.
> And when she knew Peter's voice, she opened not
> the gate for gladness...

She was so tickled to see him that she left him to
stand outside the gate. Isn't that great? So...

> **Acts 12:14b, 15a:**
> ...she opened not the gate for gladness, but [she] ran
> in [the house where they were all praying], and told
> how Peter stood before the gate.
> And they said unto her...
> ...Thou art mad. But she constantly affirmed...

She says, "But fellas, ladies, it is true. Peter is standing out..." They said, "It can't be; he's down there in
jail. Tomorrow morning he's scheduled for execution.
That's why we're praying."

> **Acts 12:15b, 16:**
> ...But she constantly [confirmed] that it was...so.
> Then said they, [well, it must be]...his angel.
> But Peter continued knocking: [He kept standing
> outside and he said, hey, fellas, let me in. Come on,

open the door. I'm here] and when they had [finally] opened *the door*, and saw him, they were astonished.

Flabbergasted. Well, what in the world were they praying for? If you are praying for something and then get an answer and it astonishes you, you better become more acclimatized to praying. But anyway, Peter knocked, and when they finally opened the door and saw him, they were flabbergasted.

Acts 12:17:
But he, beckoning unto them with the hand to hold their peace, declared unto them how the Lord had brought him out of the prison....

Who brought him out? The Lord brought him out. And, people, except the Lord battle for us, except the Lord stand in our stead, except the Lord continue His grace upon us; you and I have no life and no ministry and no voice to share.

The only purposeful existence for this ministry is the accuracy of the research of God's Word, which we are teaching to our people across the nations of the world. Otherwise, we will just be another organization, another institutionalized institute. And we have oodles of those. We have to have the Lord standing in our place.

As for Peter, he said the Lord hath done this.

Acts 12:17, 18:
...And he said, Go shew these things unto James, and to the brethren. And he departed, and [he] went into another place.

Now as soon as it was day [break], there was no small stir among the soldiers, what was become of Peter.

They could not find him. And I tell you, when they had him chained to two soldiers, what do you think those soldiers felt like when they woke up in the morning and Peter was gone? That must have been a shocker—and having gone through four sections of soldiers, and the gate still locked. No wonder this was no small stir.

2 Peter, Chapter 1, verse 13:

2 Peter 1:13:
Yea, I think it meet, as long as I am in this tabernacle,...

And the word "tabernacle" always refers to the individual believer. The body of believers, when gathered, make up what the Bible calls the temple. You are not a temple of the holy ghost, you are a tabernacle. But the whole body of believers make up the temple of the holy spirit.

2 Peter 1:13, 14:
Yea, I think it meet, as long as I am in this tabernacle, to stir you up by putting *you* in remembrance;
Knowing that shortly I must put off *this* my tabernacle, even as our Lord Jesus Christ hath shewed me.

Not only was this written many years after that experience recorded in the Book of Acts, but occurred many years later as well. This is how I know that the night when he was in that prison, scheduled for execution the next morning according to Herod, God had talked to him and said, tonight is not the night.

Because, many years later, one night, God showed him that he must shortly lay off this what? tabernacle. That, very soon now, his life would come to an end. God by revelation told him this—by word of knowledge, by word of wisdom. You see why that man could sleep in that jail that night? You see why he could walk with believing faith? Because he was operating manifestations of the spirit.

God, by word of knowledge, told him he would not die. By word of wisdom, He told him how he was going to do it. The angel came and brought him forth and marched him down that city street.

People, we should not be concerned *how* God does it, we should be concerned about the reality *that* God does it. How He does it is His business, but you and I ought to be concerned that He does it. And He can only do it when you and I use the tools which God has given us for the job. God has given us tools with which to operate. He has given us abilities wherewith to walk in this life. The doing is our task, our responsibility according to our believing faith.

In Ephesians, Chapter 3, verse 20 it says:

Ephesians 3:20:
Now unto him that is able to do exceeding abundantly above all that we ask or think, according to the power that worketh in us,

In Acts, Chapter 3, verse 6 the Word says:

Acts 3:6:
…Peter said [to the man]…such as I have give I [unto] thee:…

In Acts, Chapter 5, verse 12 it says:

Acts 5:12:
And by the hands of the apostles were many signs and wonders wrought among the people;…

By the hands of who? the apostles. By the hands of the apostles.

Peter says, "Such as I have, I give unto thee."

In Acts, Chapter 6, verse 8 it said they…

Acts 6:8:
…did great wonders and miracles among the people.

And in Matthew, Chapter 9, verse 8 it says:

Matthew 9:8:
...the multitudes saw [what had occurred]...they...
marvelled, and glorified God, which had given such
power unto men.

And in Acts, Chapter 8, you may recall when Phillip
was preaching in Samaria, that the miracles and the
signs and the wonders which he did. God has given you
ability. God has set His power within you. What you do
with it is your opportunity.

And God cannot move until you move. When you and
I know what we have in Christ; when we know how
these manifestations operate—word of knowledge, word
of wisdom, discerning of spirits, faith, miracles, and healing—when we know how these operate, then we can
believe and once again bring God's blessing to God's
people. What a tremendous opportunity!

Remember the poem:

> God has no hands but our hands
> With which to give them bread;
> He has no feet but our feet
> With which to move among the almost dead;
> We say that we are his and he is ours,
> But deeds are the proof of that, not words,
> And these are the proving hours.

Ladies and gentlemen, there has never been a time in
the history of civilization since the first century, when
men and women once again needed to hear the greatness of God's Word like they need it today. This is the
greatest privilege we have ever had. We sit right at the
crossroads of the greatest opportunities of all time because of the media, radio, television, and other avenues
that can be utilized to take the greatness of God's Word
to the multitudes in a short period of time.

And so, my people, it is God who has set us to be light. He has said that we are the salt of the earth. He has said that we are to let our light shine. He has given us the ministry. He has equipped us. He says that we are ambassadors. We are workmen. We are messengers. We are His. And as we carry the greatness of God's Word, men and women will again be blessed.

And people, to that I have dedicated my life and everything I have or ever hope to be, to help men and women who really are concerned about knowing the answers. There are a lot of things in life that I do not know, a lot of things I cannot do; but there is one thing God calls me to, and that is to teach men and women the Word who really want to know the Word. And that I can do.

Our God is no respecter of age. He is no respecter of persons, right? Our God is interested in the children, the young people, the adults. Our God is interested in every segment, every facet of our life. Because our God is not only able, but He is willing to share His abundance with His people.

And this is why we ought to rise up as a mighty army of God and really stand together on the greatness of God's Word, and stand with the people across the world who are concerned about making that Word known. Amen.

BY HIS STRIPES
YE WERE HEALED

Jesus Christ's total ministry upon earth was that we might be able to receive the abundance of that which he made available.

I want to share from the accuracy of God's Word dealing with the subject of the ministry of healing. There is a little booklet entitled, *The Cross in the Broken Body*, or *Healing in the Holy Communion*. This has in it many of the great truths that I would like to set before you. I would like to share with you the first three paragraphs in this booklet.

> Multitudes of Christians are suffering from lack of strength and physical unwholeness. This is, in most instances, due to either wrong teaching or no teaching on the subject that I have chosen for this study. There has been little teaching regarding the broken body of Jesus Christ in comparison to his shed blood. We always talk about, you know, the blood of Jesus Christ, what it accomplished for people. But how little teaching there has been regarding his broken body and its biblical significance as well as its practical significance; to the end that most Christians are thoroughly familiar with the meaning of the shed blood, but not with the broken body.

> The value of this study in abundant living depends entirely upon what position you hold regarding the Word of God. If you believe that the Bible is the Word of God, and that it is God's answer to the

needs of men, then you will be able to manifest the results in your life. According to Malachi 3:6, God says:

Malachi 3:6:
For I *am* the LORD, I change not;…

He is the same all the time. The Lord does not change His nature. What He is once, He is always. What He does once, He does always. The God whom I know, whom I teach and preach and for whom I labor, is the same God as the God of Abraham, Isaac, and Jacob. God has not become one bit weaker in all of these years.

The fruitfulness of this study, to a marked degree, depends upon whether you are seeking deliverance *from* sickness or a reasonable excuse *for* sickness. If you are not seeking complete deliverance for your life but an excuse for bondage, this study will not profit you very much. For there are people who believe that it is God's will for them to be sick. There are people who believe that God is not only the author of, but that He sends sickness, suffering, and all manner of evil directly to mankind. There are people who believe that God makes a person a better Christian by sending sickness and disease. God does not send sickness, disease, and sin into anyone's life in order to make him a more worthy or holy Christian. Nor does God send sickness or disease to prove people. For our God is a good God, and in our God (the God and Father of our Lord Jesus Christ), there is no darkness, neither shadow of turning with Him.

And the ministry of healing is perhaps the greatest ministry in the church today, and it has the least amount of teaching and understanding. People do not know the difference between the ministry of healing, praying for the sick, laying on of hands, or anything else regarding the field, basically. Most of them just talk.

The ministry of healing is to take the place of Christ here upon earth. When Jesus said, "the works that I do ye shall do also,"[1] he meant what he said, and he said what he meant. Part of the work that Jesus Christ did while he was here upon earth was to carry out a ministry of healing. To pray for the sick is one thing, to minister healing is something else. To minister healing is to take the place of Christ and to do the work that he did. It is a ministry whereby you manifest forth the greatness of the power of Christ in your life by the operation of the manifestation; specifically of word of knowledge, word of wisdom, discerning of spirits.

Therefore, the definition of the ministry of healing, as I understand the Word, is that it is your operation of the God-given ability whereby you may impart healing to others according to the revelation you have received, in the name of Jesus Christ.

Now, God uses this manifestation of healing to prove His ability to forgive sin. How do you know that God has the ability to forgive sin? You cannot go by feeling because feelings can fool you. They may come, and they may go. But the Word of God has this answer.

Turn to the Gospel of Mark, Chapter 2. It is the record of the one who was brought to Jesus with palsy. He was carried by four, and all five of them had to believe. And when we get to verse ten in this second chapter, he says:

Mark 2:10, 11:
But that ye may know that the Son of man hath

---

1. John 14:12: Verily, verily, I say unto you, He that believeth on me, the works that I do shall he do also; and greater *works* than these shall he do; because I go unto my Father.

power on earth to forgive sins, (he saith to the sick of the palsy,)

I say unto thee, Arise,…take up thy bed, and go thy way into thine house.

The proof that he was able to forgive sins was the healing of the man. The healing they could see. The man had had palsy, and God set him free because Jesus Christ ministered healing to him. And after they had seen the healing, he said to the man, "Now, you know God has power to forgive sin."

You cannot see forgiveness, but you can see healing, physical healing. And the physical healing is the proof in the senses realm that He does and can and will forgive sin.

In Mark, Chapter 16:

Mark 16:20:
And they went forth, and preached every where, the Lord working with *them*,…confirming the word with signs following….

They went everywhere preaching the Word. They did not preach their opinion, they did not preach what they thought ought to be said; they preached what God wanted said.

Mark 16:20:
And they went forth, and preached every where, [and as they preached the Word,] the Lord…[worked] with *them*, and…[confirmed] the word…[He confirmed the Word by the] signs [the miracles and the wonders that were wrought]…

The preaching and the teaching of the Word is primary. It is significant. It is singularly important because no man can believe until after he has heard the Word of

God; then, he can believe. And God confirms the Word by the signs, the miracles, and the wonders.

This ministry also builds believing for people to get saved. In Acts, Chapter 8, it says that:

Acts 8:5, 6a:
...Philip went down to the city of Samaria, and [he] preached Christ unto them.

And the people with one accord....

The words "one accord" mean unity of purpose. They are used four of five times in the opening chapters of Acts.

Acts 8:6b
...the people with one accord gave heed unto those things which Philip spake, hearing and seeing the miracles which he did.

Who did them? Philip did them. That is what the Word says, that is what it means. Philip did them. They believed what he preached, not because of the words that he used in his preaching, not because of his vocabulary, or his personality; they believed what he preached because of the miracles he did.

The miracles under the ministry of healing are the proof in the senses world that the Word of God that the man spoke was really the Word of God, because God confirmed His Word with the signs, the miracles, and the wonders following.

That is why verse 7 says:

Acts 8:7:
For unclean spirits, crying with loud voice, came out of many that were possessed...and many taken with palsies, and that were lame, were healed.

Whenever a person is possessed, it is always a devil

spirit. Christ never possesses anyone. We are not channels. We are not mediums. We are not sensitives. We are
sons and daughters of God, born again of God's spirit
by our free will. We accepted the Lord Jesus Christ, and
he never possesses us.

All possession—all possession in the Word of God,
or at any time in our society—is always from the adversary, no matter how sincere they look, because sincerity
is no guarantee for truth. Truth is truth.

Acts 8:7b:
…possessed…many taken with palsies,…that were
lame, were healed.

And verse 8 says:

Acts 8:8:
…there was great joy in that city.

There was great joy because people were being delivered under the ministry of healing. For Philip went
forth proclaiming the Word of Christ. And God confirmed
that Word by the signs, the miracles, and the wonders.

This ministry of healing not only blesses God's people,
but it glorifies God's name.

In Mark, Chapter 2, in verse 12, "And immediately…."
he told the man to rise up, take his bed and go for a
walk.

Mark 2:12:
And immediately he arose, took up the bed, and went
forth before them all; insomuch that they were all
amazed, and glorified God, saying, We never saw
it on this fashion.

They glorified God. Under the ministry of healing, it
blesses God's people, and it glorifies the name of God.

In Matthew, Chapter 15, and in verse 31, we have
this record:

Matthew 15:31:
Insomuch that the multitude wondered, when they saw the dumb to speak, the maimed to be whole, the lame to walk, and the blind to see: and they glorified the God of Israel.

You see, the manifestation of this ministry of healing proves God's ability to forgive sin, it proves the resurrection, it proves that God confirms His Word as it is spoken. It builds believing for salvation that people want to get saved, and it blesses God's people and glorifies God's name.

With the manifestation of healing, the first basic question you will have to ask yourself, and people need to be taught is: Is it for all? This is what they will be asking. So, you will hear people say, "Well, I believe God could heal so and so; I think maybe God once in a while does so and so." That's not an issue. The issue is, is healing for all individuals? If it's for one, it has to be for all. And if it's for all, it has to be for that one.

In Exodus, Chapter 15, listen to verse 26:

Exodus 15:26:
...[The Lord] said, If thou wilt diligently hearken to the voice of the LORD thy God, and wilt do that which is right in his sight, and wilt give ear to his commandments, and keep all his statutes, I will put none of these diseases upon thee, which I have brought upon the Egyptians: for I *am* the LORD that [what?] healeth thee.

Now, Chapter 23 of Exodus—I am taking you way back to the background history of the early part of the Word of God as it was written. Exodus 23, verse 24:

Exodus 23:24-26:
Thou shalt not bow down to their gods, nor serve

them, nor do after their works: but thou shalt utterly overthrow them, and quite break down their images.

And ye shall serve the LORD your God, and he shall bless thy bread, and thy water; and I will take sickness away from the midst of thee.

There shall nothing cast their young, nor be barren, in thy land: the number of thy days I will fulfil.

What a tremendous promise of the God who never changes, way back in the Old Testament time.

In Deuteronomy, Chapter 7, and in verse 13 of this chapter, listen to this:

Deuteronomy 7:13-15:
And he will love thee, and bless thee, and multiply thee: he will also bless the fruit of thy womb, and the fruit of thy land, thy corn, and thy wine, and thine oil, the increase of thy [cattle] kine, and the flocks of thy sheep, in the land which he sware unto thy fathers to give thee.

Thou shalt be blessed above all people: there shall not be male or female barren among you, or among your cattle.

And the LORD will take away from thee all sickness, and will put none of the evil diseases of Egypt, which thou knowest, upon thee; but will lay them upon all *them* that hate thee.

Deliverance promised by God way back at the beginning for people who kept His statutes, who believed His Word, who walked on it.

In Exodus, Chapter 12, in verse 7, listen to this record regarding the Passover in Egypt:

Exodus 12:7, 8:
And they shall take of the blood, and strike *it* on

> the two side posts and on the upper door post of the houses, wherein they shall eat it.
>
> And they shall eat the flesh [of the lamb] in that night, roast with fire, and unleavened bread; *and* with bitter *herbs* they shall eat it.

Before they left Egypt, God had told them what to do. They took this lamb, they sprinkled the blood thereof on the lintel of the door posts and so forth, but they ate the flesh. Now, why were they instructed to eat the flesh of the lamb? Because, if you read back in Exodus, you see it was for the healing of their bodies.

When we take holy communion in our churches, there are always two elements involved—the bread and the cup. Well, why do you take two? They did not teach me this in the seminary, and I graduated from four theological seminaries not knowing it. I was still under the opinion you came and took both of them for the forgiveness of sins. Then I started thinking, well, why do I have to do things twice? If it is good enough to do it the first time, why do I have to do it the second time?

Then I worked the Word on the subject, and do you know what I found way back in Exodus? The blood was sprinkled for the covering, and the lamb was eaten for the healing of the body. It is all written in this re-search booklet on *The Cross in the Broken Body*—I traced it all the way through the Old Testament and the Gospel period. Jesus Christ was the Lamb of God, and when Jesus Christ died for us, he shed his blood for the forgiveness of sin; but his broken body, his body was broken for the healing of our body. That is what he accomplished. He was the Lamb of God, slain from the foundations of the world. When he laid down his life, it says in 1 Peter 2:24, we were healed.

1 Peter 2:24:
> …by his stripes ye were healed.

In his shed blood, we have the forgiveness of sins—
one of the two things. Before he died, he instituted something, which is called the Lord's Supper by people. Some
people call it the Last Supper; it was not the last supper,
really. But it was the memorial that he instituted.

Paul picked it up later in Corinthians and gave us a
record of it. For he said:

1 Corinthians 11:23-25:
…the Lord Jesus [Christ] the *same* night in which
he was betrayed took bread:
And when he had given thanks, he brake *it*, and said,
Take, eat: this is my [what?] body,…
…[Then] *he took* the cup,…[and he said], This cup
is the new testament in my blood: [unto the remission of sins]…

Two things: the broken body and the shed blood. In
that bread, we have the representation of the healing of
the body of the Lord Jesus Christ—what he accomplished
for us when he died for us. But about all that any of us
ever hear taught is forgiveness of sin, remission of sin
—that his shed blood covered it. Both of them are in the
atonement. Both of them are in that which God, in Christ
Jesus, accomplished for us; and it started way back at
the Passover.

And that year when Jesus Christ died, he died at the
exact hour when the Passover lamb was slain. He was
our Passover. He died for us. He had his body broken
for the healing of our bodies. He shed his blood for our
remission of sins and for our forgiveness of sins.

When the children of Israel (about three million) left
Egypt, they travelled in the wilderness for forty years
before anybody got sick. The Bible says in the Book of
Psalms:

Psalms 105:37:
...there was not one feeble...

Among all those three million. And they were babes in arms, little toddlers just starting to walk, young people, adolescents, youth, and adults. They marched in the wilderness under the most adverse conditions, without any modern medical science for forty years; and not one feeble knee among them, which was about three million.

Now if you can find a church with ten members and not nine feeble knees, I want to see them. That's right. Everybody inside of the Church is basically sick. Why? Because no one has dared to stand up and declare God's Word, and to tell God's people again, it is God's will for God's people to be made whole.

Ladies and gentlemen, we will teach this if we die tonight. That's right. Because if we died tonight, it would still be God's will to have delivered us. We just did not have the believing to appropriate it, that's all. But this thing has become so displaced in the Church because we have lauded—you know, the drugs and the biochemists have pushed this; the doctors have pushed that—and so we have relegated the healing of the body to the medical profession. You cannot read that in the Word of God to me.

Now, there is nothing wrong with the medical profession; I did not say so. Except, if you put the medical profession ahead of the Word of God, there is something wrong with it.

There was a man by the name of Asa in the Old Testament who was a king. Let's look at the record in 2 Chronicles, Chapter 16:

2 Chronicles 16:11, 12:
And, behold, the acts of Asa, first and last, lo, they

are written in the book of the kings of Judah and
Israel.

And Asa in the thirty and ninth year of his reign was
diseased in his feet, until his disease *was* exceeding
great: yet in his disease he sought not…the LORD,
but [went] to the physicians.

And he died.

2 Chronicles 16:13:
And Asa slept with his fathers, and died in the one
and fortieth year of his reign.

You see, what we believe the Word of God teaches
is that our whole life, first and foremost, belongs to God.
And so, we always go to our heavenly Father with every
need we have, or with every opportunity as it presents
itself, according to our believing ability. We always go
to Him, first and foremost. That's right!

If I broke my arm right now, the first thing I would
do is go to my Father to see if I was jelling big enough
for Him to do the job. And if I am jelling big enough, I
am sure He is big enough to do it. But if I am jelling so
little that He isn't big enough to do it for me because I
am not jelling enough, you know what I am going to
do? I will go to the best doctor real quick to get it set.
But I never would go there first; I would always go to
my heavenly Father.

If God is first in your life spiritually, why not endeavor
to make him first physically? When you have a need, why
not go to Him? The reason we are seeing such little Christian healing today is because our believing is so low,
because we have had everything talked out of us through
the years. No one has stood up and said, "Thus saith the
Lord." We have had a few healing campaigns, but most
of those—compared to the thousands of people that are

there—are usually relatively few set free in healing, compared to the thousands that come.

And again, it is due to our times where people do not have any believing faith in God's Word that God will heal them. They hope He will. And if you come on hope, you go away sick because you get nothing by hope. That's right.

Hope in the Bible is used regarding something you cannot have now. Believing is used regarding that which is immediately available. So, I have a hope for heaven, the Bible says, because I cannot have it right now. But I have believing for salvation right now, because it is immediately available.

Now, we will not take the time to look at Deuteronomy, but sometime read the twenty-eighth chapter of the Book of Deuteronomy. You will see the greatest curse of the law is sickness. When they broke the law, they got sick.

And in Galatians, Chapter 3, verse 13 is the answer to this truth:

> **Galatians 3:13:**
> Christ hath [past tense] redeemed us [past tense] from the curse of [what?] the law, being made a curse for us:…

He has redeemed us from the curse of the law. The vast majority of the curse of the law in Deuteronomy, Chapter 28 is sickness. If Christ redeemed us from the curse of the law, then he must have redeemed us from sickness and disease; and he did just that. He redeemed us from the curse of the law, it is what he redeemed us from. So, if Christ redeemed us, are we redeemed? Even if I never manifest it or if I was not able to believe big enough in my life to appropriate it, I am still redeemed.

Anyone can get saved if they want to, but if they do

not get saved, it isn't that God could not do it in Christ; you simply were not believing for it. That's right. It is the same thing in the manifestation or the ministry of healing.

You see, the only question you logically have to ask yourself is: Is salvation for all? If you say salvation is for all, then healing has to be for all. For the same Christ who died to save you from your sins, died to save you from the consequences of them. And this is why the Christian believers ought to be the most positive—the greatest group manifesting the abundance of the life of God—of all of God's people. Remember it says:

Psalms 103:3:
Who forgiveth all thine iniquities; who healeth all thy diseases;

Healeth all our diseases. Our God is more anxious to meet our needs than we are even to pray for it. He is more anxious to give us the answers than we are even to ask the questions.

When Jesus Christ opened his ministry here upon earth as recorded in Luke 4, he said that he came to set the captives free;[2] to break the bands which had enslaved people;[3] and to break the kingdom of Satan. All of these are involved in the ministry of Jesus Christ. And his total ministry here upon earth was that we might be able to receive the abundance of that which he made available.

---

2. Luke 4:18: The Spirit of the Lord *is* upon me, because he hath anointed me to preach the gospel to the poor; he hath sent me to heal the brokenhearted, to preach deliverance to the captives, and recovering of sight to the blind, to set at liberty them that are bruised,

3. Isaiah 58:6: Is not this the fast that I have chosen? to loose the bands of wickedness, to undo the heavy burdens, and to let the oppressed go free, and that ye break every yoke?

You see, when you go to God's Word, it then becomes very plain and very simple that the manifestation of healing is for all; and that we, God's people, ought to start standing upon the integrity and the accuracy of God's Word and let the abundance of this Word of God just live within us. And one help the other, and build each other up, so that we can tap into the abundance of the greatness of the revelation that God has given to us through Christ Jesus our Lord.

Do You Will?

In order for a man to be delivered,
he has to will to be delivered.

It was a great day in my life, when many years ago, I learned from God's Word that the true God never possesses.

I had been moving into avenues and channels of learning among men and women where I was being taught that you just give yourself over to God, and that God will possess you. He will control you. He will make you speak in tongues when it is right, and when it is not you do not speak in tongues.

And I was beginning to evaluate that. People were saying, "Well, you just let God take control of you, let Him speak through you." I was singing songs like "Channels Only." Have you ever heard that chorus? Well, it is an old favorite gospel chorus, "Channels Only."

But one day, working God's Word and seeing men's experiences, the experiences did not line up with the Word. And it was a great day in my life when I learned that the true God never possesses. The adversary, the devil, always possesses. The true God simply makes it available; and man, by the freedom of his will, decides whether he wants what God, the true God, has or does not. It is like setting out a beautiful dinner, and people having the freedom to come and eat it.

It was also a great day in my life when I learned from God's Word that we are what we are because of our believing, and that no person ever rises beyond what he believes. And the reason that you believe what you believe now is because of what you have been taught. No person ever rises beyond what they are taught; no person can believe more. You could believe less, but you could not believe more.

And in order to believe, in order to learn, there has to be a center of reference outside of the individual seeking.

When a child is born, how does that child learn? You just do not allow that child to lie in its crib and sit around in the corner praying for it to learn. You pick it up and you talk to it. You whisper to it. You rock it. You sing to it. Grandma and grandpa talk to it. Brothers and sisters interact. Then the child goes to kindergarten having a teacher and playmates. All of those teachers, all of those playmates, all of those fathers and mothers, are centers of reference for learning outside of that child. That is how everyone learns. That is how you learned. That is how I learned.

And therefore, if we are taught wrongly, we will believe wrongly. You cannot go beyond what you are taught. Knowing the laws of learning which are axiomatic, most of us have been influenced by multiple centers of reference for learning. Because every person you meet, every person who talks to you, is a center of reference.

Reading is the same way, you know. If you read a book, that is a center of reference outside of you for learning. So, having been exposed to a voluminous amount of this myself, both in live person and in reading, my mind was a hodgepodge of confusion. I could quote you many men, quote you many books, but my mind was confused because I did not know what or who was true.

Then one day, understanding the great principle of learning, I came to a position for those of us who are

Christian, our only center of reference for truth is the integrity and the accuracy of God's Word.

If what Dr. So-and-so says agrees with the Word, we say, praise God! If Professor So-and-so says something and it agrees with the revealed God's Word, we say, hallelujah! But if what any man says contradicts what the Word says, we do not go with that man, we go with the Word.

It is the Word of God that is our only—I said only, and that is what I meant. It is my only center of reference for truth, for learning, outside of the individual seeking. It is mine. It ought to be yours.

The Word of God is our only center of reference outside of the individual seeking truth. And the will, the freedom of will that you have to change your opinions, your mind; the freedom of will you have to believe God's Word in our day and time is one of the inherent rights that you should never jeopardize. That's right.

That is why every time somebody is hypnotized, you have given up the freedom of your will. The person hypnotizing you has to be controlled by a devil spirit, and you allowing yourself to be hypnotized, you get controlled by one.

Do you see it? I just do not let anyone control my mind. Now, I may be stupid, but it is better to be stupid and have a free will and a free mind than to be the smartest person in the world and be possessed. That's right. Because, I have the freedom of mind, the freedom of will. Don't let anyone touch your freedom of will.

And, ladies and gentlemen, I will say it once more just so you understand it. Every time a person is hypnotized, you have lost the freedom of your will. I do not let anyone hypnotize anyone when I am around, because one of the great rights God gave to every human being is to have the freedom of will so that you could make a choice by your own will. And not be possessed, not be controlled.

There is a record in the Gospel of John that teaches us with all alacrity and sharpness. And it is that record I want to set before you now. There are many more in the Word, but this is one of them.

In the Gospel of John, Chapter 4, I want to begin in verse 43 because I want to get to Chapter 5. In order to get to Chapter 5, we have to start in Chapter 4:

> **John 4:43-45:**
> Now after two days he [Jesus] departed thence, and went into Galilee.
> For Jesus himself testified, that a prophet hath no honour in his own country.
> Then when he was come into Galilee,...

He said, he testified, that a prophet had no honor within his own country. But he went right back. Because it is not a matter of fact whether you are honored or not honored, it is a matter of the integrity of what? The Word. Whether they like you or do not like you, it is God's Word! God's Word. And Jesus went back to his own territory, to Galilee.

> **John 4:45-47a:**
> [And]...the Galilaeans received him [*dechomai'*d him], having seen all the things that he did at Jerusalem at the feast: for they also went unto the feast.
> So Jesus came again into Cana of Galilee, where he made the water wine. And there was a certain nobleman [a ruler, a head of state, a real fine man in position of authority], whose son was sick at Capernaum.
> When he heard that Jesus was come out of Judaea into Galilee, he went unto him, and besought him...

The word "besought" means begged. You know, just stayed there and said, "oh please, please…"

John 4:47b-50:
…come down, and heal his son: for he was at the point of death.

Then said Jesus unto him, Except ye see signs and wonders, ye will not believe.

The nobleman saith unto him, Sir, come down ere my child die.

Jesus saith unto him, Go thy way; thy son liveth. [Here is the great key:]…the man [did what?] believed the word that Jesus had spoken unto him, and he went his way.

He believed. He had no proof. He had no evidence. He had nothing concrete to put his teeth into, but he believed. He believed first and then he saw. He believed. He believed the word that Jesus had spoken. Did he know his son was healed? Nope. Did not know anything about it.

But Jesus had said,… Now you read it for yourself.

John 4:50:
Jesus saith unto him, Go thy way; thy son liveth.

Thy son liveth. The words that Jesus spoke were words that God had given him, therefore they were like God's Word. Here is God's Word. It means what it says, and it says what it means. This Word of God, when you read it, and you believe it, you get the results of that believing. Otherwise, you just live with consequences all your life.

Jesus said, "Go, your son liveth." And the man believed. He believed. That is what it says; that is what it means. It says so. The man believed.

He did not have a Western Union telegram or anything else, knowing that his son was alive. He simply believed that what Jesus said was true. It does not say he was possessed. It says he believed.

John 4:51:
And as he was now going down, his servants met him, [when he was going home, they ran out to meet him]...and told *him*, saying, Thy son liveth.

You see, the Word of God is the will of God. Jesus says, thy son liveth. The man believed it. When he started home, the servants met him. Did they say, "Your son is dead"? No, they said, "Your son is living!"

Then, he was a little skeptical. He wanted documentation so he could show it to the senses world. He was going to have an X-ray taken that the whole thing was healed up, you know. He enquired.

John 4:52, 53:
...[he] enquired...of them the hour when he began to amend [to be healed]. And they said unto him, Yesterday at the seventh hour the fever left him.

So the father knew that *it was* at the same hour, in...which Jesus said unto him, Thy son liveth: and himself believed, [he believed] and his whole house.

That is the family, people. You see, in biblical times whenever the father believed, the entire family believed. He sets the family pace spiritually. As he holds forth the greatness of God's Word, then the mother and children believe too. That is the way God designed it.

The father believed and all his house.

John 4:54:
This *is* again the second miracle...Jesus did, when he was come out of Judaea into Galilee.

John 5:1:
After this there was a feast of the Jews; and Jesus went up to Jerusalem.

Jerusalem? That is a terrible place to go because that is where the rulers are. That is where the top brass is. All the religious guys are up there. That is right. That is where the Sanhedrin, the seventy, the ruling body of Judaism sat. That was the center of all religion of its day, the great center. Jesus went right up to that great center.

John 5:2, 3:
Now there is at Jerusalem by the sheep market [one of the city gates] a pool, which is called in the Hebrew tongue Bethesda [the word "Bethesda" means mercy], having five porches.

In these [five porches] lay a great multitude of impotent [incapacitated] folk, of blind, halt, withered, waiting for the moving of the water.

This great multitude that lay there, all of those people were there to be healed. They were all sick. There was something wrong with them. They were incapacitated, impotent folk. Some were blind, some were halt, some were withered. They all had a need. Do you see it? And there, they are believing that someday they might be healed.

It is interesting that all of them believed in healing. All of them. Every one of them.

One of the great reasons I am teaching this is because if all of them believed in healing, then why did they not all get healed? That was a problem I wrestled with for a dozen or so years. Because when you work the Word of God, it has to fit like a hand in a glove. When it does not work with that mathematical exactness and that scientific precision, there has to be something wrong. Or if it is God's Word, it will have to fit. Now, many times I did not know the answer, but I never doubted the integrity of God's Word. I doubted my own stupidity and my own incapacity to understand and know.

The last phrase of verse 3, "waiting for the moving of the water," and all of verse 4 are deleted from the most ancient original text. So, I would like to go to verse 5:

John 5:5:
And a certain man...

It does not even give his name. It just says, a certain man was there, among all the rest of those needing to be healed.

John 5:5:
...[he] had an infirmity thirty and eight years.

Thirty-eight years he had been sick. Thirty-eight years. Do you get that? So, if you are nineteen years old, it is twice as old as you are. He was sick thirty-eight years.

Ask yourself a question: How much believing would you have left in your life if you had been sick for thirty-eight years? How much believing do you think you would have left to get healed the thirty-ninth year? Not very much, I guarantee you. Because some of us are sick three months and we do not have any believing left. This man —thirty-eight years. You know, some people are sick for one day and they say, "Oh, my God. What's the matter? Is God dead?"

Thirty-eight years. Verse 6:

John 5:6:
When Jesus saw him lie, and knew that he had been now a long time *in that case*, he saith unto him, Wilt thou [Do you will to] be made whole?

Wilt—do you will to be made whole? Where would your will to be made whole be after thirty-eight years? See it? That is the question he asked. Where is your will? What do you really will? After thirty-eight years, do you still will? Where is your will? Where is your will?

Well, I do not know if I would have had much left after thirty-eight years, do you? I marvel at these records. Thirty-eight years he was sick. Jesus said, "How is your will?"

Jesus knew he could not possess him. Jesus knew the true God would not take over making him become a channel. He says, how is your will? Do you will to be made whole?

And, ladies and gentlemen, there is a lot of difference between being delivered and being made whole. Ten lepers came to Jesus once. They were all ten healed. Jesus said to them, go show yourself to the priest. They all did. One returned to give thanks, and the Word of God says that one was made whole. Were they all healed? Yes.

There is a lot of difference between being healed and being made whole. To be made whole is to be made whole mentally, physically, spiritually, financially, and every other way. That is wholeness. And, by the way, that is the meaning of the word salvation. The Greek word is "*sōzō*," and it means to be made whole.

Jesus Christ is the complete savior. He is the whole savior. He came to make men and women whole; physically, mentally, spiritually, in every other category of their life. But we have lived so far below par. It is almost a disgrace that we call ourselves Christians because we have done nothing but degrade the truth of Christianity—if Christianity is what the Word of God says it is. And, ladies and gentlemen, if it isn't what the Word of God says it is, then who is going to define it? I am not going to listen to just anyone, I guarantee you. It is what the Word says.

How is your will? Thirty-eight years. Jesus asked him only one question. He did not say to him, when did you graduate from Harvard? He says, how is your will? Do you will? Do you will?

Look people, I do not know if you can appreciate that. It just sends showers inside of my inner self. To have will to be delivered after thirty-eight years? Did the impotent man answer and say, "Yes, sir, I want to be healed. I have the will"? No, he did not. He never answered the question! He was so beautifully human, like most of us. Jesus asked him a question, "Do you will to be made whole?" The man could have said yes or no. Yet he did not answer it. He did not answer it—just so human.

You know, God says do *you* will—if thou confess with thy mouth the Lord Jesus, thou shalt be saved. Do you say, "But, Lord, I do not believe that; I do not feel any different." See? Do *you* will to be whole?

The man never answered. Instead he said, "Oh, sir, you know, Jesus, I haven't got anybody to intercede for me. When I step down to get healed, you know what happens? Somebody else gets there before I do."

John 5:7:
...I have no man, when the water is troubled, to put me into the pool:...

Jesus never asked him about stepping down. He never asked him any such thing. He says, how is your will? See? And then the man did that beautiful psychological trip that we call rationalization, which is just a plain cop out. He just did not want to face up to it.

Now, between verse 7 and verse 8, there is a lot of deleted material and instruction that I know from the truth of the Word and how the Word operates. We see the man did not answer the question at all. And in order for a man to be delivered, he has to will to be delivered. And Jesus asking him that question, and man giving that answer, Jesus brought him around finally so that Jesus could say unto him in verse 8:

John 5:8:
…Rise, take up thy bed, and walk.

He could say to him, get up by the freedom of your will; rise, take up your bed. And this is not a bed like you think of a bed; it is a quilt or something similar to a blanket. That was their bed. Take up thy quilt or your blanket and walk.

And immediately—immediately. That is why it is a miracle of deliverance.

John 5:9:
And immediately the man was made whole,…

Made whole—not only physically, but mentally too. And, ladies and gentlemen, that is why there has to be a lot more between verses 7 and 8 than what is written in the Word. The reason there is not more written is—like the Word says—this is written that you may know eternal life and the greatness of God. That is why.

1 John 5:13:
These things have I written unto you that believe on the name of the Son of God; that ye may know that ye have eternal life, and that ye may believe on the name of the Son of God.

A lot of things Jesus Christ did are not written. The Word says, if everything be written that he did, all the libraries of Harvard could not hold it—there just would not be room. That is a figure of speech saying there would be a voluminous amount of material.

John 21:25:
And there are also many other things which Jesus did, the which, if they should be written every one, I suppose that even the world itself could not contain the books that should be written. Amen.

You know, Jesus Christ taught day in and day out, night after night, week after week. Imagine Jesus Christ, the Son of God, speaking with these people a voluminous amount of material. It never says in God's Word that this is all Jesus Christ spoke, or this is all he did. But it does say that this is what he spoke, and this is what he did. The extras are not always stipulated.

John 5:9:
And immediately the man was made whole, and took up his bed, and walked: and on the same day was the Sabbath.

Is that terrible? Is that awful? Did he not do it on the right day? You know, you can do it on Sunday and Monday, but do not do it on the Sabbath.

I love the Lord Jesus Christ, I think beyond perhaps any man living today, but do you know why I like him? Because he just broke every rule and regulation. The rule said you cannot do it on Sabbath day. So, what did Jesus Christ do? He did it on the Sabbath. He did not particularly break the rule, but a man had a need. The need always takes precedence over the day and over the place. That is the greatness of it.

And, oh, how I praise God that Jesus Christ had the audacity, the courage, to stand for truth. He ministered to that man who had been sick for how many years? Thirty-eight years. Ladies and gentlemen, if you were sick for thirty-eight years, would you care what day of the week you got delivered? Isn't that a trifling little argument—that you do not do it on the right day, or that it was not done at the right location? Maybe the right doctor was not there, and you were not counting your beads in the right way? Oh, my goodness, how terrible.

John 5:10:
The Jews therefore said unto him that was cured,...

Now, they did not talk to Jesus, they talked to the man who was made whole. And the word "whole" is sound. The word "sound" is cure. To do a cure biblically is to remove a cause. That is the doing of a cure. Now, every doctor knows that. Most Christians have never thought about it. So I know from the Word that he removed a cause, that is why it has to be a cure.

Now, there are some sicknesses that you do not have to remove any causes; then it cannot be cured. Whenever it is a cure, a cause has to be removed. Suppose you get a splinter underneath your fingernail. To remove the splinter is removing the cause. When the cause is removed, the symptom will disappear. That is doing of a cure. In the Bible, every deliverance a devil spirit has caused is a cure to the people who were possessed. And when you take the devil spirit out, the cause is removed, the symptom will cure. That is what it is talking about.

> **John 5:10:**
> The Jews therefore said unto him that was cured, It is the sabbath day: it is not lawful for thee to carry *thy* bed.

It was the Sabbath day! That is not in order. It is not legal to carry your couch, your blanket.

> **John 5:11, 12:**
> He answered them, He that made me whole, the same said unto me, Take up thy bed, and walk.
> Then [answered]…they him, What man is that which said unto thee, Take up thy bed, and walk?

And he that was healed did not know it. That is what I call love, don't you? He did not know it.

> **John 5:13:**
> And he that was healed wist not who it was: for Jesus had conveyed himself away,…

"...conveyed himself away" means he turned aside, went back, went away. The words in the text are: "turned-aside" or "gone out." That's all.

The man was healed. He just healed the man. The man was delivered. The man believed he was delivered. Jesus Christ walked away. And the man did not know who did it!

John 5:13b:
...wist not who it was:...

Isn't that something? Isn't that beautiful?

Jesus Christ did not come along and say, "Now look, before God's going to deliver you, you better put your tithe on the altar. Before God's going to deliver you, you better hang in here with us and be a certain ministry." No, he did not say anything like it!

The man had a need. Jesus Christ had a revelation; he ministered. He brought that man up, he ministered to that man's need, and the man got delivered.

John 5:14:
Afterward [after it is all over with] Jesus [found]... him...

Well, it was the only way. He did not know who Jesus was, so Jesus had to do the finding, right?

John 5:14a:
Afterward Jesus [found]...him [where?] in the temple,...

That's right. He went right to the temple after he was delivered.

John 5:14:
[And] Jesus [found] him in the temple, and said unto him, Behold, thou art made whole: sin no more, lest a worse thing come [upon]...thee.

Now, here is a record of a man who perhaps had this particular infirmity for almost thirty years because of what sin had done. Now, not every sickness is due to your sin. Could be—you could be sick, you could be in this category because of your sin, but all sickness is due to sin. There never was any sickness until after there was sin. Read Genesis.

But it does not mean it is *your* sin. It could be sin in society. And we sure have it today. One of the reasons we are not seeing the great deliverance that I am waiting to see in our country and world is because of the massive amount of unbelief in our society. Hardly anyone believes in the integrity and accuracy of God's Word, and the power of it!

In the early church, they believed. It says in Acts, as Peter was walking down the street, the shadow of Peter would pass over people, and they would be healed. There is no healing power in a shadow of Peter or the shadow —no healing power. The healing power is in believing. And they believed in those days that when Peter walked down the street, the man of God was walking there. And even the shadow of that man of God was so blessed and such a blessing, they believed that if that shadow passed over them, they would be healed; and they were healed.

We certainly have not risen to that time, have we? Neither in your community nor mine.

John 5:15, 16:
The man departed, and told the Jews that it was Jesus, [who]…had made him whole.

And therefore did the Jews persecute Jesus, and [they] sought to slay him, because he had done these things on the sabbath day.

Why did they sought to slay him? What does it say? Because it was the sabbath day. Were they interested in people? No. Were they interested in that man who had suffered for thirty-eight years who was delivered? No. One would have thought logically, if they had any decency about them, they would have stood up and said, "Well, praise God you're delivered." Thirty-eight years sick, then he was delivered, and the religious leader legislators are mad about it. These were the heads of the temple. They were the religious leaders. One would have thought they would have welcomed the man with open arms and said, "Well, praise God you're healed. You're delivered."

But no. They said, "Who did it? Who did it?"

He said, "I don't know."

"What do you mean you don't know? You got healed. You ought to know. What's the matter with you?"

He said, "Well, I don't know who did it."

"But you said it was the Sabbath."

"Yes, the Sabbath."

John 5:16:
...[they] persecute Jesus, and [they] sought to [kill] him,...

What a record for religious leaders! You are not going to have much trouble with the accuracy of God's Word among the unbelievers. You know where your problems are going to come from? The religious leaders in your community. Because they have freedom of will, many of them, but they do not will to change.

Do you will to be made whole? Do you will to change?

If I do not will to change, you know what is going to happen? I am not going to change. It is in the will. Do you will to change? When you do not have a will to change, God Almighty cannot do a thing about it. He could raise the dead again, and if you did not will to change, you never change.

John 5:16-18:

[The Jews] sought to slay him, because he had done these things on the Sabbath…

…Jesus answered them, My Father worketh hitherto, and I work.

Therefore the Jews sought the more to kill him, because he not only had broken the sabbath, but said also that God was his Father, making himself equal with God.

And the word "equal" means in the family of God. God was his what? Father. Jesus Christ was not God. He said God was his Father, and they wanted to kill him more so. He never said he was God. Even they said, he made himself to be the son of God, God was his Father. And because he said that God was his Father, they wanted to kill him.

Had Jesus said he was God, all hell would have broken loose. That would have been unforgivable. They knew better than that. That's right.

John 5:19-27:

Then answered Jesus and said unto them, Verily, verily, I say unto you, The Son can do nothing of himself, but what he seeth the Father do: for what things soever he doeth, these also doeth the Son likewise.

For the Father loveth the Son, and sheweth him all things that himself doeth: and he will shew him greater works than these, that ye may marvel.

For as the Father raiseth up the dead, and quickeneth *them;* even so the Son quickeneth whom he [what?] will.

For the Father judgeth no man, but hath committed all judgment unto the Son:

That all *men* should honour the Son, even as they honour the Father. He that honoureth not the Son honoureth not the Father which hath sent him.

Verily, verily, I say unto you, He that heareth my word, and believeth on him that sent me, hath everlasting life, and shall not come into condemnation; but is passed from death unto life.

Verily, verily, I say unto you, The hour is coming, and now is, when the dead shall hear the voice of the Son of God: and they that hear shall live.

For as the Father hath life in himself; so hath he given to the Son to have life in himself;

And hath given him authority to execute judgment also, because he is the Son of man.

What a tremendous record! Here is a man who is impotent, sick for thirty-eight years, and the one thing Jesus wanted to know is, do you will to be made whole? He did not possess him, he did not control him. The true God never possesses. The true God never controls. You are never a channel for the true God. You are never a medium. The true God never does anything through you. He works within you to will and to do His good pleasure by your believing.

Do you will to be made whole? He brought him to that place that he willed. Why were not all the rest of them healed? Because Jesus Christ had no revelation to minister to the rest of them. In all those porches lay a whole multitude of the sick and impotent folk. They all believed in deliverance, but only one was healed.

Why? Did Jesus Christ not love the rest? Sure he did. Then why was one healed? Because only one at that moment could rise to that place of believing. Do you will to be made whole?

Now, it does not say that no one else rose up later, but at that particular time there was only one who willed to be made whole; that is why only one was delivered. They all believed in healing, but only one was made whole because only one could rise up to that believing privilege to be made whole, and he is that one that Jesus ministered to! And he had been impotent and incapacitated for thirty-eight years. Jesus never possessed him, he never controlled him. He never took advantage of him.

And what a great day it is in our lives when you too learn that you, by the freedom of your will, decide how far you are going to go with God. Are you going to believe God's Word or are you going to believe what people say about it? Are you going to will to believe God's Word, or you are just going to will to believe what others say?

You are going to believe *something*, because everybody believes. The question is not *do* you believe, but *what* do you believe and *whom* do you believe? And knowing that all learning requires a center of reference outside of the individual seeking, I challenge you to believe God's Word as that center of reference outside of you for truth. Not Plato, not Aristotle, not Socrates, not Freud, or Playboy, or anything else, but what? The Word! The Word!

Do you know that Thomas Paine said he would live to see the day that nobody read the Bible or believed it? Ladies and gentlemen, historically, Thomas Paine is dead and gone, and there are at least a few of us that still read it, and we are still living. Our God is alive now. We have got the proof of it because we got the manifestation. We are born again of God's spirit. We have Christ in us the hope of glory. And, ladies and gentlemen, we are heaven bound and all hell is not going to stop us from getting there.

And no matter what men may say, think, or do, this Word of God is going to be fulfilled; every jot and tittle of it is going to be fulfilled. It is God's Word and it speaks to our day and our time. And we are again saying to people all over the world, "Thus saith the Lord!"

There are only two things mankind can do: they can either believe it or reject it. But, praise God, at least they have the privilege to say yes or no. And I thank God for that freedom.

That is freedom of the will—do you will to be made whole?

I do not know any greater record than this. There are others in there, they are all great, but this one just sets it like a diamond. Thirty-eight years—that is what blew my mind. I have known people sick for three months who cannot stand it anymore. This man, thirty-eight years, finally got to the place that he was able to do what? believe. By the freedom of his will to be made what? whole.

Maybe there is still a little opportunity for some of us, right? The joy of believing, the joy of changing. Do you will to really believe God? Do you will to be made whole? You determine how far you are going to go with God and the things of God.

THE HEALING WHOLENESS
OF GOD'S LOVE

*You can look up verse after verse of scripture on love,
and in every one of them you will see how love contributes
toward making you whole physically.*

The greatest healing I know is spiritual. And that healing is the new birth. While the healing is spiritual,
the spiritual is so dynamic that it overflows and affects
the physical. And it is basically in believing. Even those
people of the Old Testament who could not be born again,
if they were properly taught and believed what they were
taught, then believing brought a lot of healing to them.

In our day and time, this is what I am going to be
teaching and setting before men and women across the
country and world:

Romans 10:9, 10:
That if thou shalt confess with thy mouth the Lord
Jesus, and shalt believe in thine heart that God hath
raised him from the dead, thou shalt be saved.

For with the heart man believeth unto righteousness;
and with the mouth confession is made unto salvation.

That, I believe, is the greatest healing. Accompanying
this birth of Christ within is speaking in tongues, building
up that inner man, that spiritual man.[1] For it is God which

---

1. The gift of holy spirit is called the "new man" in Ephesians
4:24 and Colossians 3:10; it is called the "inner man" in Ephesians 3:16; and it is called the "inward man" in 2 Corinthians 4:16.
These are set in contrast with flesh, which is called our "old man"

worketh in you both to will and to do of *his* good pleasure (Philippians 2:13).

Now, that spirit of God working within us has never been analyzed as to how much that does physically for us. But the Word of God says that He worketh within us to will and to do His good pleasure. And one of His good pleasures along with His will must be 3 John 2—prosper and be in health.

3 John 2:
Beloved, I wish above all things that thou mayest prosper and be in health...

Now, it is not just to be born again, it is to be born again with the renewed mind on what are our sonship rights, and what we have in Christ;[2] because there are a lot of people who are born again, but nothing happens to them physically. The reason nothing happens to them physically is because they have never put on the mind of Christ or known and believed what really happened to them spiritually when they were born again. Therefore our teaching ministry is so dynamically urgent. Just teach, teach, teach!

I believe the greatest thing I know in all healing is love. You know the foundation is done, but then in practice, is that love. 1 Corinthians, Chapter 12, verse 27, says:

1 Corinthians 12:27:
Now ye are the body of Christ, [whether we like it

---

in Romans 6:6, Ephesians 4:22, and Colossians 3:9; and called the "outward man" in 2 Corinthians 4:16.

2. As a result of being born again of God's spirit, the believer becomes a son of God. Because Jesus Christ gained our redemption and salvation on legal grounds, we now have certain rights and privileges as members of the family of God, blessings we refer to as our "sonship rights."

or not, we are the body; and we are] members in particular.

Not everyone is a sore thumb in it; not everyone is a pointing finger; not everyone is an eye. But every part of that body is very important.

1 Corinthians 12:28-31:
And God hath set some in the church, first apostles, secondarily prophets, thirdly teachers, after that miracles, then gifts of healings, helps, governments, diversities [*genos*] of tongues.

Are all apostles?...prophets?...all teachers?...all workers of miracles?

Have all the [*charismata*] of healing? do all speak with tongues? do all interpret?

But covet earnestly the best gifts: and yet shew I unto you a more excellent way [than coveting].

Chapter 13 is the greatest chapter in the Word on the love of God in the renewed mind in manifestation. You see, God so loved, according to John 3:16, that God gave His only begotten Son.[3] Now you and I are sons of God, and we must so give that others can learn to live. For as we give, they live. If God so loved that He gave, the least that you and I can do is so love that we give.

You know, it is so easy to criticize. It is so easy to find fault. It is so easy to see wrong because that is the natural man, how we were born and raised. That was the culture and environment we came out of. But now we are born-again believers, being motivated by the greatness of God's Word. We have to drive ourselves to get over criticism, fault-finding, seeing the wrong all the time. God so loved that He what? gave.

---

3. John 3:16: For God so loved the world, that he gave his only begotten Son, that whosoever believeth in him should not perish, but have everlasting life.

I remember Moses, Abraham, David, and many others in the Old Testament that God so loved that He gave. And in the New Testament, I remember Paul; God so loved that He gave.

If we could discipline our minds to never say anything but that which is positive and on the Word, what a day that would be. If we cannot say anything good about someone then we better look at ourselves, because everyone has something good that we can share.

In 1 Timothy 6:10, it says:

1 Timothy 6:10:
...the love of money is the root of all evil....

If the love of money is the root of all evil, then the love of God in the renewed mind in manifestation must be the root of all good, by sheer logic. The love represents the world, the power, the structure. There is nothing wrong with the world, the power, and the structure; except once they get money, they never get enough of it. That is why the love of it is the root of all evil.

The love of God in the renewed mind in manifestation will never get enough of the love of God. We can always use more love. Spiritually, He has given us all of it, but I have not put it all in the mind.

Just picture for a moment and remember the healing that came when someone really loved you with the love of Christ. Not that possessive, egotistical type of love; not that "get something out of you" type of thing called love—no, no, no. Picture where they just opened their heart to you, and tenderized you with the love of God in the renewed mind. I do not know anything more healing than to be loved—than to just gather someone into your spiritual arms, so to speak; into your heart, into your mind—and tenderly sharing your dynamic love with them (the Christ that is in you).

You know, anyone can raise hell, but very few people who are Christian ever get to the place of really exuberating love, tenderness, kindness, forgiveness, understanding. Think how healing it is when someone walks up to you and takes you by the arm, and says, "I sure love you." That is a lot more healing than someone taking you by the arm and saying, "Well, what is the matter with you?"

You see, we have heard the negative side, but we seldom take a look how healing a place can be where there is a believer with that love of God. Yes, you are the greatest arm of God's healing in the world today. You heal just by loving people, by tenderizing them, by taking them in.

Now, you may not agree with what they are doing; they may be wrong. You may have to show them some Scripture, but you can do that lovingly too. God is our Father. We are His children. If God so loved, we are His children, then we love.

There is no other way of bringing great healing, and I am not just speaking spiritually; I am speaking physically —physical healing. Because that love does something to people that makes their blood flow better, muscles function better. I do not know what happens in the physical body, I just know it happens. It warms them inside.

They say that worry gives you ulcers because it does something to your bloodstream that eats out your stomach or your intestines, so you get ulcers. Well, if that poison in the bloodstream is from worry, think of the sweetness of love in there. Then love would be healing. Love would tenderize. Love would bring that blood to flow better. You know, when you lose your temper, and you jump up and down yelling, just think how sick you feel on the inside; how your heart pumps like crazy and you get red in the face—just the opposite of what love does. Love will settle the heart down, and it will beat normally, unnoticed. I doubt if any of us have ever really looked at the healing wholeness of love.

When you spell it all out from God's Word, the Word says: how can we say we love God if we do not love our brother.[4] God so loved that He gave.[5] You can look up verse after verse of scripture on love, and every one of them you will see is contributing toward making you and me physically whole. Nothing is as healing as that love.

I looked up a few verses of scripture I want to share about health and healing beginning in Proverbs, Chapter 12, verse 17.

Proverbs 12:17, 18:
He that speaketh truth sheweth forth righteousness: but a false witness deceit.

There is that speaketh like the piercings of a sword: but the tongue of the wise *is* health.

So, there are two ways: one is the love way, the other is the opposite. "Speaketh like the piercing of a sword." You know, loud voices and yelling at each other or at someone is like the piercing of a sword. It cuts. It injures. But the tongue of the wise—not piercing but love—speaketh truth, sheweth forth wisdom; that brings health.

Proverbs 16:24:
Pleasant words *are as* an honeycomb, sweet to the soul, and health to the bones.

Pleasant words come from the heart of love. And the heart of love is the heart that has been tenderized with the love of God in the renewed mind; where we put on

---

4. 1 John 4:20 If a man say, I love God, and hateth his brother, he is a liar: for he that loveth not his brother whom he hath seen, how can he love God whom he hath not seen?

5. John 3:16.

the mind of Christ, and we speak, and we walk with that mind, and with that love.

It says also in Proverbs that death and life are in the power of the tongue.[6] All sickness is death in whole or in part. All healing is deliverance in whole or in part as needed. Death and life are in the tongue. So, the life that is there must be the life of the love of God in the renewed mind in manifestation.

Proverbs 13:17:
A wicked messenger falleth into mischief: but a faithful ambassador *is* health.

Faithful ambassadors holding forth God's Word bring health. I could minister healing every night but that is not the greatness of what I believe. I believe it is wonderful to minister healing, but I think the greatest ministry is the ministry of the Word. It is that Word that liveth and abideth forever. It is that Word that brings healing, and people have to get confidence in the Word, not in a man. See it? Confidence is needed in God and His Word. The man is only a vessel. A faithful ambassador brings health by teaching the Word and by loving people.

In spite of the shortcomings of all of us, we still have the greatest amount of love radiating of any people any place in the world. There is no greater love being made known in the world than through this ministry. And, as ambassadors holding forth the love of God, it will bring health to people. It is the Word you want to promote. You talk the Word! A man says something, read him the Word! Do not explain your ministry stands for this or for that; tell him what the Word says. It is God's Word.

Isaiah 58:7, 8:
It is not to deal thy bread to the hungry [talking

---

6. Proverbs 18:21 Death and life *are* in the power of the tongue: and they that love it shall eat the fruit thereof.

about the fast], and that thou bring the poor that are cast out to thy house? when thou seest the naked, that thou cover him; and that thou hide not thyself from thine own flesh?

Then [then if you do, then] shall thy light break forth as the morning, and thine health shall spring forth speedily: and thy righteousness shall go before thee; the glory of the LORD shall be thy rereward.

Do you know what that means? Sometimes men are prone to help someone else, but they will not help their own children. They are sweet on everyone else's woman except their own wife; sweet on everyone else's man except their own husband; sweet on helping the poor heathen in India and not the next-door neighbor. That is what that verse means.

Look at it again:

Isaiah 58:7b-9:
…when thou seest the naked, that thou cover him; and that thou hide not thyself from thine own flesh?

Then shall thy light break forth…[then] health shall spring forth speedily:…

Then shalt thou call, and the LORD shall answer;… and he shall say, Here I *am.*

If we get things in proper order with the new birth, the manifestations, speaking in tongues, studying to show ourselves approved by rightly dividing the Word of God, putting on the mind of Christ, rightly dividing it—and then just have that love of God in the renewed mind in manifestation—the healing, physical healing, is fantastic among a group of believers, because it is built on the Word. And the Word delivers; the Word heals.

APPENDICES

*By other teachers who served with
Dr. Wierwille's ministry and with the
same heart for the Word of God.*

APPENDIX 1

A MERRY HEART

Often the healthiest people you know are those who smile and laugh a lot. But what about when we face negative situations?

Have you ever noticed that often the healthiest people you know are those who smile and laugh a lot —not those who frown and complain all the time? God's Word tells us that a cheerful attitude has a positive effect on our health. Proverbs 17:22 says:

Proverbs 17:22:
A merry heart doeth good *like* a medicine: but a broken spirit drieth the bones.

Let us look more closely at this verse. First of all, the word "merry" means "glad" or "joyful." The word "good" has a broad meaning and is therefore properly supplied. The word "medicine" is more accurately translated "cure." It comes from the Hebrew word "*gehah*," which means to thrust away a bandage that is no longer needed. Another translation of this verse reads, "A merry heart makes the body healthy…"

Proverbs are usually structured in parallel sentences, and in this case, a merry heart parallels a broken spirit.

The word "broken" means "wounded or smitten." In this context, the emphasis is more on being disappointed, downcast, or discontented as a general state, as opposed to being hurt by a single event. The word "drieth" is used literally of wet things that dry up. It is also used metaphorically of sapping strength and vigor. The word "bones" is singular, not plural, in the Hebrew. We know that blood, which contains the soul life, is manufactured in the bone. The entire verse properly reads: "A glad heart makes the body healthy, but a wounded life saps the strength from the body." Rotherham's translation has it: "A joyful heart worketh an excellent cure, but a stricken spirit drieth up the bones."

Isn't that a terrific verse to know? A merry heart works an excellent cure, making for a healthy body.

We want to look at a few examples in God's Word of people with a merry heart. We will see how important our attitudes are in getting this merry heart.

Luke 12:16-19:
And he [Jesus] spake a parable unto them, saying, The ground of a certain rich man brought forth plentifully:

And he thought within himself, saying, What shall I do, because I have no room where to bestow my fruits?

And he said, This will I do: I will pull down my barns, and build greater; and there will I bestow all my fruits and my goods.

And I will say to my soul, Soul, thou hast much goods laid up for many years; take thine ease, eat, drink, *and* be merry.

But what did God say? God has the final word, right?

Luke 12:20, 21:
But God said unto him, *Thou* fool, this night thy soul shall be required of thee: then whose shall those things be, which thou hast provided?

So *is* he that layeth up treasure for himself, and is not rich toward God.

If we want to be "rich toward God," we need to have the right attitude. We can see in this parable that the rich man thought only of himself and that he would be in charge for the next few years. But God had a different answer for him. We should live our lives being rich toward God. We see that it is the attitude, respect, and reverence toward God that is important, not material increase.

Remember the parable of the forgiving father in Luke 15? The younger son asked his father for the inheritance due him, which was quite legal to do in that culture; so the father divided it to him, and the son went into a far country where he wasted all his inheritance. A great famine arose in that country, and having no funds left, he was forced to take the most degrading job in the Judean culture—a pig feeder. Formerly living like a rich man's son, he now found himself eating with pigs. Suddenly he became aware of where he was and the state he was in.

Luke 15:17, 20, 22-24:

And when he came to himself, he said, How many hired servants of my father's have bread enough and to spare, and I perish with hunger!

And he arose, and came to his father. But when he was yet a great way off, his father saw him, and had compassion, and ran, and fell on his neck, and kissed him.

...the father said to his servants, Bring forth the best robe, and put *it* on him; and put a ring on his hand, and shoes on *his* feet:

And bring hither the fatted calf, and kill *it;* and let us eat, and be merry:

For this my son was dead, and is alive again; he was lost, and is found. And they began to be merry.

Isn't that a wonderful occasion for having a family together and having that merry heart?

From these two records in God's Word—the rich man and his storehouse, and the parable of the forgiving father —we have two examples of a merry heart. One man had a merry heart because he was rich for himself; the other because he was rich toward God. For our lives to be fulfilled and our hearts to be truly merry, we must be rich toward God in our attitude of heart.

When things are going well it is easy to maintain a merry or joyful heart. But what about when we face negative situations? I think especially of a parent's concern for his child's health. When a parent becomes fearful, he has reached a dangerous point. We know from the Power for Abundant Living class that fear is wrong believing which issues in wrong results. The account of Job vividly illustrates this point. Job was a parent who feared for his children's well-being. His fear was the "hole in the hedge" of his believing, bringing on negative results.

Job 3:23, 25:
Why is light given to a man whose way is hid, and whom God hath hedged in?

For the thing which I greatly feared is come upon me, and that which I was afraid of is come unto me.

By claiming the promises of God and acting upon God's Word, Job received deliverance from mental and physical pressures. We must do the same.

We know that if we have any kind of fear, we have to get rid of it. We can claim God's promises and take positive action upon His Word. As believers, we never react negatively to a situation because we know we are in control. We have these promises in God's Word:

3 John 2:

Beloved, I wish above all *things* that thou mayest prosper and be in health, even as thy soul prospereth.

Romans 8:37:

...in all these things we are more than conquerors through him that loved us.

2 Corinthians 2:14:

Now thanks *be* unto God, which always causeth us to triumph in Christ, and maketh manifest the savour of his knowledge by us in every place.

2 Corinthians 9:8:

And God *is* able to make all grace abound toward you; that ye, always having all sufficiency in all *things*, may abound to every good work:

What do we do? We do not have a passive attitude, and we do not go to the doctor thinking he is going to do it all. Many people have been disappointed by that kind of action. We decide the action we need to take to have that merry heart restored again. It is important to our well-being. We must keep a cheerful heart, a merry heart, a quality of mind which will take the weight off us.

Running out of energy, money, and time are three things I know of which can weigh us down. I know that I had a tendency to be late. I used to think, "How am I going to get over this?" I would always be running out of time, which eventually made me late for meetings. Sometimes I would be ready to go out the door, and the phone would ring or somebody would come by. I had to learn to organize my life. I started leaving home early enough so that those last-minute phone calls did not happen—I was not there to answer them. As for running out of energy, many times we have things we need to do but, because we are tired, we do not have a positive outlook on handling the situation. We cannot let ourselves get into these situations where we run out of time, energy, or money. We prevent them by planning ahead. We take action so that these things which could weigh us down, which could keep us from having a merry heart, do not happen.

Laughter is a great key in maintaining a merry heart. I have seen numerous articles written in magazines that deal with laughter as a key to healing. One such article that a believer lent me says:

> Laughter may indirectly aid in decreasing pain in inflammatory conditions associated with such physical problems as arthritis, for instance. Evidence is beginning to suggest that laughter sends a message to the brain requiring that it produce more alertness hormones called catecholamines. The release of this alertness chemical then stimulates secretions of the body's own painkillers, which are the endorphins, and the perception of pain decreases. The bottom line is that laughter may be a painkiller and the increase in catecholamines has been linked to a decrease in inflammations. There is also evidence that laughter is one method the body employs to relax. When you laugh heartily and the humor spasm stops, your pulse rate drops below normal and skeletal muscles become deeply relaxed. The body is revitalized. The relaxation response has been found to last approximately forty-five minutes after the last "Ha." The greater the intensity of laughter, the larger the decreasing tension and the more long-lasting the effect. Laughter also allows the muscles to go limp and is an effective agent for reducing stress.[1]

A joyful heart worketh an excellent cure and has a

---

1. See also Norman Cousins, *Anatomy of an Illness* (New York: W.W. Norton & Co., Inc., 1981), pp. 39 and 40.

definite effect on the body. It is interesting to note that science is catching up to what we already know from God's Word.

I have had difficult physical situations to face. At these times I would know I had to restore my merry heart because I did not want the adversary to steal from me. I turned to God's Word, and one of the things that I put in my mind and in my life was Psalms 94:19:

Psalms 94:19:
In the multitude of my thoughts within me thy comforts delight my soul.

I would think about the comforts that are mentioned in God's Word. I would think, "Well, what is going to delight my soul from God's Word today?" I would think about Exodus 3, verse 14:

Exodus 3:14:
And God said unto Moses, I AM THAT I AM:...

Research has taught that this verse means: "I shall become what I shall become." God is going to be there to take care of us in every situation. We rest in the Word of God we know. We can relax and believe it and let it happen. God will take care of the rest.

There are always different verses I give to people when they call me on the phone. I know that ministering healing to them is what will help them, but they also must have something to put in their minds. I tell them, "Read Romans 8 or Ephesians 1." Ephesians 1 reveals what God has already done for us.

He has made our bodies so that their nature is to heal themselves. As we claim the promises in God's Word and act upon them, we can truly have a merry heart.

Exodus 15:26:
...I *am* the LORD that healeth thee.

APPENDIX 2

WORD-STUDY: *HUGIAINŌ*

I pray that you will be led in a good way and be healthy in word, healthy in teaching, healthy in doctrine, healthy in believing, healthy in the family faith, and physically healthy according as your soul is led in the good way.

If you look around the world with ears to hear and eyes to see, then you have been confronted with all the fear, all the negatives, all the things the adversary is working overtime to inundate in people's minds. His motivation is to get you full of fear with doubt, confusion, and worry.

Certainly, there is a lot of sickness in the world. There is plenty of physical sickness, but I mean sickness of the soul—a great sickness. There is a great void of truth.

The number one thing you have to realize is that you need to teach God's Word, hot and heavy. You see, because your vitality, the dynamics of your continued fellowship with God is dependent upon your relationship with His written Word; if your relationship with His written Word is dull, lifeless, and boring, what kind of fellowship do you think you are going to have with God? Dull, lifeless, and boring.

The written Word is electrifying! I call it "hot Bible." And God's primary will is for total deliverance in every aspect and every facet of our lives. God is concerned with the entire gamut of human life. And our God is a God of deliverance.

But so many times, people limit God in their mis-understanding or misuse of a word or verses from the Bible. I would like you to look at a verse in 3 John. Recently, I realized as I looked at this verse, how many times we have quoted it, talked about it, and how often it comes up. I also realized that I had never worked this verse in depth. So, I decided to do it, and it totally opened up my eyes of understanding to what God's will is regarding a certain aspect of our life. And that verse is 3 John 2:

3 John 2:
Beloved, I wish above all things that thou mayest prosper and be in health, even as thy soul prospereth.

I began to think, what is God's heart here? What is involved? Too many times, for most of our believers, being in health means not being sick—how limited. For most, when we say or think of this verse, we think of two things: money and not going into the hospital. But that is so limiting as far as what God really has said in this verse. By the time we are done working this verse, it is going to blow your mind how much is involved with God's heart and will.

I began by looking up that word "prosper." That is what started it all—prosper and health. What is it all about? And the word "prosper" is the Greek word "*euodousthai*" which comes from the Greek root *hodos*. And *hēgéomai* means "to be led in a good way." To have a prosperous journey. It is translated like that in Romans, Chapter 1.[1]

And it is only used four times in the New Testament: twice here in this one verse, which makes it interesting; once in Romans;[2] and in 1 Corinthians 16 where it talks

---

1. The lexical form is *eudothesomai* in Romans, Chapter 1.
2. Romans 1:10: Making request, if by any means now at length

about abundant sharing, according as the Lord has prospered you.[3]

So many times, we think of it strictly in financial terms, but the beauty is "to be led in the good way." And this really began to work on my mind when I had the privilege to share God's Word and the theme was: God can make a way where there is no way.

As I worked it, it blew my mind how much was in there—to be led in a good way.

3 John 2a:
Beloved, I wish above all things…

The word "wish" is the Greek word "*euchomai*." And it is used for prayer. It means to pray. So, this is one of God's prayers. If you have ever done any work in studying the prayers in the epistles, you will find how much power, how much heart, how much love, how much abundance there is in God's heart toward His believers.

And here is a prayer that God has given to the Apostle John by revelation. He says: Beloved, I pray above, or I pray concerning all things—all things considered, all without exception. What I consider everything about human life—my prayer for you, my people—God says, is that you are to be led in a good way and be in health even as thy soul prospereth.[4]

Now, the words "to be in health" are one Greek word; it is the Greek word, "*hugiainō*." And *hugiainō* comes from another Greek adjective which is *hugiēs*. And *hugiēs*

I might have a prosperous journey by the will of God to come unto you.

3. 1 Corinthians 16:2: Upon the first *day* of the week let every one of you lay by him in store, as *God* hath prospered him, that there be no gatherings when I come.

4. 3 John 2: Beloved, I wish above all things that thou mayest prosper and be in health, even as thy soul prospereth.

is an adjective, and that means to be healthy or to be sound, to be whole. And *hugiēs* is used 14 times in the New Testament, the Gospels through Revelation.

Hugiēs is interesting because it is always used of persons or their individual members—like an arm or a leg or your gall bladder—that you as a person are physically sound and whole, or your members are. But *hugiainō* has a much broader understanding to it.

As a matter of fact, when I started looking at that word, I began to see 3 John 2 in the light of leadership. It is broad, it is general, it is to all believers, but a leader in the ministry should be specifically and exactly attuned to this.

I began to find that *hugiainō*, after I had looked through the uses and usages of it, came to be used 12 times in the New Testament. Now after checking the uses and usages of *hugiainō*, I began to see a purpose for everything God says—where He says it, when He says it, how He says it, to whom He says it. God knew we were going to be working the Word. God knew we would be checking out every angle. So, when God uses a particular word or phrase just a certain amount of times, then a lot of times it has a significant meaning.

Whenever you work a word, you want to get as far back and as much information on it as you can. So, I checked out how this word *hugiainō* was used by the Pythagoras, like Plato, Homer; how it was translated to into the Septuagint; how it was used in the New Testament; how would they call, theologically, the post-Apostolic Fathers used it. See the whole history and etymology of that word, because it will help you.

Now, many times God will use a word without any regard for those things. And the first thing you want to do is let the Word speak for itself, but they can help you in the overall understanding of some of those things.

Now, *hugiainō* is a verb derived from *hugiēs*, the adjective. And the profane Greek sources like Plato, Aristotle, and Pythagoras used it not of physical health, but to describe mental health. Rational thought. Or something that was firm, reliable, constant. That was that *hugiainō* word. And to show you that it did not have just a purely physical meaning, many times *hugiainō* was included in a customary farewell wish on gravestones. Now, when you are dead it does not do anyone any good to hope that you are healthy out there. But you see, *hugiainō* as a farewell wish on an epitaph had far more than just a merely physical meaning, do you understand? Because the physical life was over. In the Greek mythology, they were talking about beyond.

So *hugiainō* did not have nearly as much emphasis on the physical aspect of it as it did on the mental. *Hugiainō* came to be used to describe the Pythagorean theory of harmony. Well, Pythagoras was that mathematician and he had this theory on the harmony of the universe. His usage of *hugiainō*, health, rests on a balanced mixture of many different qualities. This defining of healthy as a mixture of different qualities and a balance of extremes was adopted and applied in every Greek age.

Plato used *hugiainō*. He defined health using *hugiainō* as the highest of human goods as opposed to divine goods. In other words, the highest goods a man can achieve is *hugiainō*, health. And in his work on responsibility, Plato wrote that, "One can tell the sick what manner of life will make him well." Not what medicine, not what therapy, but what manner of life will make him well. And he states that virtue follows or springs from health of the soul, where vice is its sickness. Sickness of the soul will yield vice.

And look around. Do you see vice? Sure. The adversary is working up a storm. There is sickness all around because peoples' soul life are full of corrupt, diseased teaching.

Health of the body is not the goal of *hugiainō*. Health of the body is the result. It is the result of *hugiainō*, this mental health.

Now, *hugiainō* in and of itself means to be healthy, to be sound, to be in good health. As you look at these, you will find that of the twelve uses in the New Testament, eight of them are in the pastoral epistles. Fully two-thirds of all the uses of that word are in the pastoral epistles. The pastoral epistles are your leadership epistles. They are instruction from God to leadership on what to do. How to rule within the Body of Christ. How to work so that things go according to God's will.

Take a look at the uses of *hugiainō* and see what categories the usages break into, because use and usage are different.

Sound (Healthy) Doctrine

In 1 Timothy 1:9, we will look at some of these.

1 Timothy 1:9, 10:
Knowing this, that the law is not made for a righteous man, but for the lawless and disobedient, for the ungodly and for sinners, for unholy and profane, for murderers of fathers and murderers of mothers, for manslayers,

For whoremongers, for them that defile themselves with mankind, for menstealers, for liars, for perjured persons, and if there be any other thing that is contrary to sound doctrine;

The word "sound" is *hugiainō*—healthy doctrine. Now, the word "doctrine" is interesting because it is the Greek *didaskalia*. And *didaskalia* means teaching. There is another Greek word, "*didache*," which means teaching also, and there is a neat shade of difference in the two. Because *didaskalia* does not involve just the act of teaching, but it also emphasizes the result of teaching. In other words, what is taught and the result of that knowledge, hence doctrine as well as teaching.

And God says that His will is here. He gave the law to go against anything that is contrary, opposed to healthy doctrine. So, therefore there must be healthy doctrine. Look at some other uses.

HEALTHY TEACHING

Healthy doctrine in 2 Timothy, Chapter 4.

> **2 Timothy 4:2, 3a:**
> Preach the word; be instant [all the time] in season, out of season; reprove, rebuke, exhort with all long-suffering and doctrine.
>
> For the time will come when they will not endure [*hugiainō*, healthy teaching and healthy doctrine]

The time will come when they will not endure healthy teaching, which produces healthy doctrine. They will not endure it.

> **2 Timothy 4:3b:**
> …but after their own lusts shall they heap to themselves teachers, having itching ears.

They are going to have teachers who will tickle their ears and tell them what they want to hear. Unhealthy teaching producing unhealthy believing. Doctrine is right believing, how to believe rightly. There is healthy right believing, and there is unhealthy believing; there is a contrast here.

Look at Titus, Chapter 1. We are in the pastoral epistles. Verse 9, is another familiar verse:

Titus 1:9:
Holding fast the faithful word as he hath been taught, that he may be able by [*hugiainō*] sound doctrine both to exhort and to convince the gainsayers [contradictors].

Sound doctrine—healthy doctrine. Look, disease cannot attack successfully a healthy organism. A healthy organism can successfully withstand the attack of disease. And here in God's Word, the healthy doctrine is able both to exhort and convince the contradictors—healthy teaching and healthy doctrine. Our believers are not going to believe all of the junk on TV, but an unhealthy believer might consider it and wind up like Eve did. That was her first mistake, remember? But a healthy believer, one who has healthy right believing, is not prone to the disease of unbelief. That is the adversary's disease—unbelief. The adversary's outreach plan is to steal, kill, and to destroy. And he uses fear to get the ball rolling, and that is disease.

But a healthy believer is not prone to the fear disease. He can withstand it because he is healthy. Pests are not going to attack a healthy plant. You farmers know that, so you keep them healthy. Healthy animals are not going to get attacked by hyenas or vultures. It is the dead or dying ones, right? Same thing with believers.

And see, you people as leaders should have your ears open. But people, every one of us in the household of God is a leader, because we are all committed; we have committed unto us the ministry of THE leader, Jesus Christ, THE way. That ministry of his is committed unto us, and we are leaders.

We are the physicians of the world. Do you understand? We are the true physicians of the world, as the Great Physician was when he was upon earth. All of us are commissioned by God to go out and teach health, promote health. But not just physical health. So far, we are at healthy doctrine and healthy teaching.

Look at Titus, Chapter 2, verse 1:

Titus 2:1:
But speak thou the things which become sound [*hugiainō*] doctrine:

Sound is *hugiainō*—healthy teaching and believing; right doctrine. "...speak thou the things which become..." health—not disease, not fear. Get caught up in the greatness of God's Word and the health of that Word—healthy teaching.

Didn't you always want to know you were right? Well, here it is. This is health! This is the guidebook to health. Healthy teaching, healthy doctrine.

So, there we have two categories already. Healthy teaching—we are commissioned as God's people to teach healthy teaching because healthy teaching will produce healthy doctrine—healthy right believing. So, you see that we have two categories there of *hugiainō*. Not anything physical yet. It is involving teaching and doctrine. Do you see it?

HEALTHY WORDS

Now, look at another one. If we are going to have healthy teaching, producing healthy doctrine, what are we going to have to be able to do? What do you do when you teach? speak. So, what are you going to be able to speak?

Well, look at 2 Timothy, Chapter 1, verse 13:

2 Timothy 1:13:
Hold fast the form [the pattern, the *tupos*] of [*hugiainō*] sound words, which thou hast heard of me, in faith [believing] and love which is in Christ Jesus.

Hold fast like a rock. Hang on to it. Tenacious believing in love. Healthy words. I immediately think of Peter in the Gospels where Jesus said, are you going to leave now, too? And he said, Lord, unto whom shall we go? For thou hast what? the words of life.[5]

People, here they are: the words of life, the words of health. Something that is healthy has life. Something that is diseased is dying. These are the words of life, therefore they are healthy words. There are healthy words, and we have to hold fast to them in believing and love —hold fast, tenaciously.

Look at 1 Timothy, Chapter 6:

1 Timothy 6:3a:
If any man teach otherwise [contrary], and consent not [or splits not, splits out from] wholesome [*hugiainō*, healthy] words,...

He is proud? Well no, that is the next verse. If he does not consent to healthy words, what are healthy words?

1 Timothy 6:3b:
...*even* the words of our Lord Jesus Christ, and to the doctrine which is according to [*eusebeia*] godliness;

Godliness—a real true, vital, spiritual relationship with God, as opposed to religion, which is man-made.

The words of life, the words of health, even the words of our Lord Jesus Christ, the words in the book about him—those are healthy words. And we are to speak them. If you do not speak them, if you are contrary to them, if you are split out from them; you are proud, knowing nothing, and all the rest of those wonderful things there.[6]

---

5. John 6:68: Then Simon Peter answered him, Lord, to whom shall we go? thou hast the words of eternal life.

6. 1 Timothy 6:4, 5: He is proud, knowing nothing, but doting about questions and strifes of words, whereof cometh envy, strife, railings, evil surmisings,

Healthy words—there is the third category. We hold fast with believing in love to the pattern, the form of healthy words. And then we teach healthy teaching based on the healthy words. And the healthy words and the healthy teachings would produce healthy right believing in God's people. And when there is healthy right believing, there is going to be unity. There will be oneness.

It is unbelief that causes division. Unbelief is a disease. Fear is unbelief. Where does it come from? It is the devil's disease called unbelief. And unbelief, which causes division in God's ranks, cannot attack a healthy believer because he is going to fight it off. Those beautiful little white blood cells in the Body of Christ—good words, the healthy words, the healthy teaching—the healthy right believer will say, "No. That is not true. That is ridiculous. Get out of here." And that is it for that little germ of the devil. See?

Healthy words will yield healthy teaching; and that will produce healthy right believing, which will protect the believer, and therefore the Body of Christ, from the disease of unbelief, which is the devil's outreach.

But that is not all. So far, we have got healthy words, we have healthy teaching, and we have healthy doctrine or right believing, right? So far, I have not seen one usage here that involves physical health.

Do you see how limiting we are in our misunderstanding and misuse of 3 John 2? Because so far, just in the first three categories, it involves: all the words are the words of life, all the healthy teaching, and the categories of sound, right believing.

HEALTHY IN BELIEVING

Now take a look at another usage of *hugiainō* in Titus,

Perverse disputings of men of corrupt minds, and destitute of the truth, supposing that gain is godliness: from such withdraw thyself.

Chapter 2. We are in the pastoral epistles, written to leadership. Leadership is responsible for the protection, the guardianship, of that deposit. And you guard that via manifestations of the holy spirit. And you promote that with the words of health, the teachings of health, the right believing of health.

In Titus, Chapter 2, verse 1:

Titus 2:1:
But speak thou the things which become [*hugiainō*, healthy believing] sound doctrine:

Why?

Titus 2:2:
That the aged men be sober, grave, temperate, sound [*hugiainō*] in faith, in charity, in patience.

Healthy in believing. Healthy in love. Healthy in patience. So, healthy words, healthy teaching, and healthy doctrine; what do you think you are going to be in the believing category? healthy—a big, robust believer spiritually. That is right. Because healthy words, healthy teaching, and healthy doctrine will produce healthy believing. Do you know what healthy believing is? You just read the record in Luke, Chapter 1 of Mary sometime. Mary knew the stigma of an illegitimate child. Mary knew she could be stoned. That is why Joseph wanted to put her away secretly so at least she would live, remember? But the beautiful thing, in spite of all those odds culturally against her, in Luke 1:37 the angel said, "For with God, nothing is impossible." That is what it says in King James. But, do you know what the Greek says? The Greek reads, "There is no word from God that is void of power." And that is how Mary got pregnant. God spoke the word by the angel.

And the very next word in verse 38, Mary said, "Be it unto me according to thy word." First she says, "Behold the handmaid of the Lord." You know what the word "handmaid" is? It is the feminine form of *doulos—doulē*. Behold, the slave of the Lord. I am ready to go with you, God—be it unto me, according to thy Word.

And I want to tell you, I am sure thankful for Mary's believing. Because one woman's believing—one woman's believing enabled God to change the shape of human history forever. Because if she would have said no deal, I guess maybe there would have been someone else; I do not know, but I am sure glad I do not have to worry about it.

Believing changed the course of history. What about your believing? Do you want to be healthy in believing like Mary, or do you want to be diseased in believing? Healthy believing separates truth from error. Healthy believing spots a lie. And healthy believing says, it does not compute. Get it out of here. So healthy words, healthy teaching, and healthy doctrine will produce healthy believing. See it?

Now, we have four categories so far: healthy words, healthy teaching, healthy doctrine—right believing, and then healthy believing. And believing is action. So we are going to be taking healthy actions then. If we are believing healthily, then our lives will produce and manifest the fruit of that healthy believing—1 Corinthians 15:33. You should work some of the words in there: Be not deceived; evil associations corrupt good morals (good ethics; the Greek word is *ēthē*). Where you hang out is going to have an effect on how you are doing spiritually.

Look, this is what it is not to be healthy. In Peter, it talks about Lot who was vexed with the filthy behavior of the wicked.

2 Peter 2:7
…just Lot, vexed with the filthy conversation of the wicked:

That word "vexed" is *kataponeō*. It means to be wearied from heavy labor, to get worn out. Lot got worn out by all the devilish things that were going on around him. He should have never been in Sodom and Gomorrah in the first place if you ever heard the Word. He had a fight with Abraham.

And then the next verse says that he vexed his righteous soul in seeing and hearing. It does not say in doing the evil. It does not say in partaking of it. Just in seeing and hearing the evil that was going on around him, it says it vexed his soul.

2 Peter 2:8
(For that righteous man dwelling among them, in seeing and hearing, vexed *his* righteous soul from day to day with *their* unlawful deeds;)

That word "vexed" is a different Greek word. It is the Greek word *basanizō*. And *basanizō* means to torture or afflict with pain. He tortured his righteous soul with pain just by seeing and hearing.

So healthy believing, you are going to avoid vexing your soul with the conversation of the wicked, the behavior of the wicked of the seeing and hearing. You are going to be where there is health. You are going to be promoting health. And if you go someplace where there is not health, you are going to be the doctor. Do you understand?

The Great Physician Jesus Christ came to heal. He committed his physicianship to you and me in this sense. We take the place of the absent Christ until the Return.

Do you love God enough to put yourself in a position where you are forced to discipline yourself to carry out your vocation as a son of God with all power? I hope so.

That is healthy believing. When you are healthily believing, you are going to be moving ahead. You are going to be driving with the Word in all health. Healthy words, healthy teaching, healthy doctrine, healthy in believing.

HEALTHY IN THE FAMILY FAITH

Now look at Titus again, Chapter 1, verse 12:

Titus 1:12, 13:
One of themselves, *even* a prophet of their own, said, The Cretians *are* alway liars, evil beasts, slow bellies.
This witness is true...

How would you like to get a letter by revelation from your leader that people in your fellowships and Bible Studies are always liars, wild beasts, evil beasts and slow bellies—this is true.

Imagine that. So, you know what he tells him to do?

Titus 1:13:
...Wherefore rebuke them sharply, that they may be [*hugiainō*, healthy] sound in the faith.

Healthy in the family faith. That is a beauty, because God has called you to the Body of Christ, and you have answered that call. You are born again. Therefore, there is some unique thing. You are the only person like you that there ever has been in all the history of the world. There is no one else exactly like you living today, and there will not be anyone else exactly like you for the rest of history until Christ comes back. How much are you worth then? And add to that, God has put His treasure in that earthen vessel. Oh, what a vision! What beauty, spiritually! That is fantastic!

And He has called you to that Body of Christ because you supply something completely unique; because you are the only one of you there ever is, ever was, and ever will be. And He has put the spirit of Himself in you for you to manifest in that own unique, beautiful way, supplying to the overall Body of Christ that effectual working and the measure of every part which maketh increase of the body unto us—the edifying of itself in love.

And God designed the body to function at maximum with all the pieces working. If I had my arm amputated, I could still live, but could I function as well as I do with it? Some of you might say, yes, you probably could. But, I could not—same thing.

And that is why every individual member of the Body of Christ is extremely important. And if one splits out of the family, we cannot operate as well as if everyone was standing. We are not doing so terribly, but how much more could we do? That is why each member is important.

Look, that is why I want them healthy in the family faith. I want each member of that Body to be healthy, that the whole Body is functioning at maximum; healthy in the family faith, so that each member is producing that uniqueness which God called us to the Body to supply, so that we can have increase in the Body unto the edifying of itself in love. Isn't that beautiful?

Now look at these five categories we have of *hugiainō:* healthy word, healthy teaching, healthy doctrine, healthy in believing, and healthy in the family faith. We have not even seen physical health yet. You see, when each member and that Body of Christ is healthy within that family of faith, how healthy is the overall body?

When the Body of Christ is healthy, the devil can unleash all hell on our backs and we are going to stand. The only antidote, the only medicine for the sickness and the disease of unbelief and fear that the adversary has afflicted the world with is the medicine of God's Word.

A faithful believer is going to be healthy in believing, healthy in words, healthy in all that stuff. He is going to promote health. He is going to carry out that spiritual physicianship. And then we have healthy in believing and healthy in the family faith. You see, there are the eight uses in the pastoral epistles. You see how much leadership is involved in that? Do you see it? Healthy words, healthy teaching, healthy doctrine, healthy in believing, healthy in the family faith.

All right. Well, what about physical health? We are not finished with all the uses. We started in 3 John 2. We covered eight in the pastoral epistles. That leaves us three more. And it is uniquely beautiful to me where those three uses occur. They occur in the gospel, but it is not like one in John, one in Matthew, one in Mark. All three are in Luke.

Luke, the beloved physician—the physician who wrote about the ministry and life of the Great Physician, emphasizing his life and ministry as the son of man, the compassionate healer. Do you see it? And that is where you find those three uses of *hugiainō*. They give you a complete picture of God's heart, even in the Christ Administration. Let's look at them.

For the first one, Luke, Chapter 5, starting in verse 27:

Luke 5:27-31:
And after these things he went forth, and saw a publican, named Levi, sitting at the receipt of custom: and he said unto him, Follow me.

And he left all, rose up, and followed him.

And Levi made him a great feast in his own house: and there was a great company of publicans and of others that sat down with them.

But their scribes and Pharisees murmured against his disciples, saying, Why do ye eat and drink with publicans and sinners?

And Jesus answering said unto them, They that are

[*hugiainō*] whole need not a physician; but they that are sick.

Look at the very next verse about the primary aim of his physicianship.

Luke 5:32:
I came not to call the righteous, but sinners to repentance.

And how do you do it? Healthy word, healthy teaching, healthy doctrine, healthy believing. Do you see it? Jesus Christ is the Great Physician who is ministering to mankind (those with sickness of sin and unbelief) by calling them unto repentance.

The allegory is not emphasizing physical health, but the mental health of the soul. That is the first use in Luke.

PHYSICAL HEALTH

Now, Luke, Chapter 7. Remember the centurion?

Verse 7:

Luke 7:7:
Wherefore neither thought I myself worthy to come unto thee: [because he is not an Israelite, he is a Roman centurion] but say in a word, and my servant shall be healed.

Just say a what? word. Now, if Jesus Christ is speaking diseased words, what is it going to do for somebody who is sick? It would not help him. But he is not speaking diseased words.

Luke 7:7b:
…say in a word, and my servant shall be healed.

Verse 9:

Luke 7:9, 10:
When Jesus heard these things, he marvelled at him,

and turned him about, and said unto the people that followed him, I say unto you, I have not found so great [believing] faith, no, not in Israel.

And they that were sent, returning to the house, found the servant [*hugiainō*] whole that had been sick.

Healthy that had been sick. Well, we finally got our physical wholeness in there, didn't we? Praise God. So, we find that physical wholeness is a part of it. But of all the uses of *hugiainō*, that is the only one that talks about physical health.

Like I told you at the beginning, the goal of healthy words, healthy teaching, healthy doctrine, healthy in believing, healthy in the family faith—the goal is not physical health. That is the result. Physical health is the result. It is almost taken for granted. And that is what the Platonists and the Peripatetics, these classical Greek writers wrote. That is exactly why *hugiainō* took on that meaning for them. They assumed physical health if the soul was healthy. See it? Rational, whole thoughts. That is why Plato said, you can tell the sick what manner of life will make them whole. It is not a medicine. It is a way of life.

So, you are either living a healthy way of life or a diseased way of life. And I want to tell you, believers, we do not have any time to hassle with disease. Get rid of it. Take a shot in the arm of the Word and cast out any disease of doubt, worry, fear, and unbelief. We cannot afford, as God's people, to allow the disease of unbelief, the adversary sickness, to attack any part of your life.

And your life is important to the life of the whole. That is why I fight for believers. Because if that guy gets sick, then part of my body is sick. When you smash your thumb with a hammer, you cannot just rip the thumb off your hand and say, "Stay there until you stop hurting." Your whole body is going, "Ouch!"

The same thing applies spiritually. That is why we fight as believers to keep every one of us healthy in the family faith. So that we as a Body stand together fighting the adversary's disease.

The physical health is a part of *hugiainō*. So now we have six beautiful categories of that word. Look at it: healthy word; healthy teaching; healthy doctrine; healthy in believing; healthy in the family faith; and physical health. Six—what an amazing number!

You know, I thought of six after looking at all the uses. And it does have some interesting significance. So, six is the number of man—the human number—the number indicating man's weakness, man's frailty; the defiling influence upon human nature because of the adversary.

And God says, "Look, I know you are weak. I know you are susceptible to the devil's disease. That is why I have given you health!" Healthy words, healthy teaching, healthy doctrine, healthy believing, healthy in the family faith and physical health—isn't that beautiful?

The final use of *hugiainō* is in Luke 15. Only the Gospel of Luke, of the four, has this parable recorded in it. The prodigal son you have heard. Well, it is actually the prodigal of the forgiving father, and the son comes home.

Verse 22:

Luke 15:22-27:
...the father said to his servants, Bring forth the best robe, and put *it* on him; and put a ring on his hand, and shoes on *his* feet:

And bring hither the fatted calf, and kill *it;* and let us eat, and be merry:

For this my son was dead, and is alive again; he was lost, and is found. And they began to be merry.

Now his elder son was in the field: and as he came and drew nigh to the house, he heard musick and dancing.

And he called one of the servants, and asked what these things meant.

And he said unto him, Thy brother is come; and thy father hath killed the fatted calf, because he hath received him safe and [*hugiainō*] sound.

This is a beautiful parable. Jesus Christ utilized parables to teach truths about God. Have you ever heard the phrase that when someone gets born again that God has a great party in heaven? There is a parable that substantiates that beautifully.

Look, this is one of the most beautiful, poignant teachings on God, the Forgiving Father, that I know. Look at it and think of it as your own, about you. You, being out in hog country. Look at verse 24. Think of God saying this when you became born again.

Luke 15:24a:
For this my son was dead, [in trespasses and sin, but now he's] alive again;…

Hallelujah! He was lost and is now found. Isn't that beautiful? Now, once again, you are safe—saved and healthy. What a beautiful usage to put that in there. And so beautiful to me that the only usages of *hugiainō* outside the pastoral epistles and John are all in the gospel of Luke; the physician who wrote about the ministry of the Great Physician, and emphasizing his life as the son of man, the compassionate healer.

Just a coincidence? No way. You begin to see how God in His foreknowledge set the beauty of the Word for us.

SUMMARY

That is what I mean by "hot Bible." And every time you read it and work it, it is going to do that for you. That is the beauty of our Father's book. Remember in *Power for Abundant Living*, "This is not an age of devotion, this is life!" and then it fades out. You know, I almost fell off the edge of my seat the first time I heard it—wow! These are the words of life, health, strength.

It is not enough to know the world is sick, because every one of you knows it. But what are you doing to heal it? The physicianship of Jesus Christ has been committed unto us, and first things first, let us take care of the family. Understand? You do not sit there and see a brother killing himself spiritually with all sorts of junk and say, "Well, I'm glad that's not me." That is rejoicing in iniquity. And the love of God renewed by manifestation does not do that. Get over there and give them the medicine: healthy words, healthy teaching, healthy doctrine. Get him healthy in believing so he will stay healthy in the family faith.

We have to fight for each other. When this Body is healthy, and we are together; they can scream at you, they can spit at you, they can fire you and it just does not bother us. I am healthy. And I can thank God for my health.

Uncle Harry always used to pray and thank God for a healthy body and a sound mind. Think about it in the broader terms of the Body of Christ. I want so much to be able to pray, honestly, and thank God for a healthy Body of Christ.

And I am convinced beyond any shadow of a doubt that the great heart, the highest practitioners, the most skilled surgeons, the most skilled physicians are the "spiritual physicianship" that God has committed unto us in our ministry, by God's grace. You know why?

Because I do not know anyone who really in their heart loves the Word more and desires more to dig it and get to its greatness. You are the most prestigious physicians in the world. Get out there and do some surgery, you know, speak the Word and witness.

I have been telling people what Daniel did as a POW, prisoner of war. In Daniel 6, verse 3, he operated holy spirit. That is what got him to be "the top brass." Verse 4, he was completely faithful to God. Never used anything illicit or illegal to enhance or protect his position. Verse 10, he had God before life and job. God was primary. When they made the Word illegal, he stood. Verse 14, he did not let Darius, who was the king of the whole world, be his sufficiency or his deliverer. Darius tried to but could not. Verse 16, he witnessed. Because Darius said, your God whom you serve continually is going to deliver you, won't He? How did he know? Daniel must have been witnessing.

And from Hebrews 11, we know also that Daniel did it all by the manifestation of believing. The manifestation of believing comes into operation once you have received revelation. In order to receive revelation, you have to believe. The greatest cargos of life come in over quiet seas. So, Daniel, must have had his seas quiet and kept them that way.

So that is what you need to do, believers. Operate holy spirit; get out there and operate all nine manifestations. Stay absolutely faithful to God in every facet of life. Keep God before life and job. Trust Him only as your sufficiency and your deliverer. Witness and cultivate your seas and keep them quiet. And the only way you are going to do that is to stay healthy. And this is how you stay healthy, *hugiainō*. That's right.

Now back to 3 John. See, the Word of God assumes that the teaching of Christianity is correct instruction. It is correct instruction because it is reasonable—it is absolutely reasonable—and it appeals to sound intelligence. And that is what *hugiainō* is all about.

Out of the previous times you read 3 John 2, from now on I think you should have a little broader perspective of it. Take a look at it now:

3 John 2a:
Beloved, I wish above all things…

My prayer concerning all things—when I consider everything, God says, I pray that you are led in the good way. And you are *hēgéomai*. That word comes from the word "*hodos.*" *Hodos* means way. When used literally, it means a highway, a way of going; when used metaphorically, it means a manner of action or a method of proceeding.

And that is a word that Jesus Christ called himself: "I am the way," the *hodos*. I am the way, the proper method of proceeding. I am the right action to take to have access to God. Follow me. And God's prayer above all things when He considers everything is that we are to be led in the good way. Imitators of Christ.

That is what it means to prosper: to be led in the good way, the way of the Word, and be in health. Not being sick? Oh, how limiting. Be in health. Be healthy. Healthy in word, healthy in teaching, healthy in doctrine, healthy in believing, healthy in the family faith, and physically; even as, or according as, your soul is led in a good way.

And who determines which way your soul is led? You do. And how do you do it? That is what it is all about, renewed mind. Renew the mind. Set these principles deeply in your heart and life. Look at that verse!

My prayer concerning everything, when all is said and done, God's prayer for us is: I just pray that you will be led in a good way and be healthy in word, healthy in teaching, healthy in doctrine, healthy in believing, healthy in the family faith, and physically healthy according as your soul is led in the good way.

What a gorgeous verse! Do not ever limit God again. It involves the entire gamut of our lives. And at the very center, that is what should be there—the greatness of God's Word.

God can make a way out of whatever the devil throws out. Look, when you were dead in trespasses and sins, without God, without hope in this world, completely lost; God made The Way, The *Hodos*, Jesus Christ. And God can absolutely make *A* way, after having made *The* way for all time. You are the ones who are going to decide by your renewed mind believing whether you want health or disease.

What do you want? Health? Then get your nose in the Book. Revel in the words of life. Hold forth the words of life. Teach them. Cling to the words of life. Be healthy in your believing, stay healthy in the family faith, and physical health is just about guaranteed. It is the result. Do you see it? Physical health is included.

Yes, part of God's will is for us to be physically healthy. But look at all the other things, in that Word "be in health" that God has in store for us. See it.

You are a healthy human being in the Lord's eyes. God has given you the physical, mental, and spiritual; and pronounced you healthy. Grade A, God inspected. So, walk that way, okay? Otherwise, we are going to get sucked into the sickness of the world. God's view of health is that big. Never limit Him again in your understanding of it.

And look at the perfection and the beauty of that word. It is absolutely great! Don't you just love God for giving you the Bible? Just sit there and read it and say, "Thank you, God. I love you. I'm so glad you wrote me this." And people, now is the time more than ever before, get your nose in this Book. Drive it into your head. Live it. Think it. Eat it. Sleep it. Share it. Go to Bible fellowships. Study it. Stand. And we are going to take the Word over the world!

Let's have a word of prayer: Father, I thank you in the wonderful name of Jesus Christ for the greatness of your Word; its accuracy, its precision, its tremendous beauty, Father. How much you see for us, how much you have envisioned for we your people, to be these great physicians of your Word and minister to a sick and dying world, Father, with the greatness of the truth of your Word.

I thank you that we too can be disciplined physicians who can stand together by: holding fast and believing in love those healthy words; teach abundantly (healthily); cling to healthy doctrine; be healthy in our believing; stay healthy in this beautiful family of faith you have called us to; and even stay physically healthy, Father.

We surely thank you for everything you have done for us in your son, Jesus Christ. And I thank you God that he is our example, and that is how we are, that is how we can walk. I thank you, Father, for the continued strength and health, *hugiainō*, in every believer world-wide. To your glory and the outreach of your word until the return of your son, Jesus Christ, to bring us home to you.

And we thank you for the reality of that hope, ever present in our minds, that we just stand like rocks and get rid of the sickness, Father, in the world.

We love you, God, and thank you for all things that you have given unto us. Through Christ Jesus, our Lord, Amen.

APPENDIX 3

THE WORD BRINGS HEALING

When we put on His Word in our minds, when we absorb it, when we begin to live it; we receive the greatest healing I know.

It says in God's Word that God sent His Word and healed people. For many years I did not understand what that meant: "God sent His Word and healed people." Then, as I got deeper and deeper in the working of the Bible, I began to see that literally *God's Word* is healing. When we put on His Word in our minds, when we absorb it, when we begin to live it, we receive the greatest healing I know.

Yet, on a greater plane, what does it profit a person to be healthy a lifetime and still lose his soul in the end because he was not born again? Jesus came that all of us might have complete wholeness. "Salvation" and "wholeness" come from one Greek root, *sōzō;* thus salvation means wholeness, and wholeness means salvation. When Jesus Christ cleansed the ten lepers, he sent them to the Temple to show themselves to the priests so that the priests could acknowledge, according to the law, that they had been healed. After going to the priest for a clean bill of health, only one returned and gave Jesus Christ credit and thanks. Jesus said that leper was made whole. All ten were healed, but only one was made whole. So, there is a lot more to living than just physical health and well-being.

Jesus Christ came that we might have life to the fullest. I know that by his death on the cross, by his shed blood, we have both our remission and forgiveness of sins. Also, by his stripes we were healed. Therefore, the potential for wholeness physically and spiritually is available in Christ Jesus.

Now, the thing we as informed believers do—and I see this thing happening or beginning to happen in our community and our country—is to help the spiritual temperature of believing God's Word rise.[1] As we hold forth God's Word, and the believers receive that Word and put on the mind of Christ, believing expectation goes up. And when that temperature rises sufficiently, people are delivered mentally, physically, spiritually, financially, and every other way so that they are made whole.

This time I want to look for healing at that part of God's Word found in Mark 3. It seems that Jesus Christ could get into what we might consider messy situations without effort. The Pharisees had criticized Jesus, as recorded in the second chapter of Mark, for "working" on the Sabbath. Jesus responded directly that the Sabbath was made for man and not man for the Sabbath. From that confrontation, Jesus went into the synagogue. It seems like every time he entered into a synagogue, he found himself confronting the religious leaders. The reason he had problems with these leaders is that he was endeavoring to put new wine into old bottles. After

---

1. We can see in the records of the believers' walks and the growth of the Church in the Bible that believing is "contagious"—as more and more people believe God's Word and act on it, they see more and more answers to prayer, more promises of God coming to pass, and more of God's deliverance in their lives and those of others. As these results of believing are more and more visible and shared and talked about, it builds more believing, inspires believing in others, and that produces more and more results. Dr. Wierwille termed this spiraling growth in believing a rise in the "temperature of believing."

all, Jesus Christ had a ministry, and that ministry was to Israel. So, he had to go into the synagogues, that is where the people of Israel were to be found. He had to give them an opportunity to hear what he had to say. The account in Mark 3 takes up when Jesus entered into the synagogue in Capernaum. There he found a man who had a withered hand.

Mark 3:2:
And they [the Pharisees] watched him [Jesus], whether he would heal him [the man with the withered hand] on the sabbath day;...

Now here is a man who has a real need; his hand is withered. The man had a need, and he was in the synagogue. That is the place where the Word of God was to be. That is where that sweetness, that tenderness, that love, that kindness, that understanding, that forgiveness was to be. He put himself, a layman, right at the place where greatness should have been. The man did his best.

Jesus had just told the Pharisees that the Sabbath was made for man; and since the Sabbath was made for man, then the man with the withered hand had the right to have his need met any day of the week including Saturday, the Sabbath. Jesus had just explained this to the religious leaders when he went into their synagogue, yet they still watched him to see if he would heal on the Sabbath day, that they might do one thing—accuse him of dealing with a man's problem. Just how devilish and mean can people get? Jesus Christ, God's only-begotten Son—who had not done anyone any harm and had always done the will of God—wanted to help a person who needed help, and yet the religious leaders were only interested in accusing Jesus of acting unacceptably to them.

This rends my heart, people, that at the very place where we ought to be able to get help, people sit around to find fault and accuse. It seems to me it is high time that we as Christians bind together and fight the devil instead of fighting each other, because frequently we are just as guilty as the Pharisees when we are caught up in matters other than God's Word and His love.

Now this man in Capernaum had a real need. He was at the place where he should have been to have his needs met, but the people there were not interested in meeting his needs; they were interested in arguing as to whether Jesus operated in the right way at the right time with the correct protocol, and all kinds of things that did not matter under the circumstances. Jesus was not stupid. He knew that they were watching him as to what he would do. But, you see, he did God's will all the time. Had he not ministered to that man after he had revelation, Jesus Christ's ministry would have failed, and he could not have been your redeemer and mine. He was the perfect savior because he walked perfectly before God. So, do you know what Jesus did?

Mark 3:3:
...He saith unto the man which had the withered hand, Stand forth.

First of all, it took tremendous courage on Jesus' part to do it. Secondly, put yourself in the shoes of the impaired man. If those Pharisees and leaders are going to be unfair with Jesus, what do you think they are going to do with this man? Look at the courage it took to stand forth, to stand up.

Then Jesus looked around on the people—

Mark 3:4:
And he saith unto them, Is it lawful to do good on the Sabbath days, or to do evil? to save life, or to kill? But they held their peace.

The observers were not going to open their mouths. They remained silent because they could not answer that question without looking foolish.

It took me years to believe the verse which begins:

Mark 3:5a:
And when he had looked round about on them with anger...

Jesus Christ looked about on those leaders with anger. He was angry. He was, in our terminology, mad. He was not just some wishy-washy push-over. He was God's man. He stood. Jesus looked on the unbelievers that day in Capernaum, he stood up for what he believed, and he was angry. Do you know why? Because of the hardness of their hearts. The hardness of people's hearts to God's Word does not break our hearts, but it does hurt. Jesus Christ only wanted to share the greatness of God and His Word, but the people in that synagogue who were responsible for that synagogue and its operation had hardened their hearts.

Let's read on:

Mark 3:5:
And when he had looked round about on them with anger, being grieved for the hardness of their hearts, he saith unto the man, Stretch forth thine hand.

Jesus was angry when he said to the man, "Stretch forth thine hand." So, God did not heal that man because Jesus was angry. Is that right? You have not read the record, then.

Jesus said to the man, "Stretch forth thine hand." That is all the Word of God that man had. His hand was withered. He could not do anything with it when Jesus commanded him to stretch it forth. Now ladies and gentlemen, that is an impossibility. But we've got a *possible*

God. And God is bigger than all impossibilities, for with God all things are possible. He makes us more than conquerors; He gave us eternal life. I hear people say, "Well, I want to see a miracle. I want to see a person healed." You've seen the greatest miracle in the world if you will just look in the mirror. For when you got born again, you were raised from death unto life. And to raise a dead person is no small miracle, is it?

I do not understand a lot of things, but I know from the Word that our God is able to deliver. I do not care what the fiery furnaces of life may be, our God is able to deliver. I learned long ago that all of us have our furnaces. Many times when you see a person in a wheelchair, or you see a blind person, you immediately think what poor shape they are in. I never think that. I only see the potential of the greatness of our God. Besides, a lot of people I have not seen in wheelchairs, I have read about shortly afterwards in the obituaries, while the person in the wheelchair was still alive.

You see, really, I do not know very much; but I know God, and God knows a lot. I know a God that is a God of love; I know a God who is a God of forgiveness, a God of understanding, a God of peace, a God of righteousness; a God that puts joy in the soul of a man or a woman and makes it possible for him or her to lay down at night without any fear or frustration and get a tremendous night's sleep.

Four words is all that man in Capernaum had: "Stretch forth thy hand." That is all he needed. But you know something? Those were just words. He could have responded to Jesus' command by saying, "Look, my Mom's been telling me to do that for years." But he didn't. He believed that the words of Jesus Christ were truth to him, that Jesus Christ meant what he said and said what he meant. Jesus said to the man with the withered hand,

"Stretch forth thine hand. And he [the man] stretched *it* out..." Do not ask me to explain it. That is all I know about it. That is the Word. I do not know any more. He said to the man, "Stretch forth thine hand," and he stretched it forth. Then—

Mark 3:5 continued:
...his hand was restored whole as the other.

And right then and there the heads of the synagogue had a meeting. They immediately—

Mark 3:6:
...went forth, and straightway took counsel [not only with themselves, but with the king's men] with the Herodians against him, how they might destroy him [Jesus].

All Jesus had done was to be good to a man in need. He did not hurt the man, and he did not steal from the synagogue's collection plates. He did not do that, yet all they wanted to do was to destroy Jesus. The Herodians, the top brass in government, and the leaders of the synagogue, tried to figure out how they might destroy this one man who was doing nothing but good.

Mark 3:7-12:
But Jesus withdrew himself [because he was afraid? —no, because of revelation] with his disciples to the sea: and a great multitude from Galilee followed him, and from Judaea,

And from Jerusalem, and from Idumaea, and *from* beyond Jordan; and they about Tyre and Sidon, a great multitude, when they had heard what great things he did, came unto him.

And he spake to his disciples, that a small ship should wait on him because of the multitude, lest they should throng him.

For he had healed many; insomuch that they pressed [rushed] upon him for to touch him, as many as had plagues.

And unclean spirits [that were in some of those people], when they saw him, fell down before him, and cried, saying, Thou art the Son of God.

And he straitly charged them that they should not make him known.

Why did he do that? word of knowledge. It does not say that Jesus cast out the devil spirits at that time, does it? Unless you understand word of knowledge[2] and the other manifestations of the spirit, the Bible is so unclear. But when you see the walk of a man of God like Jesus Christ, just walking with the Father in alignment and harmony, knowing what is going on but not having the go-sign to take any devil spirits out; we see how only God knows and must give us instructions for each situation. He simply charged them "…that they should not make him known." The devil spirits had made him known by saying, "Thou art the son of God."

Mark 3:13-15:
And he goeth up into a mountain, and calleth *unto him* whom he would: and they came unto him.

And he ordained twelve, that they should be with him, and that he might send them forth to preach,

And to have power to heal sicknesses, and to cast out devils.

As soon as Jesus had delivered the man with the withered hand, followed by healing many others, the

---

2. The manifestation of word of knowledge is your operation of the God-given ability whereby you may receive from God, by His revealing it to you, certain truths or facts concerning any situation about which it is humanly impossible for you by your five senses to know anything.

Herodians started to apply pressure to stop Jesus. But God simply said to him, "You had better leave town and go up in the mountains." Jesus did not go up because he was afraid. He went because he had revelation.

According to verse 13, Jesus called people up to the mountain with him:

Mark 3:13, 14:
…and they came unto him.
And [out of that group that came] he ordained twelve, that they should be with him…that he might send them forth to preach.

Later on, in the Word it says that Jesus sent the twelve out. Wherever these men went, they brought deliverance to people because they were speaking the Word. And wherever people truly hear the Word, they are delivered.

Does it say in Mark 3, regarding the man with the withered hand, that Jesus laid his hands on him? No, he never touched him. I believe he simply said to the man, "Stretch forth thine hand," and the man believed what he said and did it. Jesus did not touch him. That is why later many were healed, as it says:

Mark 3:10:
For he had healed many;…

He healed many in that synagogue because of the level of the believing temperature—in spite of the leaders. The leaders could not control the people's believing. It is the common folk that raised the temperature. No matter what the leaders said, the signs, miracles and wonders continued. Even though the leaders went to political leaders, they couldn't deter Jesus from doing God's work. God's healing will move when common people, just like us, believe and begin to move. The greatest healing I know is the hearing of God's Word. When the

Word is taught, and people believe that Word, then they get deliverance. The Word brings healing. There is no man living that could minister to all of you; I know I would never get the job done. But a person can teach God's Word to thousands, and thousands can be delivered when that temperature of believing rises so when they hear the Word, they appropriate it to themselves. Do you understand what I am saying? It is that simple. I want you to see from the record in Mark 3 that Jesus Christ ministered to the man simply by giving him God's Word. After that, many more were healed because of the spiritual temperature, the whole level of believing, was so fantastic after they heard the Word. That is what I expect to see among believers—those who have a need in a category can have the need met just with the teaching of this wonderful Word of God.

APPENDIX 4

TOTAL MAN

As a human being, you are: the food you eat, the water you drink, the air you breathe, and the thoughts you think. That is total man.

INTRODUCTION

When you begin working God's Word, start living for God, and trying to do the best you can for people, you get involved in a lot of different things, because the Word of God will get you to the place that you see you have a spiritual need that has to be met, and God meets that need. Then you see how you have to renew your mind. There are things that your old man nature has which you have to get rid of. So, it is not only a spiritual matter when you really love God, it is a mental one too. You renew your mind with God's Word, and it is in another realm, the physical.

I do not know if there is any scientist interested enough to ever follow it out, but I know from having lived, observed, and worked the ministry that one of the reasons people do not "think good" is because they are not eating good food. Therefore, you really have to get God to cover a lot—really fantastic.

Dr. Poesy in Samoa told me they never had any communicable diseases on that island until they introduced Western food, the canned goods. Usually, if there is something on the outside of a can you do not understand, it is poison. And a lot of the things they are pouring into us is the same ingredients you use when a person is dead to preserve him so you can look at him for three days.

Now, I am not a food fanatic; I am a God fanatic. However, I happen to know if you put into your mind certain reading material, you are going to begin manifesting it. And I know when you put into your physical body the wrong kinds of food, it will contribute toward your life in manifestation physically. One of the great things I have learned about physical living is do not overeat. Just never eat too much, period. I think this is very important in physical living that you just do not overload the machinery.

Another important aspect to life is breath—breathing. You can take any person and in a period of one or two weeks improve their whole breathing so fantastically that their whole life takes on a new dimension physically. One should participate in physical fitness or exercise; never overdo it, but always go beyond your ability at that moment. In other words, we always drive ourselves just a little further than where we thought we could go. And I do this mentally, as well as spiritually. I just keep moving on. That builds your breaking point in life, whatever that is. You can build yourself up to be a much better man or woman than you ever thought you could be.

Now you can never have any better physical food than the soil that grows it. That is just axiomatic and plain common sense. If you do not have a good soil, you cannot grow a good plant. If you cannot grow a good plant, you cannot eat a good plant because it is not there, right? And all of life, *physically*, has to come out of that soil because out of the soil you eat. Suppose you had a glass of milk today. Well, some cow had to produce it because you do not get milk from a bull or even from a crabapple tree. You get milk from cows. And someone had to go "utterly" to work to get that milk. But now suppose you feed that cow a low type of nutritional plant. What kind of milk are you drinking?

We have men and women who are committed to the kind of ground and soil and the things that develop in that soil which can be produced. Like for instance, we grow all our things organically. It is all, again, to produce fruits and vegetables and plants and animals that have real value in eating. And when we have extra food available, people can pick it up; anyone is welcome to it. This is part of the life that you get into with the accuracy of God's Word. Because man is a complete being —mental, physical, spiritual. He is a complete being. You cannot isolate the spiritual by itself. It has to be one.

SOIL—PLANTS—FOOD

Isn't it wonderful to be part of a ministry that believes in the total man and teaches the total man all the way? I have been associated with churches practically all of my life, and never once have I ever seen such a total ministry.

We enjoy sharing the greatness of God and what He has made available for us. Because truly He is a big, wonderful God! He has made everything possible for each and every one of us. Many times, we get carried away by a lot of the scientific knowledge that man has today. I have nothing against scientific knowledge, but many times, it leaves God out of the picture. It is test tube results. You know, I have gone to people in the agriculture departments, and I tried to share this story that I am going to share with you. Telling them what this program has been doing for us—how we are enjoying life abundantly, how farmers all over the United States are enjoying it. And I have testimonials stacked high of farmers that voluntarily give us testimonials. They want other people to know and to share what it is doing for

them. And you know the first question agriculture departments ask me? "Where is your scientific evidence that
it works?"

"Well," I said, "here I have all these testimonials from
our farms. We would like you come out and look."

And you know they laughed at me right in my face.
They said, "You think we would take a farmer's testimo-
nial? You think we would take anything from a farmer?
It has to be proven in a test tube before we will believe
it."

And I come right back and ask them the question
kindly: "How do you test nature in a test tube?"

You see, the things I believe in I have never seen, but I
know they are real. Do you think Jesus Christ is coming
back again? Yes? Have you ever seen him? No? We
believe it. So many times, it is hard for the natural man
to see the spirit of things.

We are farm people. And I am going to talk to you in
a farmer's language because that is all I know. I am
going to tell it just the way that I have always lived. We
are farm people, and I am proud to be a farmer. I believe there is no better place in the world to live and to
raise a family where you can really be close to God
every day with the freedom that you have out there.

Living in Iowa within two miles of where we started
farming, our main desire in life was to enjoy life, to
raise a family, and to be an asset to our community, and
to love God. Those were our desires in life. In our early
marriage, we enjoyed this very much. After about eighteen years, we decided we wanted to take things a little
bit easier on the farm. We were farming quite a bit of
land and a lot of cattle, so we decided to make some
changes. And about that time, we were first introduced
to what they called the commercial fertilizers. Now many

of you probably do not know too much about agriculture, but I will try to explain it. That is the reason I am going back before I get into the meat of it.

Chemical fertilizer is what they call a plant food approach. Where they make man-made chemicals and feed a plant directly to make it stimulate the growth, mainly to grow bigger yields—bushels, bails, tons. And of course, you know everyone is interested in that because that is where they measure their dollars and cents. Well, when they first introduced this program to us, I got excited because that was the same time they said I could increase the yields. I figured out really quick that we could make a little bit more money. So, we decided we would follow their program. Now the first thing they recommended is that we get our soil tested. You have to go out in your fields and take different samples of the fields, send the soil in, and let them do the testing. And they will tell you what you need. So, we did. Well, first thing they said we needed was some fertilizer, these chemicals. So, we got a plow and broadcast them—spread them out on the land, and worked it in the land. Then we got ready to plant the crops; they said we had to put a little fertilizer in the row with the seed to stimulate that growth. They told us we needed some nitrogen. So, we applied all this fertilizer to the soil, and we really got a yield. We got excited. I thought now we have it made. So, we took on the dealership and we started selling these chemicals and fertilizers to our friends and to our neighbors.

This went along fine the first few years. We enjoyed these yields. But pretty soon we started having some problems on our farms that we had never had before. Now they did not seem too disturbing at the time, but yet, I knew there was something wrong. The first thing we noticed was with our cattle. We had about eighty stock cows, all our little calves, and a lot of young cattle around. But the first thing wrong we noticed was water started running out the of the eyes of these animals in the middle of summer. And then the flies would get around the eyes, and sometimes they would even go blind. We had to start using ointment to treat them. Before, they were always nice and healthy, and we would put them in the feed yard. Everything was going fine, but pretty soon, not only the watery eyes, but our little calves started getting scours,[1] and they got pneumonia. And we had to start using these drugs, medications in the needle to give them shots to even keep our calves alive. Well, they came out with these wonder drugs at that time. Give them a shot or two to get them over it, and everything was looking pretty good again.

But about the same time, we started having a weed problem. We could always handle our weeds all these years with the proper cultivation and rotation with our land. We could always handle our weeds. We started having giant foxtail[2] and weeds like that; we could not figure it out. Well, they came out with sprays for the weeds.

I believe the same problem is true with the soil. There is no shortage of potash,[3] phosphorus, nitrogen, or any

---

1. Scours is a term for diarrhea; another term that may be applied to this disease is "enteritis," which means inflammation of the intestinal tract. While cattle of any age can develop diarrhea, most cases of calf scours occur under one month of age, with the majority occurring between roughly 3 and 16 days of life. (http://veterinaryextension.colostate.edu/menu2/Cattle/Calf%20Scours%20101.pdf)

2. A foxtail is a spikelet or cluster of a grass, that serves to disperse its seeds as a unit. Thus, the foxtail is a type of diaspore or plant dispersal unit. Some grasses that produce a foxtail are themselves called "foxtail," also "spear grass." They can become a health hazard for dogs and other domestic animals, and a nuisance for people. (https://en.wikipedia.org/wiki/Foxtail_(diaspore))

3. Potash is a potassium-based product that is often bonded to other chemicals. It is predominantly used as a fertilizer to encourage

part of it—I don't believe that. We have been on a natural program for fourteen years on our farms. And when we started on the program of building soil, the test of our soil had to have all these I was telling you about and more every year. If anyone wants to take any test of any of our soil and any one of our farms, you will find out that it is a balanced soil now; it needs nothing. It has everything it needs. There have been samples of that soil sent in saying it is equivalent to grow 250 bushels of corn per acre if you had the moisture and weather to go with it. And we have never bought any out of the bag and added with it either; we have let nature do it.

You see what is happening to soil today with many of these chemicals? Things are getting tied up or locked up. And then, you see, any time you destroy any phase of life in the soil or disturb it in any way, it does not function the way it should function. Then it cannot make available a potash, a nitrogen, etc. You talk to any fertilizer man, he will tell you that you have all kinds of nitrogen, phosphorus, and potash in the soil, but he will tell you it is not available. But he has never told the farmers why it is not available.

You know what the key is to make it all available in the soil? L-I-F-E. Isn't that simple? You see it is so simple, the things that we talk about that it is hard to believe. God's Word is simple isn't it? But how people make it complicated and get it all twisted up! Isn't that right?

Same thing with the farmers. It has to be test tube tested. It has to be soil tested, you know, really complicated.

---

water retention in plants, increase yields, improve taste and help plants resist disease. The two most common potash fertilizers are sulfate of potash (SOP) and muriate of potash (MOP).
(https://investingnews.com/daily/resource.../potash-vs-phosphate-whats-the-difference/)

Then they have great big names for it; have you ever noticed that? And they are getting so many diseases now, they start calling them viruses. You know what a virus means? You look it up in your dictionary. It is unknown, something they still do not know. They do not have an answer for it, so they call it a virus. Everyone has got a virus nowadays, have you noticed that? Get sick and go to the doctor.

I would like to tell you a little story that I believe ties in with the whole thing we are talking about. A number of years ago my wife and I had the privilege (and our son) to go way back in Canada fishing. Now the only way we could get up there was to fly in with a pontoon airplane. We stayed with a trapper and his wife in a little trapper shack back in that wilderness. And they told us they had lived there for forty-two years. So, you could imagine some of the stories the trapper had to tell.

One of the stories he told that I will never forget was about these caribou. Every spring he said the caribou would migrate by his cabin by the thousands. He said it would take days for those herds to get by his cabin. And they would go up what they call these moss beds. And of course, that is what these caribou feed on is moss. They would have their young ones up there. Then in the fall they would come again right by the cabin. Then they would get their rifle out and shoot whatever was needed for the winter supply of meat. But they do not have any caribou anymore. I asked, what happened?

He said, right after World War II, the Canadian government got the idea that these timber wolves were killing too many caribou. So, they ordered the trappers to poison the wolves. And when he said that he jumped up and said, "I was against that!"

And I said, "Why would you be against something like that? If those wolves are killing off some of your caribou I could not see any reason (at least at that time) why not to get rid of those wolves!"

You know what he said? "Nature put that wolf up here for a purpose. He's got a job to do."

I said, "What could that be?"

"Well," he said, "the wolves only destroy the sick and weak caribou. The healthy ones always get away and then they reproduce. That is how nature keeps the health in the herds." And he said, "We had thousands of caribou. You cannot believe how large the herds were. But we had to poison the wolves. It took about two years before they noticed the caribou started getting sick. Disease started to set in those herds and they started to die." And he said, "Today we do not have any caribou anymore; they died off with disease.

Now I am going to ask you: do you think those wolves were good? Or were they bad? They were good, right. That is the reason God put them there!"

Other stories like that have been written which I have read in the *Outdoor Life* where they have tried the same thing in Alaska. Different areas, and the same thing happened. They moved the wolves back in, then within a few years the caribou and wild game came back again. Nature always has a way to keep its balances.

You remember a little bit ago when I said every living thing is good? That is a pretty big statement to make, isn't it? I am sure you can think of a few insects and a few bugs you do not like, but God put them here for a purpose. I do not know all the reasons and why, but every phase of life has a purpose, a place, and a job to do. Now if that is true, what about all these insects? What is the purpose of an insect?

Well, back on our farms when we first started having our first little problem with insects, they called them root worms. That is something that eats the roots off of the corn, and then the corn just falls down. The insect does not go up and eat the ear, the good part; all he does is chew the roots off. Well, these people I was doing business with at that time said do not get excited, we have something for you. And they called it Aldrin.[4] They put that out with the corn and that really fixed the root worms. They said I had to keep using it so the next year we put it on, just like the year before. What do you suppose happened the second year? The little root worms came back again, only this time they were stronger, and I believe they were more mad than they were the year before. I could not believe it. I went out in that field, and the corn was falling this way and that. Looked around, and sure enough, the root worms were eating the roots off. So, I called those people and told them what was happening. They said they were sorry about that, but they learned a little from that. They said the root worms were getting resistant to that poison. We were going have to make it stronger. So, the next year they came out with a stronger poison. Then the little insect got stronger. Then they made the poison stronger; the insect still got stronger. And those poisons the farmers are using are many, many, MANY times stronger than they were in the beginning. In fact, they are so deadly today, that right on the container or the cans, there is a big warning that says "POISON"— big letters. It says when you apply it, be careful. You have to wear gloves, you have to wear goggles, you are supposed to wear a respirator. It says right on the containers. And when you have all these containers emptied out, then you are supposed to smash them, dig a hole, and bury those empty cans 18 inches deep away from your

---

4. Aldrin is an organochlorine insecticide that was widely used until the 1990s, when it was banned in most countries. It is a colourless solid. Before the ban, it was heavily used as a pesticide to treat seed and soil. (https://en.wikipedia.org/wiki/Aldrin)

water supply. But spread the poison all over your farm, I guess that's alright. Just go ahead, put it on, but look out for the empty cans, they're dangerous!

And you know something, we have more insects than we have ever had in the history of farming. We have more weeds, more diseases, and more problems on the farm than there has ever been in the history. Let us stop and think a little bit. You know, people don't *think* anymore. Most people are followers. Have you noticed that in the world? They just follow along; blind leading the blind, many times. How many years now has the farmer been using chemicals? Five, ten, fifteen, twenty or more? Don't you think by this time that we would have all the insects killed? We should have had all the weeds killed. Those farmers should be on an easy street if that program is an answer. But it isn't. They have got more problems than ever before. You see, when we try to fight nature, or fight God, we are fighting the greatest power there is, isn't that right? And I am going to ask you, how in the world can you win when you are fighting a power like that? It is impossible. The sicker we get it down here, the more problems we are going to have. When that soil gets sick, we get sick plants, animals, and people. You see, as a human being, you are: the food you eat, the water you drink, the air you breathe, and the thoughts you think. That is total man.

And the food that you put in that body of yours, be very careful what you feed it. You would not think of taking your automobile that burns gas and put kerosene or diesel fuel in it, would you? You would not go very far, for very long at least. But so many times, people do not realize how important food really is so that you can have a healthy body, be able do a day's work, and be able to think clearly. It takes total man—a balance. If we are going to enjoy the more than the abundant life, I believe it has to be a total balance. It cannot be out of balance.

Many farmers in the agricultural business today are in a rut. They are looking for answers. They know they have problems. They realize what they are doing is not right, but they have nowhere to turn. That is why I get such a joy of sharing this with people. Reminds me of a little story, about two little frogs living at the pond. One day they decided they were going to take the day off to visit their friends over at the other pond. They get up real early that morning. They are hopping along through the meadow just having a good time, but they come to a road with two deep ruts. Well, like little frogs are, I suppose, trying to show off a little bit, one little frog says, "Let me show you how I can jump over that big rut."

So he backs up and takes a run. Just about the time he was going to leap, he slipped and fell down in that deep rut and he could not get out.

The other little frog worked for the longest time trying everything to get his little friend out of that rut, but it was just too deep. Finally, the sun started going down and it was getting dark. And the little frog said to him down there, "Friend, I am going to have to leave you. When it gets dark, I can't even find my way, then we're both lost."

"So," he said "Why don't you go on your way." So, he bids his little friend goodbye, and real sad like, he goes hopping along. He gets out there a ways, and he thought he heard a noise. He looks around, and who do you suppose he saw? His little friend. Here he comes, just hopping for all he is worth. And when he caught up with him, he said "Now tell me, please, how in the world did you get out of that deep rut?"

"Well," he said, "a wagon came along, and I had to."

You see, there is no problem so big that there isn't an answer. Isn't that wonderful! Even man's problem. Always an answer. God is always giving us a way out.

There is always an answer for every problem in life. I shared this program with farm people. And do you know the joy of putting together these meetings? People came up to me after the meeting, and they said "What makes you so excited? My goodness, you really believe don't you?"

"Well," I said, "I took a class one time called *Power for Abundant Living.*"

When I say *Power for Abundant Living*, they say, "What's that?"

And I start explaining without getting into it too deep. I am always excited about it though, "You just have to take it. That is the only way you really understand it. It does not make any difference what denomination or church you go to. I believe that it really teaches the Word so that you can really understand it." You see people are ready. They want answers, in all dimensions.

You know, as I look at the commercial fertilizer chemical program, it looks to me like it is one of the greatest tools that the devil is using on the farmer—on all of us. If he can get you to eat food that is contaminated with poor quality so that your health is bad, and you are physically weak, that is a pretty good start for him, isn't it? To me, that program, as I look back, that I used to be on was a destructive program. How can a farmer enjoy life and enjoy that farm on a destructive program? Can you have life and destroy life? If I had thirty cows out there in a pasture, and every day I went out and destroyed one, how long would I have thirty cows? But if I turn a bull out there in that bunch of cows, that is a different story.

You see, farmers do not realize that their soil is a living thing. And I hope each and every one of you share this with people, tell them how important it is because many of you do not live on a farm. You have to buy what you buy out of the store. You see, when you promote life, you shall have more life. And you know, that is an absolute law of nature; that is the law of the universe. (Like when you promote life, you shall have more life.) And I found out something else: every turn that we have made for nature on our farms, we have been paid back tenfold. Those farms out there are producing crops that people come from thousands of miles all over the United States and even foreign countries to see what we are doing. That soil is a living reality of life so that man can enjoy life in all dimensions. And people, we never want to forget that God is our creator. He has made all things possible, and He wants us to live the abundant life. He does not want any of you sick. That is why He has given us soil. And everything I am sharing with you is in the Word. Be good stewards of the soil, take care of the soil, work with the soil, and you will never be short-changed. You will always get bonuses.

What really carries me is our families back home. You know, we are a close family. We all live there on the farms, and we are so thankful for that. When I am home, there is not a day goes by that those grandchildren (at least one or two or more) come over, and I love them. But I spend about 90% of my time away from home now sharing this message so that farmers can enjoy more life; so that you can enjoy more life. I am interested in the future of our children and our grandchildren. I am interested in your future. And we start building from the foundation. You see, if you are going to build a good home, you have to build a good foundation first.

Now, if you are to learn that Word as we have been taught, if that Word is really going to mean the abundant part of you, the foundation has to be there first. And that is a good, healthy body, a temple for God.

APPENDIX 5

THE SECRET OF
RADIANT LIVING

Looking within will make us miserable—looking around will cause us to be distracted—but looking unto Him is the great secret of radiant Christian living.

The awe-inspiring abilities latent within the human mind are indeed wonderful and important to the believer. One of these great abilities is mentioned in the book of Colossians:

Colossians 3:2:
Set your affection on things above, not on things on the earth.

Here we are exhorted to set our thinking (the word "affection" is *phroneō*, mind) on the things of God. Your mind has the ability to concentrate upon a specific thing, and to remain in that state of concentration for a considerable period of time.

In the Word are specific things upon which we, as believers, should concentrate our thinking. We are also blessed with several records of men who concentrated on things other than what the Father intended. As we examine these, we can learn by their mistakes. The records clearly show what was the outcome of their concentration upon inferior things, and, above all, how these men were brought back to a right understanding of what they should concentrate upon.

HOW TO BE MISERABLE

Asaph, the psalmist, gives us our first insight into this subject in Psalm 77. He tells us of the time in his own life when he faced serious problems. His autobiography in this psalm tells us:

Psalms 77:2:
In the day of my trouble I sought the Lord: my sore ran in the night, and ceased not: my soul refused to be comforted.

His mind refused to be comforted. In the midst of tremendous trouble he says:

Psalms 77:3:
I remembered God, and was troubled: I complained, and my spirit was overwhelmed.

He briefly remembered the greatness and the goodness of God to him in past days, and yet he was troubled. He could not conceive why this particular problem was upon him, nor why, as he thought, God had left him alone. As his mind went from thinking about the great things of the past days to the terrible problems of the present, his spirit was overwhelmed. So much so, he tells us in verse 4:

Psalms 77:4b:
…I am so troubled that I cannot speak.

Psychologically, this description speaks of tremendous depression.

Even though we do not speak, the human mind is always active. Asaph found that while his problem was so great he could not speak, yet his mind began recalling some of the events prior to this crisis.

Psalms 77:5:
I have considered the days of old, the years of ancient times.

He remembered the goodness of God in past days.

Psalms 77:6a:
I call to remembrance my song in the night:…

That great time when through the sheer exuberance of joy, I sang in the darkest night.

Psalms 77:6b:
…I commune with mine own heart: and my spirit made diligent search.

Why has this happened to me?

Psalms 77:7:
Will the Lord cast off for ever? and will he be favourable no more?

Has my day of grace ended? Has my wonderful fellowship with the Father somehow come to an end? Does He not like me anymore?

Verse 8 continues in the same questioning vein—the human mind at work in the midst of trouble.

Psalms 77:8:
Is his mercy clean gone for ever? doth *his* promise fail for evermore?

Are God's promises finished with now? Does this mean that everything God has promised will no longer come to pass? The questioning continues:

Psalms 77:9:
Hath God forgotten to be gracious? hath he in anger shut up his tender mercies? Selah.

If we were honest, we would admit that many times our mind has followed a similar pattern. Undoubtedly, each one of us could write as graphic description of the working of the mind in the midst of trouble as this psalm. However, what is written here is written for our learning.

We should now carefully observe how this man was able to get on the right track once again. In his autobiography, he says:

> **Psalms 77:10-14:**
> And I said, This *is* my infirmity: *but I will remember* the years of the right hand of the most High.
>
> I will remember the works of the LORD: surely I will remember thy wonders of old.
>
> I will meditate also of all thy work, and talk of thy doings.
>
> Thy way, O God, *is* in the sanctuary: who *is so* great a God as *our* God?
>
> Thou *art* the God that doest wonders: thou hast declared thy strength among the people.

What made the difference? What caused this sudden statement of thanks and praise to God? This man had found that as long as he looked within, as long as he sat there and let his mind ramble on in the field of negative thinking, just so long would he be miserable. But the moment he started thinking about the greatness and the goodness of God, and this was spoken out in a positive confession, at that moment the problem sank into insignificance.

We, too, should be careful about what we concentrate upon. To concentrate upon yourself, your own unworthiness, your supposed inability, will always drag you down. Multitudes of Christian believers are constantly exhorted to search their hearts and examine themselves. How far greater it would be if we spent our time considering what God has done for us in Christ Jesus, considering how we can manifest in a greater measure the more abundant life that Jesus came to give us. Let us learn the lesson well, that as long as we look within, we shall be miserable.

How to be Distracted

Another autobiography that will help us in our quest is given in Psalm 73. This honest and factual account of the working of the human mind should again be noted carefully. This particular man did not spend time looking within, but his error was equally as bad. Looking back upon the incident, he starts with a positive statement.

Psalms 73:1, 2:
Truly God *is* good to Israel, *even* to such as are of a clean heart.

But as for me, my feet were almost gone; my steps had well nigh slipped.

He felt very insecure, as if he was perhaps slipping rapidly into insanity.

The interesting thing to us in our current search is that he clearly tells us what caused this state. Verse 3 commences with the word "for," giving us the reason for the statement of verse 2:

Psalms 73:3:
For I was envious at the foolish, *when* I saw the prosperity of the wicked.

With this particular man, the problem was not of looking within, of feeling unworthy, of feeling unable to do things; his problem was looking at other people. These people had no faith in God, were out to make every penny they could, and were people to whom it seemed nothing ever went wrong.

He lists carefully his observations in verse 4 and following. He notices first their good health and abounding strength, causing them to swell with pride.

Psalms 73:4-6:
For *there are* no bands in their death: But their strength *is* firm.

They *are* not in trouble *as other* men; Neither are they plagued like *other* men.

Therefore pride compasseth them about as a chain; Violence covereth them *as* a garment.

Their own ability to supply their needs and greeds makes them people whose:

Psalms 73:7:
...eyes stand out with fatness: they have more than heart could wish.

Because nothing ever went wrong with them, or so it seemed.

Psalms 73:8b:
...and speak wickedly *concerning* oppression....

They did not mind what they said or to whom they said it.

Psalms 73:8c:
...they speak loftily.

In fact, so sure were they of their position, they spoke against the heavens itself, against the greatness and goodness of God.

Psalms 73:9, 11:
They set their mouth against the heavens, and their tongue walketh through the earth.

...How doth God know? and is there knowledge in the most High?

In verse 12, he seems to conclude the whole matter:

Psalms 73:12:
Behold, these *are* the ungodly, who prosper in the world; they increase *in* riches.

His accurate observations sound like the twentieth century. People with health and prosperity, but without ethics, morals, and above all, without a knowledge of God.

The observation of these things cause this man to literally sit down and wring his hands in despair all day long. He tells us that when he thought to know these things, it was too painful for him. This man learned that when we look around we are distracted from the major emphasis of life. We are distracted from the attitudes, beliefs, and concepts which should characterize the believer. Looking around will always cause distraction, even as looking within will cause us to be miserable.

We must continue further in this autobiography and discover how this man got back on the right track once again. The great secret of his change in thinking is given in verse 17:

> **Psalms 73:17:**
> Until I went into the sanctuary of God; *then* understood I their end.

Until he went to the place where God's Word was spoken, where God's praise was given, he could not comprehend the situation. There in God's house, he thought and dwelt upon the greatness and goodness of God. He then realized that the situation was actually the reverse of what he had been thinking.

In verse 2, he told us his feet had almost gone and well-nigh slipped. But in verse eighteen, he states clearly to God:

> **Psalms 73:18:**
> Surely thou didst set them in slippery places: thou castedst them down into destruction.

The situation was exactly the reverse. Instead of his feet being slippery, he was the one who was secure. But they, the wicked and prosperous ones, were indeed slippery.

Psalms 73:19:
How are they *brought* into desolation, as in a moment! they are utterly consumed with terrors.

The secret is obvious. Spend time searching the Word, filling your mind with the great thoughts of all God has done for you in Christ Jesus. Then you will see things from God's point of view and not from the point of view of this world.

This man saw the error of his ways for he tells us in verses 21 and 22:

Psalms 73:21, 22:
Thus my heart was grieved, and I was pricked in my reins [in my mind].
So foolish *was* I, and ignorant: I was *as* a beast before thee.

But he says now:

Psalms 73:23, 24:
Nevertheless I *am* continually with thee: thou hast holden *me* by my right hand.
Thou shalt guide me with thy counsel, and afterward receive me *to* glory.

To look within will make us miserable; to look around will make us distracted. Then where should we look? Upon what should we concentrate our thinking?

HOW TO BE RADIANT

To understand the positive viewpoint as to what we should concentrate upon, we will look at several verses in different parts of the Word. Since we have used the Psalms for our material so far in this study, we will look first at Psalms 34:5:

Psalms 34:5a (American Standard Version):
They looked unto him, and were radiant;…

This statement of fact is given by David, following his testimony of God's goodness in his life.

Psalms 34:4:
I sought the LORD, and he heard me, and delivered me from all my fears.

He then states, "They looked unto him, and were radiant," to show that this situation is common to all God's people who will adjust and control their thinking.

The result of looking unto Him is to become radiant; to have a smile on your lips, a thrill in your heart and a spring in your step. Since God is Spirit, this looking unto Him cannot mean a physical look. It means concentrating upon the nature and acts of a loving Father.

In the book of Hebrews, we are exhorted to look to Jesus.

Hebrews 12:2:
Looking unto Jesus the author and finisher of *our* faith;...

The impact of the words "looking unto" is interesting and vital in the Greek. A more literal translation would be, "Looking away from all else unto Jesus." Not just a brief glimpse or a fleeting thought, but a continued, prolonged concentration upon what God did for us in Christ Jesus. We should look unto Jesus, for he said:

John 14:9:
...he that hath seen me hath seen the Father;...

The next verse in Hebrews 12 gives added light on this subject.

Hebrews 12:3:
For consider him...lest ye be wearied and faint in your minds.

Both verses two and three signify an action that we are

to do by an act of our will. There is a choice involved; we can do it, or we can choose not to do it. We can choose to look unto him and be radiant, or we can choose not to consider him, and thus become wearied and faint in our minds. There is only one intelligent and logical choice for the believer: to look away from all else unto Jesus.

A similar exhortation is found in Hebrews 3:1:

Hebrews 3:1:
Wherefore, holy brethren, partakers of the heavenly calling, consider the Apostle and High Priest of our profession, Christ Jesus.

Again, we are exhorted to consider Christ, especially in relation to what God did for us in Christ Jesus and freely made available to every born-again believer. How great, how wonderful, how thrilling it is to fill our minds with the greatness of the Word.

The important things in life are not those things which we can see but rather eternal, spiritual things which cannot be observed by the human eye. In 2 Corinthians 4:18 we read:

2 Corinthians 4:18:
While we look not at the things which are seen, but at the things which are not seen: for the things which are seen *are* temporal; but the things which are not seen *are* eternal.

Again, the exhortation is given to fill our minds with spiritual things. Undoubtedly, as we live our natural lives in a material world, there are many things we must think upon. However, the real, lasting things are the spiritual. Surely if these are the things that are going to count then we should spend much time concentrating upon them.

Let us consider one more verse that will help us in understanding the object which should fill our minds.

Isaiah 26:3:
Thou wilt keep *him* in perfect peace, *whose* mind *is* stayed *on thee.*

This perfect and constant peace is something to be desired by every believer. It is available as we spend time keeping our mind, our thoughts upon God.

Considering unitedly all these great promises we find the secret of how to be radiant. It is simply looking unto God; looking unto Jesus; looking not at the things which are seen, but the things which are not seen; staying our mind upon Him.

Let us remember, looking within will make us miserable; looking around will cause us to be distracted; but looking unto Him is the great secret of radiant Christian living.

HE SENT
HIS WORD

HEALING WORD VERSES

He sent his word, and healed them,...

Psalms 103:1-5:

Bless the LORD, O my soul: and all that is within me, *bless* his holy name.

Bless the LORD, O my soul, and forget not all his benefits:

Who forgiveth all thine iniquities; who healeth all thy diseases;

Who redeemeth thy life from destruction; who crowneth thee with lovingkindness and tender mercies;

Who [satisfies] thy mouth with good *things; so that* thy youth is renewed like the eagle's.

Psalms 1:1-3:

Blessed *is* the man [whose]....

...delight *is* in the law of the LORD; and in his law doth he meditate day and night.

...he shall be like a tree planted by the rivers of water, that bringeth forth his fruit in his season; his leaf also shall not wither; and whatsoever he doeth shall prosper.

Psalms 23:1-3:

The LORD *is* my shepherd; I shall not want.

He maketh me to lie down in green pastures: he leadeth me beside the still waters.

He restoreth my soul: he leadeth me in the paths of righteousness for his name's sake.

Exodus 15:26b:

...[He] will put none of these diseases upon thee,...: for I *am* the LORD that healeth thee.

Psalms 30:2, 12:

O LORD my God, I cried unto thee, and thou hast healed me....

To the end that *my* glory may sing praise[s] [unto] thee, and not be silent. O LORD my God, I will give thanks unto thee for ever.

Psalms 31:1-3:

In thee, O LORD,...I [have] put my trust; let me never be ashamed: deliver me in thy righteousness.

Bow down thine ear to me; deliver me speedily: be thou my strong rock, for an house of defence to save me.

For thou *art* my rock and...fortress; therefore for thy name's sake lead me, and guide me.

Psalms 31:5:

Into thine hand I commit my [soul]: thou hast redeemed me, O LORD God of truth.

Psalms 31:24:

Be of good courage, and he shall strengthen your heart,...

Psalms 107:13, 20, 21:

Then they cried unto the LORD in their trouble, *and* he saved them out of their distresses.

He sent his word, and healed them, and delivered *them* from their destructions.

Oh that *men* would praise the LORD *for* his goodness, and *for* his wonderful works [unto] the children of men!

Isaiah 53:4, 5:

Surely he hath borne our [sicknesses], and carried our [griefs]:...

...he *was* wounded for our transgressions, *he was* bruised for our iniquities: the chastisement of our peace *was* upon him; and with his stripes we [were] healed.

Isaiah 58:8:

Then shall thy light break forth as the morning, and thine health shall spring forth speedily: and thy righteousness shall go before thee; the glory of the LORD shall be thy [rewarder].

Acts 4:29, 30:

And now, Lord, behold their threatenings: and grant unto thy servants, that with all boldness they may speak thy word,

By stretching forth thine hand to heal; and that signs and wonders may be done [in] the name of thy... child Jesus.

Acts 10:38:

...God anointed Jesus of Nazareth with the [holy spirit] and with power: who went about doing good, and healing all that were oppressed of the devil; for God was with him.

1 Peter 2:24:

Who [in] his own self bare our sins in his own body on the tree, that we, being dead to sins, should live unto righteousness: by whose stripes [we] were healed.

3 John 2:

Beloved, I wish above all things that thou mayest prosper and be in health, even as thy soul [prospers].

John 14:6a:

Jesus [said]…, I am the way, the truth, and the life:…

John 6:63c:

…the words that I [have spoken] unto you,…are spirit, and…are life.

1 John 5:4:

…[whosoever] is [begotten] of God overcometh the world: and this is the victory that [hath] overcometh the world, *even* our [believing].

1 John 4:4b:

…[for] greater is he that is in you, than he that is in the world.

Matthew 8:17:

That it might be fulfilled which was spoken [through] Esaias the prophet, saying, Himself took our infirmities, and [bore] *our* [diseases].

Ephesians 2:10:

…[you] are his workmanship, created in Christ Jesus…

1 Peter 5:7:

[Cast] all your care[s] upon him; for he careth for you.

Philippians 4:19:

[And] my God shall supply [every need of yours] according to his riches in glory [through] Christ Jesus.

Philippians 4:10:

I can do all things through Christ [who strengthens] me.

Philippians 4:11b:

…for I have learned, in whatsoever state I am, [I am self-adequate].

Romans 8:37b:
...in all these things we are more than conquerors...

Romans 8:32:
He that spared not his own Son...how shall he not with
him also freely give us all things?

Colossians 2:10a:
...[you] are complete in him,...

Colossians 1:13:
[For he] hath delivered [you out of the authority] [and]
power of darkness, and...translated [*you*] into [his
own] kingdom [by the work] of his dear Son:

Revelation 12:11a:
...they overcame him [the adversary] [because of] the
blood of the Lamb, and [because of] the word of
their testimony;...

1 John 2:1b:
...we have an advocate [a defense attorney] with the
Father, Jesus Christ the righteous [one]:

Ephesians 1:3-23:
Blessed *be* the God and Father of our Lord Jesus
Christ, who hath blessed us with all spiritual bless-
ings in [the heavenlies] in Christ [Jesus]:

According as he hath chosen us in him before the
foundation[s] of the world, that we should be holy
and without blame before him in love:

Having predestinated us unto [sonship]...by...Christ
[Jesus] to himself, according to the good pleasure
of his will,

To the praise of the glory of his grace, wherein he
hath made us [lovely and acceptable].

In whom we have redemption through his blood, the
[remission] of sins, according to the riches of his
grace;

Wherein he hath abounded toward us in all wisdom and prudence;

Having made known unto us the mystery of his will, according to his good pleasure which he hath purposed in himself:

That in the [administration] of the fulness of times he might gather together in one all things in Christ, both which are in heaven, and which are on earth; *even* in him:

In whom also we have obtained an inheritance, being predestinated according to the purpose of him who worketh all things after the counsel of his own will:

That we should be to the praise of his glory, who... trusted in Christ.

In whom ye also *trusted*, after...ye heard the word of truth, the gospel of your salvation: in whom also after that ye believed, ye were sealed with [the holy spirit] of promise,

Which is the earnest of our inheritance until the redemption of the purchased possession, unto the praise of his glory.

Wherefore I also, after I heard of your [believing] in the Lord Jesus, and love unto all the saints,

Cease not to give thanks for you, making mention of you in my prayers;

That the God of our Lord Jesus Christ, the Father of glory, may give unto you the spirit of wisdom and revelation in the knowledge of him:

[That] the eyes of your understanding being enlightened; that ye may know what is the hope of his calling, and what the riches of the glory of his inheritance in the saints,

And what *is* the exceeding greatness of his power to us-ward who believe, according to the working of his mighty power,